Today I'm Alice

Today I'm Alice

Nine Personalities, One Tortured Mind

ALICE JAMIESON

with Clifford Thurlow

PAN BOOKS

First published 2009 by Sidgwick & Jackson

This edition published in 2009 by Pan Books
an imprint of Pan Macmillan Ltd
Pan Macmillan, 20 New Wharf Road, London N1 9RR
Basingstoke and Oxford
Associated companies throughout the world
www.panmacmillan.com

ISBN 978-0-330-51303-6

1 3 5 7 9 8 6 4 2

A CIP catalogue record for this book is available from
the British Library.

Printed and bound in the UK by
CPI Mackays, Chatham ME5 8TD

Visit **www.panmacmillan.com** to read more about all our books
and to buy them. You will also find features, author interviews and
news of any author events, and you can sign up for e-newsletters
so that you're always first to hear about our new releases.

Contents

For all of the staff at my local Accident & Emergency Department who have always treated me with respect, acted with the utmost professionalism and never judged me whenever I have fallen under their care having overdosed or self-harmed. Especially to two nurses, Dave and Chris, who, with other members of staff, literally saved my life in January 2008. Thank you for fighting for me and for my survival.

Since then, at an uncertain hour,
That agony returns,
And till my ghastly tale is told
This heart within me burns

The Rime of the Ancient Mariner
Samuel Taylor Coleridge

Acknowledgements

My story has been written with Clifford Thurlow, who has patiently drawn my memories from me to collaborate on this book. Collaboration for me was easy. I have been collaborating with the 'alters' most of my life.

Lots of people have helped with this book. They know who they are and I thank them from the bottom of my heart.

A few people I would like to acknowledge here, first and foremost my best friend and soulmate, Alec, for his unwavering support.

Also Iris Gioia, my trusting friends Marie, Lynette, Vicky, Alison, Graham and Jeremy, for believing in me; the Gestalt-psychotherapist Marsha Chase, for her wise and professional comments on the manuscript; the psychiatrist Dr Joan Coleman, of RAINS (Ritual Abuse Information Network & Support), who is constantly there when I need support; analytical psychotherapist Remy Aquarone, Secretary of ESTD (European Society for Trauma and Dissociation) and former International Director of ISST-D (International Society for the Study of Trauma and Dissociation); the team at Sidgwick & Jackson led by my imperturbable editor Ingrid Connell, and our agent Andrew Lownie, who put the puzzle together.

Alice Jamieson
March 2009

Foreword

In April 1993, at the age or 24, I was diagnosed with Multiple Personality Disorder, also known as Dissociative Identity Disorder. I have alternative personalities who manifest unexpectedly and at random, changing my character, my voice, my age. I lose time and lose myself.

All through my childhood I suffered sexual, physical and emotional abuse. I told no one. This book describes how I developed 'mechanisms' to cope with the abuse as a child and how, as an adult, I have struggled to lead a normal life through periods of psychosis, mental breakdowns, drug addiction and self-harm. I make no apologies for the uncompromising language and the blunt truths that need to be told.

The abuse of children is unimaginable for those who have not experienced it. It is hell for those who suffer the daily feeling of shame, the nightly fear of the door opening and that man, it is nearly always a man, entering their bedroom. The abuse more often than not takes place in the home and usually involves close family relatives, fathers, brothers and others.

Since its launch in 1986, ChildLine has helped many thousands of children who have called about sexual abuse. But the children who make that call are only the tip of the iceberg. The vast majority are too damaged, too isolated, too afraid to pick up the telephone. It is estimated that nine out of ten[1] abused children remain silent and maintain their silence as adults.

I hope my book will encourage others who have been abused to speak out, and will give further insights into the telltale signs of child abuse that social workers, teachers, health professionals and family members often miss. There is nothing in this life worse than child abuse and if this book helps just one person it will have been worthwhile dredging up my most painful memories to write it.

Names and places have been changed to protect the privacy of others. It is, however, a true and highly personal record of the events of my childhood and how those events continue to haunt my life as an adult.

1 Kevin Browne, Professor of Child Psychology, University of Liverpool, *The Guardian* 27/09/2008.

CHAPTER 1
Fragments of Memory

My memory is like a large vase that has been dropped from a window. All the pieces are there, some large, some small, some smashed to dust. As I try to put the pieces back together, joining one memory to another, parts of the story become clear and lucid, but lots of blanks and lost time remain. My first day at school? Gone. Family holidays? Nothing. My favourite book? When I first learned to ride a bike? All impossible to find among the long dark shadows that stretched through my childhood.

This is what I do recall.

We were the model nuclear family: Father, Mother, me and my brother Clive, a sensible four years my elder. We were Radio 4 people: conservative, well mannered, educated, thrifty, a bit old-fashioned, outwardly kind and nice.

We lived in a four-bedroom house with a circular drive around a giant oak tree in an affluent area of the Midlands where neighbours said good morning, children were polite and people kept their dogs under control. My father worked as a solicitor in Birmingham. He changed his car every year; always a top-of-the-range Rover, and played golf on Sunday mornings. Mother worked as a secretary for an estate agent and drove a pale-blue Triumph two-seater.

The house was built of pale sandy brick with a red roof

and French doors that opened on to a stone patio. The kitchen led to the breakfast room, beyond which was the long back garden where holly trees hid the shed where my father kept spiders in jam jars. Upstairs there were four bedrooms, a large bathroom and a separate toilet. We each had our own room. The top landing was like a dividing line, Father and Clive on one side, at the front, Mother and me at the rear with windows overlooking the back garden.

At the end of the landing was the box room known as the Bird Cage because of its ornate domed roof. It was in this room I kept my toys and went to hide when my parents had one of their shouting matches. When I was a little girl, the room seemed like a giant doll's house, a magical place where I played alone. At other times, the Bird Cage really was a cage and, when I tried to open the door, I was unable to get out. The rows between my parents usually ended with my mother storming out of the house and I remained locked in the box room until she came home again. The Bird Cage contained an air vent to take cooking smells from the kitchen. After rowing with my mother, my father would often cook something.

This is one very clear memory I have from this time: I am locked in the Bird Cage, the smell of food from the air vent making me hungry. I rap, rap, rap on the locked door. 'Daddy, I'm hungry. Daddy, I'm hungry.'

My father responds by opening the door and giving me a tin of spaghetti hoops, before locking me in again. I stare at the tin, which, of course, I cannot open. This was my punishment. It must have been my fault my parents had argued. I was being disciplined for upsetting them. In an act of rebellion, I bang the tin repeatedly against the wall.

On other occasions I would be really naughty and draw on the wall. Before I could write, I would scribble on the unpainted plaster, messages that meant something to me, that no one ever read.

Mother would come home. Father would let me out of the Bird Cage, and everything would go back to normal. Normal was the watchword. We were, after all, the perfect family, each boxed in our own room.

Mother was a petite, pretty woman with blonde highlights in her brown hair and generous lips that smiled easily. She was, in her own way, quite glamorous and aware of it, too. She had a forceful personality, a sharp tone to her voice, and tended to get her own way. She was impulsive, a doer more than a thinker, sporty in her powder-blue car. Neat and fastidious, she moved with long strides, and was always busy. This sometimes gave her a distant air in complete contrast to her flamboyant blouses and designer skirts that swayed rhythmically as she hurried along in her high heels.

She spent about an hour in the morning on her hair and make-up, while the rest of us ran round making breakfast and trying not to get under each other's feet. Father would go to work first. Clive would set off for school on his bike, and when I started school aged five, Mother would drop me off on her way to the office.

One morning I was sitting on the table in the breakfast room, Mother flitting about collecting her things, when she stopped and asked me, 'Do you think I should leave him?'

She was talking about her husband, my father. I knew that, although I didn't know what to say. At five you live in your own world. The world of mummies and daddies is beyond your understanding. 'Oh, it doesn't matter,' Mother added with an impatient sigh, and we carried on, hurrying out to the car, my shoes polished, her hair lacquered to hold her curls in place.

Mother and I clashed. She called me an impossible child. I was a chatterbox. I asked too many questions. I was hyperactive, full of energy, always eager for her attention. When she made cakes, as she did when I was small, I would clamber up on a stool, anxious to join in. 'Mummy, can I do the mixing? Mummy, can I break the eggs? Mummy, can I lick the bowl?'

I was being impossible. She overcame the impossible by letting me help, but a part of me felt I was being a nuisance. My mother hid her feelings and I, at my mother's knee, learned to hide my own. We lacked an essential communication when I was a little girl and by the time I reached puberty I had constructed my own wall, a front that covered my shaky self-esteem, which Mother could not penetrate.

My brother had got his personality and quick agile movements from our mother, his looks from her father, our grandpa. Clive was engrossed in his own world. He rarely brought friends to the house. I don't recall him raising his voice, getting angry, playing his music too loud. He was aloof, guarded, private. But in summer when the sky was blue and the light stayed longer in the sky, he became more friendly and when older brothers are friendly, that means teasing. I was desperate to be teased.

Clive knew I adored my collection of cuddly toys, the teddies, the big soft Mr Happy and my Snoopy dog with the lopsided grin. Sometimes I would be sitting in the living room playing, and Snoopy would appear outside the window, dangling on a bit of string from my mother's bedroom. I'd go running upstairs, by which time Clive would have dropped Snoopy and hidden in the hall. When I burst into Mum's room, he'd be outside the French doors downstairs, threatening to give Snoopy a bashing.

I squealed with pleasure. It took so little to make my life

complete. I yearned for Clive to be friendly and playful all the time, but had to make do with the occasional teasing. He never swung me in his arms or took me for a ride on the crossbar of his bike. Clive didn't have the fraternal urge to pull me on his knee in front of the television. Mother didn't either. That was Daddy's role.

My father was a tall man with strong features, thick dark eyebrows and dark hair that gleamed like coal under its coat of Brylcreem. His parting was as straight as a line drawn by a ruler, and he had a bald patch on his crown that he would pick at, flakes of dry skin wedging under his fingernail. When I was on his lap, watching TV, or when he was reading his newspaper, he would scratch his head then put his finger in my mouth and I would suck it.

Father harboured vague disappointments and considered himself a cut above the neighbours. He liked people to know he was a member of the best golf club, although he only played once a week. He sometimes looked wistfully at the more cosmopolitan life of his brother, a stockbroker in London. My father seldom travelled except to the faraway places he reached on his short-wave radio, the sound of its whistles and whirs behind his bedroom door was the sound-track to my childhood.

It is easy now as an adult to see how I craved my father's attention when I was a little girl. I was afraid of my father and drawn to him as metal things are drawn to a magnet, as children are drawn to leaning over long drops and crossing the road without looking.

When my father worked in the garden in summer I would run around barefoot, just in my knickers. He would scoop me up in his arms and carry me into the shed with its smell of sawdust and cut grass, its air of calm and order, the light softened as it came through the small dusty windows. Tools with wooden handles hung from brackets, and arranged on the shelves were jars of nails, screws, washers and spiders, the tops drilled with holes so the spiders could breathe.

He'd sit me down on the bench and playfully wave a warning finger. 'Don't you dare move,' he'd say, and I'd do as I was told. I'd sit there, shoulders rigid, teeth gripped, my little fists clenched.

My father loved this game and we played it lots of times. I would be all hot and sweaty from running about and now I'd feel cold fear like icy fingers running up my spine as he tipped the creepy crawlies out of their jars on to my belly. I'd watch, frozen in terror as their hairy legs crept over my skin. I tried not to move but the spiders tickled and I couldn't stop myself. I'd wriggle and squirm and that night I would dream that someone was in my room. They'd close the door, throw my teddies from the bed, pull back the bedclothes and run their fingers like spider legs over my body.

Spiders frequently dropped in on my dreams when I was little and, as I got older until I was about twelve, in one dream that came to me often I saw flames swirling about my feet, heating my toes without actually burning them. I am naked from the waist down, lying flat and kicking my legs like a baby on its back.

I wake in a cold sweat and, in that disorientated moment, I'm almost certain I can see the image of a man running the flame of a cigarette lighter in circles around my toes. The picture is hazy and quickly disappears. What remains is a chemical taste in my mouth like sour milk. I put on my dressing gown, lock myself in the bathroom and clean my teeth. I have the cleanest teeth of any twelve-year-old girl in England.

When these dreams came flashing back into my mind, my stomach would clench as if someone's hand was clutching at my insides and that same bitter taste would rise like bile into my throat. It would often sting when I went to the toilet, although I was used to that; it had happened since I was very small. What was worse was the fuzziness in my head, a feeling that some small part of myself had been misplaced or rearranged in the night, that as I sat there on the loo in the morning I was me but in my dreams I was someone like me but not me.

It was very confusing and I always planned to tell my mother about the cigarette-lighter dream. I wanted to ask her what she thought it meant. But there was never a good time. We were always in a rush. We didn't talk about personal things. I tried my best to push the thoughts and images out of my head by immersing myself in frenetic activity.

I had got into the routine of rushing home from school and doing an hour of homework with the teddies watching me from their place piled on the bed and on the shelf in my bedroom. I would cook for Clive and my parents and have the food ready for them when they got home. They didn't arrive at the same time, and didn't eat together, so I'd prepare three separate evening meals, cooking and washing up each time, then doing it all again.

I wasn't made to do the cooking. I did it because I wanted to. To keep busy. Homework. Housework. Slicing tomatoes. Washing lettuce. Whisking eggs. Sometimes when I was making an omelette for my father I'd find myself adding more and more butter and not know why I was doing it. In fact, it felt sometimes that it wasn't my hands cutting off chunks of butter but the hands of a stranger.

I was filling each fleeting second doing things, the flood of activity pushing my bad dreams further and further back into the gloom until, like shadows, they absorbed each other.

The ugly visions that obsessed me were set against the shiny light of Sunday afternoons when Mum took Clive and me to

7

visit her parents in Erdington. Father rarely came and we seldom saw his family.

Visiting my grandparents was like going on holiday. Erdington was like a different country, more modest, more honest in a way. Just as my father didn't think much of the neighbours, I'm sure he regarded his wife's parents in their modest semi as a little beneath his grand status as a member of the best golf club, solicitor, a man of substance. My father's father had died before I was born. His mother, on peering down on me in my cot as a newborn, had said sniffily to my mother, 'She must be a throwback from your side of the family.'

This woman, whom I seldom saw, was called Granny.

My grandma was my mother's mother, a lively, industrious woman who was only happy when she was busy. She had bouncy curls of white hair, matronly hips and red hands from being constantly in and out of water. She was like the grandma in *Little Red Riding Hood* with her button nose and twinkly eyes that gave the impression there was more going on behind them than she let on. She worked part-time in a department store in Birmingham until she retired. She knitted cardigans and had been a good needlewoman until arthritis made her fingers knobbly and bent.

She taught us how to make toffee and little cakes shaped like pasties she called apple envelopes, bustling around doing ten things at once: warming the pot for the tea, turning the gas down under the tray of toffee, arranging the apple envelopes on the Doulton china plates with gold rims round the edges. The lingering revulsion from my bad dreams would lift from my mind and I'd feel happy to be alive in that kitchen with the long windows looking over the garden with its rose bushes and flower beds. The garden must have faced in the opposite direction to our back garden because it was always filled with coppery light.

Grandpa would come in from pulling up weeds, grinning as he changed out of his work shoes into a pair of polished brogues, bending from the waist to give me a peck on both cheeks. Grandma I adored, but Grandpa was my soulmate. According to family legend, when I was born he held me in his arms, looked into my eyes and said, 'This little one's been here before.' I was told this story so many times it has stopped being folklore and become memory.

My grandfather had clear blue eyes, and they looked at me with pure unconditional love. I didn't have to do anything or be anything to be loved by Grandpa. I just had to be me, and that was different from life at home where I felt that the burden was on me to hold our family together. Our house with its dividing lines and closed doors, with the four seats round the table in the breakfast room only ever occupied by one person at a time, was like the Rubik's Cube that preoccupied my brother, an unbearable puzzle no amount of twisting and turning would ever put right.

Grandpa was going deaf but that only made his other senses more acute. There was wisdom and I suspect a hint of sadness in those perceptive blue eyes. When we left to go home, he would hug me so tightly it was as though he didn't want to let me go.

We were a family who avoided *personal* things, typically English with our secrets and sense of getting on with it. But when I look back through the tangled, addled mess of my memories I can't help but wonder if Grandpa grasped in his canny way that all was not well behind the tall wooden fence at home on the posh side of the Midlands.

Grandpa had worked as a draughtsman. When he retired at age sixty-five, he took on a part-time job cataloguing the plans and drawings for a civil engineering company. He was a copper-plate engraver and a competent artist with a light stroke and confident hand.

I'd say, 'Grandpa, draw me something,' and he'd grab his sketchbook and draw as a child draws, naturally without preparation, an impressionistic landscape coming to life as his pencil danced across the page. Through years lost to drugs, psychiatric hospitals, sofas in forgotten flats, in the homes of forgotten friends, I managed to hang on to Grandpa's *The Waving Palms of Tropic Isles*, an ink drawing of two palms on a distant horizon, and I think of those two palms as me and Grandpa somewhere far away and safe.

Grandpa belonged to that time when men made sure they had a sharp crease in their trousers, a clean white shirt and a tie with a Windsor knot. He kept loose change piled in columns on the dressing table in his bedroom in order to have the right money for the conductor on the bus. He didn't have a car and didn't want one. On a bus you could chat with other passengers or sit upstairs on the top deck and watch the world go by. He wore suits when he went out and favoured Grandma's chunky cardigans at home, the pockets bulging with lengths of garden twine, boiled sweets, a balled-up handkerchief, his packet of Senior Service. He would tap the cigarette on the packet, firming the tobacco before lighting up, the aroma of that strong sweet smoke the smell of Grandpa.

I don't recall my grandpa ever saying an unkind word about anyone. He always had a smile and made me roar with laughter when he told his stories, no matter how many times I had heard them.

When I was twelve, I got the chance to go on a Mediterranean cruise to Israel with my school. Grandpa paid the £200 deposit. When he gave me the cheque he went down on his knees against the living-room wall, rocked back and forwards and wailed in the way of believers at the famous Wailing Wall in Jerusalem. I laughed until tears ran down my cheeks.

We left by plane for Split in the former Yugoslavia, then climbed on board the SS *Bolivia* and set off in a force 11 gale across the Aegean Sea for Haifa in Israel. The sea was so rough, the ship lurched drunkenly from side to side and we watched from our bunks as our luggage shot back and forth across the dormitory floor. Most of the girls threw up, but I seemed to have good sea legs and enjoyed the sense of adventure, the sense that the ship was battling against the odds and we would come through the storm together. It was the first time I had been away on my own and, in those angry waves, while the girls around me were getting seasick and hysterical, I had never felt more relaxed in my life.

On board the *Bolivia* there was no past, just that moment. My head was clear. The bad dreams had floated away on the wind, sunk to the bottom of the sea. It felt as if the bags and rucksacks in the dormitory were the thoughts normally rattling round inside my head and they had been released to slip and slide freely across the floor. I screamed because all the girls were screaming, that's what girls do, but secretly I was really happy.

The sea seemed to reflect my thoughts and when the ship docked in the port of Haifa on Christmas Day it was calm. We scrambled on to the waiting coach and I watched the Holy Land unfolding before my eyes as we wound our way through the ancient landscape to Jerusalem. The Wailing Wall came into view and I giggled to myself as I remembered Grandpa going down on his knees. I would look back on that day many times and I came to realize that Mother had a sense of humour too. She laughed as loudly as me when her father played the fool, as she put it, and she admired him because he had the confidence to be himself.

We journeyed to Bethlehem to visit the Church of the Nativity, the site of the birth of Christ, returned to Jerusalem to see the chamber of the Last Supper and then made our way to the church built on Mount Calvary, where Jesus is thought to have been crucified. After a donkey ride, I was starving and we had a late lunch on the Mount of Olives where Jesus is said to have fed the 5,000 with two loaves and five fishes.

We were in the cradle of civilization, with historic connections to the three great religions of the western world: Judaism, Christianity and Islam. It seemed shocking to me as a twelve-year-old that these holy places were patrolled by armed Israeli soldiers. World affairs had never touched me before, but travel broadens the mind, and it occurred to me during that school trip that the broader the better; the more information you collected, the less room there would be for bad dreams and distorted memories.

I telephoned my parents using the ship-to-shore radio to wish them happy Christmas as we sailed to Rhodes, the Crusaders' island, famed for the Lindos Acropolis, a 375-foot climb up stone steps cut into the hill over the Old Town. A sight 'once seen never forgotten', I read in my guidebook. We crossed the Mediterranean to Turkey where I gorged on authentic Turkish Delight made with rosewater, dusted with copra and flavoured with mint, pistachio and cinnamon. The words and tastes were new to me, as were the sights of veiled women in long robes, the minarets above the mosques, and noises like the cry of the muezzin calling the faithful to prayer, a sound so like the verses chanted at the Wailing Wall it could have been an echo.

The huge siren blasted on the *Bolivia* and we steered a course across a placid sea to the island of Santorini. In a snaking line, we climbed the jagged footpath to gaze spellbound at the crescent-shaped lip of the largest volcanic crater in Europe, the supposed location of the lost city of Atlantis. On New Year's Eve, we arrived at Heraklion in Crete, where we spent the day exploring the ruins at Knossos and I bought presents for my family: a woven bag for Mum, a belt for Clive, a ceramic ashtray for Grandpa, something for Dad, something for Grandma.

Our final stop on New Year's Day was Valletta, a port town, the capital of Malta, and I returned home with my rucksack crammed with rolls of film and my head vibrating with all the dates and archaeological wonders I was dying to share with Grandpa.

I rushed into the house smiling, but Mum looked as if she was in one of her moods and sat me down in the kitchen. Now what? I thought. She told me that Grandpa had suffered a heart attack on Christmas Eve and was fighting for his life.

'Why didn't you tell me?'

'What, and ruin your holiday?'

I broke down in tears.

Grandpa was fighting for his life. The phrase was terrifying and I could hardly bear the wait before we could visit him in hospital later in the day. I unpacked, and when I found Grandpa's ashtray broken it seemed like a bad omen.

As soon as the double doors opened at visiting time, I rushed into the ward wearing a Turkish fez. Grandpa was pale and looked older lying there in his striped pyjamas. But the moment he saw me, he pushed himself up in the bed, grabbed the red fez and put it on his own head. He took my hand. 'What would I do without my little poppet?' he said, and from that day on he started to get better.

CHAPTER 2
Running and Starving

It often felt as if I were playing a role, that we were all acting out parts in a television soap: the father who works hard to support his family, a mother who loves her husband, emotionally balanced children without a care in the world. The little ups and downs served as minor conflicts that were quickly resolved, progressing the drama to some inevitable but unclear conclusion. Except for when I was with my grandparents, my smile was always false. I was constantly watching myself, forever trying to see myself as everyone else saw me. It was never natural, always a sham, and the other players seemed just as good at playing their roles as I was at playing my own.

The family we pretended to be was perfectly normal, with our birthday celebrations, watching television together, barbecues in the garden. In summer during Wimbledon, Clive would rig up a net using the washing line and we'd play tennis. My father showed me how to serve, holding me in the right position. 'Do it this way ... no, no, no, you have to follow through ... Not like that. Stretch your arm. Curve your back ... No. No. No. Do it again'. I was attuned to the subtlest change in tone, the feel of my father's hands on my arms, his body pressing against my back. Mum would clip-clop up the garden path on her heels carrying a tray of lemon barley with ice cubes rattling in the glasses. We'd take a break, standing there panting, then run off to find the lost balls.

But something felt wrong. Something was missing. I knew this, and sensed that the rest of my family did too.

Mother looked happy when she went to work and looked happy until the moment she pulled into the drive, locked the car in the garage and made her way into the house. Her happiness was outside those four walls. Father always seemed as if he were on the verge of saying something; that gagging noise in his throat was going to be some life-changing disclosure, but the moment of revelation remained in the airless vault of his mind until it withered and died.

Now that Clive was coming up to seventeen, he made the journey to see our grandparents less often. He had more pressing interests, including a girlfriend. I went every Sunday and wouldn't have missed it if I'd had a dozen boyfriends, not that I actually had any at all. Grandpa was getting better. It seemed like a personal reprieve and I couldn't help wondering if it had been my tour of the Holy Land that had stirred a guardian angel to action.

After his heart attack, Grandpa was diagnosed with diabetes and had to change his diet. Grandma stopped baking apple envelopes. She prepared white fish, stocked the larder with fresh fruit and vegetables, and checked the calorie and sugar contents on the backs of all the jars with a magnifying glass. When I arrived at their house, Grandpa would hurry me down the garden to show me what he was growing in the greenhouse. He'd shut the door and act like a spy as he pulled out a slab of toffee. He'd break it up and have a piece himself.

'Don't tell Grandma,' he'd say.

'But you shouldn't, Grandpa, it's against the rules.'

'Life's too short for so many rules,' he'd grumble, and we'd both stand there sucking our toffee.

At these moments, the dreams that haunted me seemed particularly warped and obscene. I was forever picturing a man coming to my room and taking off my clothes in the middle of the night, running his hands over my body, pulling at my limbs, touching me in places where he shouldn't. As my eyes flickered open in the morning, I would see in those first fragmentary moments fleeting, half-formed visions of things that were so hideous I rushed to the shower to burn the images out of my brain below the hot water. I was a bad person for letting these dirty thoughts into my mind. I stood in the greenhouse trying to tell Grandpa about the horrible things I imagined, but I was like my father in that one respect at least and let the words wither to dust in my throat.

If I appeared downcast for a moment, Grandpa would instantly give me a hug. I didn't like physical contact of any sort – the way girls link arms in the school corridor, or a stranger sits too close on the bus. I flinched and pulled away from everyone except Grandpa. I felt safe with his arms in the sleeves of a woolly cardigan round me.

'Are you happy, poppet?' he'd ask.

'Yes, yes. Very happy, Grandpa.'

'Here, have another piece of toffee. I don't want you wasting away, you're about as thin as a breath of fresh air.'

I grinned and ate more toffee. 'I'm always happy when I'm here,' I said.

'Yes, I know, but are you happy the rest of the time?'

'Yes, of course I am,' I replied.

'That's the spirit. You know what I always say: don't let things in life embitter you, let them enrich you.'

I remember those words so clearly.

During our daily visits to Grandpa before he came out of hospital, Mum and I had become closer and, even though the nightmares were growing more frequent and more vivid, I didn't want to ruin that closeness by trying to describe them. At twelve, I didn't have the words to explain what I was seeing, because what I was seeing was fleeting and out of focus. It was like flicking through the pages of a picture book or a comic, the images running into each other. If someone had asked what I had seen, I wouldn't have been able to describe anything conclusively, just random bits as if from a collage: a tongue, an eye, a pair of big hands, a cigarette lighter circling my feet so that my toes looked bright pink in the darkness.

It was best to say nothing. Perhaps it will all go away. Perhaps this was part of growing up, of being prepared for the adult world. Mother had seemed depressed before Grandpa's heart attack and, if that were the case, she had come through it and was more content. She was dressing with ever greater flair, brighter colours, more uptown, less provincial. She tried to encourage me to do the same. We'd go shopping and look at pretty dresses, although dressing in dresses was just about the last thing on my mind.

I turned thirteen and it felt as if I were losing something, or something I'd already lost would never be regained. I was losing a sense of who I was within my own body. The only way I could retain some control was through what I put into my mouth, which grew less and less and eventually became almost nothing at all.

Several times a day I would find myself unexpectedly in my father's room, a dark, masculine place I wouldn't normally dream of going. But for some reason a set of bathroom scales stood in the corner and I would stare down at the revolving dial to make sure I hadn't gained any weight in the intervening hours since the last weigh-in. I skipped breakfast and lunch, except perhaps the odd bit of fruit, and stuffed myself with a salad sandwich without butter for dinner.

Mum was worried that I was so thin. Her worry turned to

terror when one of her friends suggested, after seeing adverts on television about drugs, that I might be a heroin addict.

'Heroin?' I said. 'What's that?'

That calmed my mother down and I popped off to the bathroom where I could strip in private and stare into the long mirror to make sure I hadn't put on any unnecessary weight. At thirteen I was growing breasts and one of the upsides of anorexia is that it delays the process of puberty. For a year I didn't have a period. I saw sexual images in my dreams, I didn't want to see them in the mirror. I hid myself in baggy T-shirts and jeans. I was a whiz at hockey, running the ball down the wing like a streak of lightning. I wanted to get really fast and took up a strict regime of jogging.

Every morning I was up at seven regardless of the weather and hammered round the streets for an hour. I'd shower and gorge myself on a banana and half an apple, drink lots of water and rush off to school where I never had to be told to work hard. At Dane Hall Secondary I was the clever girl, the swot, the prize-winner, who always envied the easy-going girls who chatted about boyfriends and pop stars.

That didn't mean I was out of touch with my times. Oversized sweatshirts were all the rage. They suited me. The trendy girls were strutting about in neon tops and leg warmers, the boys in acid-washed jeans, the cuffs rolled up on their blue school blazers copying Don Johnson from *Miami Vice*. Through the early eighties, everyone was listening to Depeche Mode, Human League, Spandau Ballet, new-wave bands that used synthesizers and drum machines.

I was already considered eccentric and thought of as being *totally* weird in my attraction to The Who and Pink Floyd. I listened to their songs over and over again on my Walkman; it seemed as if they had been written just for me.

There was in my family a desperate sense of hanging on:

Father to his futile air of superiority, Mother to the empty shell of her marriage, me to my lost childhood, Grandpa to dear life. I hated going to bed at night, dreaming bad dreams, sexual dreams, ugly dreams, waking another day older, jogging through the dawn, growing thinner. Sometimes I felt like a shadow that would vanish when the sun rose over the rooftops.

Days and months slipped by in spirals of unremembered activity: the A-plus for a piece of homework studiously written, instantly forgotten; the goal scored at hockey; the prize Clive won for bowling out three opponents in a school cricket match. The garden changed its coat of colours at the end of summer. Christmas presents were carefully bought and exchanged with artificial emotion. The soap opera's seasonal special was broadcast.

Another birthday. Fourteen. In some cultures I would be a woman. I feel like a woman. I feel like a child. I feel like an infant. I have different feelings at different times and I have no idea how I should feel and what feeling belongs to the *me* that *is* me.

My father had become a complete stranger, talking to me only on rare occasions and then in a way that made me feel uneasy. When I had something to do after school, or went to a birthday party at the weekend, he had got into the habit of asking me if I'd got off with anyone. 'What do you do at these parties? Have you got a boyfriend? Is he a good kisser?'

I'd mumble an embarrassed response. As a young teenager, sex was the furthest thing from my mind. On the contrary, while girls were getting interested in make-up and boys, I wanted to screen myself from all such thoughts. I filled my life with intense activity. I was still cooking dinner most evenings. I worked so hard at school I couldn't help but be top of everything. I read until my eyes hurt, and ran and played hockey until I dropped exhausted in my bed at night hoping that the dreams would stay away and leave me in peace

They didn't. The nightmares ran in cycles, disappeared, and others took their place. I was still waking with a bad taste in my mouth and would stare at the bottle of aftershave on the shelf in the bathroom as I cleaned my teeth. The smell of my father's aftershave seemed to fill the house. It permeated my bedroom, clinging to the fur of the teddy bears. I stared at that bottle and had visions of smashing it in the bath, but of course I never did.

Father haunted the house like a ghost, arriving late, eating alone, shutting himself behind his bedroom door with the short-wave radio, the whistles and whirs conjuring up scenes in my head that were so sordid and surreal they could have been murals painted by Salvador Dalì. I had surges of conflicting emotions, feeling sorry for my father, who seemed lonely and reclusive, and experiencing attacks of inexplicable hatred when I woke in the dark night from a bad dream and found myself whispering a prayer: 'I wish you were dead. I wish you were dead. I wish you were dead'.

One sunny day at the end of May, rounders practice was cancelled and I went home planning to do my homework early and get it out of the way. I realized as I cut across the front garden that I had forgotten my key. There was a car in the drive, so I knew someone was in. I pressed the bell. There was no answer. I pressed again, holding my finger down. After what seemed like an eternity, Mum opened the door. Her hair, always rigidly in place, was tossed about, her eyes were shiny and, as she made her way towards the breakfast room, I noticed that the zip of her skirt was open.

'I had a migraine; Stephen brought me home,' she said

casually. Stephen was her boss. 'He was going to dictate some letters.'

Strange activity for someone with a migraine, I thought.

At that moment, I heard Stephen coming downstairs whistling. He entered the kitchen grinning. His hair was wet and swept back, and he wasn't wearing his jacket and tie.

'Hi, you're home,' he said.

I didn't answer.

I left the kitchen, climbed the stairs and went to my mother's room. The bedclothes were pulled back. I ran my hand over the bottom sheet. It was still warm. I don't know why I did that. And I don't know why I felt sickened by this discovery. I felt betrayed. I'd known, deep down, since I was five years old, that my mother was having an affair. But it felt wrong finding out like that, seeing her with her skirt unzipped, the feel of warmth on my palm as I ran it over the sheet. It felt as if my mother had been cheating on me, rather than my father.

In my bedroom, I tipped my books out on the bed and wrote an essay about the Roman conquest. Running. Starving. Submerging myself in work. I had an arsenal of devices to stop myself thinking about the present, or dwelling on the past. I was living in my head, punishing my body, running, it seemed, in circles and getting nowhere.

When Stephen left, Mother tiptoed up the stairs and knocked on my door before entering.

'Everything all right?

'Why shouldn't it be?'

'You don't seem yourself today.'

'I'm never myself,' I said.

She gave that impatient sigh mothers reserve for teenaged daughters and when she'd left the room, I thought about that exchange.

'You don't seem yourself today.'

'I'm never myself.'

It was about the most honest thing that either of us had ever said to each other. It was my 'self' I was trying to find. Sometimes I would close my eyes and pretend I was someone else with a mission to explore the corridors of my brain in search of answers to obscure riddles, the source and meaning of my dreams that were growing more lucid, less fragmented, the clips of film splicing into a narrative. I resented Mother, not because she was having sex with Stephen, but because it had allowed the spectre of sex to open the front door, climb the stairs and enter her bed. Sex was ugly, repugnant, horrifying; it was the ghost no one had ever seen, but everyone sensed its presence.

The following weekend, sex came to haunt me again. My father had a friend who would come to show off every time he bought a new car. I had heard Mother say that he was a 'flash bastard' and she didn't like him. But my father was impressed by this man. He was the managing director of a local company and a member of the same golf club.

They had been outside looking at the Jaguar, which was sleek and black. I was in the lounge and, when they came in, Father left me alone with his friend while he went to get something. The man was loud, self-confident, full of smiles. He came forward as if to say hello, but immediately put his arm round me and fondled my breast.

Mum happened to walk in at that moment and she crossed the room like lightning.

'Hey, you, back off,' she screamed.

He just laughed and moved away. I went running up the stairs and did something I hadn't done for long time. I hid in the Bird Cage.

I didn't eat anything that night. Next morning, after jogging, while Mum was upstairs getting ready for work, I took a beaker with a screw top from the kitchen and filled it with a cocktail of whisky, gin, vodka, brandy – taking shots from each bottle in the drinks cabinet so no one would notice it was gone. My heart was fluttering. A tic in my neck was kicking. I'd seen on TV shows that after accidents the victims needed a whisky or a brandy to settle their nerves, and that's just what I needed to get me through the day.

At school, I took sips of my secret concoction and the feeling was intoxicating. My brain was numb. I felt happy. At home, it seemed as if I were surrounded by all things raunchy and suggestive. Women on television wiggled across the screen with exposed cleavages. There were ads for the new film *Splash* showing Daryl Hannah all but naked. Clive's girlfriend made a rare appearance, knocked on my door, and entered my bedroom wearing a tight top and jeans that showed the shape of her bum.

'What's wrong with you?' she demanded.

'There's nothing wrong with me. What's wrong with you?'

'Why don't you eat properly?'

'Why don't you mind your own business?'

It was a conversation full of questions and no answers. She turned and took her cute figure out of my room and I sat in the corner with Mr Happy, not feeling happy at all.

Sex was everywhere, in the crude images stalking my dreams, in the memory of my mother waltzing through the house with her skirt unzipped, of Stephen with his wet hair and cheery whistle. The combination of these scenes, together with the strain of puberty and anorexia, created a constant feeling of confusion and pain.

Alcohol eased that pain. Next day I filled the beaker again. And the next. And the next. Time for me is and always has been vague, capricious, unpredictable, not a continuous stream, more like a tide ebbing and flowing, impossible to check or measure. I took small nips; I watched the levels go down and, abracadabra, the spent bottles disappeared, new ones reappeared, and no one ever discovered it was me dipping into the drinks cabinet with my plastic beaker.

All good things have their downside. With drinking it's hangovers. Friends and teachers began to smell alcohol on my breath and notice that I was often withdrawn and depressed. Another problem with the drink is that it makes you sleepy and on one occasion the star pupil was discovered snoring through double maths.

Like tankers at sea, schools move slowly, but after several weeks, Mr Keating, the head of year, called me to his office and gave me a cutting from the local newspaper about children who had parents with drinking problems. He had assumed I was imitating my parents, the first in a lifetime of wrong assumptions, misdiagnoses, of missing the point.

Mr Keating made an appointment for me to see a clinical psychologist and accompanied me to the Child and Family Unit at the Naydon Clinic, an annexe to the adult day hospital. I didn't tell my parents about the appointment, and didn't feel inclined to explain my newly acquired taste for alcohol to the psychologist, a tall pale woman who sat in her small, low-ceilinged office like an apparition with the wintry light behind her. Mr Keating remained with me at first, but then the tall woman asked him to leave so she could ask me some questions in private.

She made a spire from her fingers while I sat on a low chair with my navy-blue school skirt across my knees, my fingers picking at the blue and red stripes on my Dane Hall tie. The woman wanted to make a family tree and I watched her draw a complex sequence of circles and arrows that touched some deep dark hidden memory and made me feel uncomfortable. She used her fingers to specify what she wanted me to talk about:

My relationship with my mum and dad.

How I felt about them.

What I thought they felt about me.

And, *most important*, what I thought about me.

It was ridiculous. I had been trying to answer these questions since I was born and couldn't suddenly put a shape to the mess inside my head. She asked me about my dreams and the mere mention of them was so agonizing I told her I was one of those people who never dreamed at all.

'Ah, but everyone dreams.'

'But not everyone remembers.'

'Or wants to remember?'

'Yes, that's right,' I said.

I made another appointment, which I didn't keep. I thought the whole exercise was a waste of energy and had no intention of going again.

What the psychologist didn't know, and would never learn, because I never told her, was that her questions had inadvertently flicked on the light in my head. That night, when I lay in bed hugging Mr Happy, the cigarette-lighter dream beamed into my memory.

I am two years old. The bedroom door opens and, in the dim glow of the night light, I watch a man enter the room. He pulls back the bedclothes, holds his finger to my lips and, with the other hand, flicks the wheel of my mother's cigarette lighter. He moves the flame close to my toes. I kick and wriggle as he does this. I want to get away but I can't. He's too large, too strong, his big finger presses against my lips. He leans forward and, in the glow of the blue flame, for the first time I recognize the face of my father. The weird thing is I am not surprised or terrified. I am comforted by the sense of familiarity.

When he puts the cigarette lighter away, he smiles. I smile back. He takes off my pyjamas and plays with me, tickling me. He wets his finger and runs it between the lips of my vagina. He then unzips his trousers and takes out his willy. He supports the back of my head. I open my mouth without being told and he puts his willy in my mouth. He jerks it back and forth and fills my mouth with a bitter liquid that tastes like sour milk.

I see this scene very clearly. I feel it is familiar somehow, that it has happened many times, the detail varying just slightly. Sometimes he puts his willy in my mouth to make it wet, then climbs on my bed and pushes his willy into the entrance of my vagina. Sometimes he rolls me on to my tummy and puts his willy in my bottom. It really hurts. My face is pushed into the pillow. I try not to cry out because I don't want to make my daddy unhappy.

Over the next few weeks I kept deconstructing the dreams of him coming to my room and it was like shifting shapes in a kaleidoscope, changing the pattern, analysing the parts and putting it back together hoping the picture would look different. Because now, for the first time, I was starting to wonder if these were not dreams, if this had really happened.

I was trying to hold on to something tangible, something more than a feeling, and the more I tried, the more it seemed like make-believe. If these things had taken place how could I have forgotten? You don't forget these things. It's not possible. I told myself over and over again that it wasn't true.

CHAPTER 3
Four Faces

On 3 March 1985, the telephone woke me in the early hours of the morning.

Doors opened and closed. Under the gap below my bedroom door the light came on in the hall. I got up and glanced out of my room as Mum left the bathroom brushing her hair.

'It's Grandpa,' she said, and hurried down the stairs. 'I'm going to the hospital.'

'Wait for me,' I called.

'There's no time, Alice.'

The front door slammed. I listened to her car pulling out of the drive and was still lying awake listening an hour later when she returned. I heard the key turn in the lock. My heart was pounding as she climbed the stairs. She could only have been in the hospital for a short time. That meant it was either good news or bad news, and I remained in bed trying to decide which.

When I finally went to her room, Mum was already in bed. She looked exhausted. She had puffy eyes and no make-up. She pulled back the covers. I stood immobile at her bedroom door considering this sudden display of affection and knowing what it must mean.

'Come,' she said.

I just stood there.

I had a sudden pain in my stomach. My head was spinning.

Mother smiled weakly. She patted the bed and I crawled into the warmth of her sheets. She put her arms round me and held me tight. I didn't know if she was holding me for me or for herself. I could feel the shape and heat of her body. I had dropped to six stone in weight and felt like a baby returning to the womb, a baby kangaroo swaddled in her pouch. It was hard at that moment to think about Grandpa.

'He had another heart attack,' she whispered. 'It was quick.'

'Quick?'

'Grandpa's gone.'

'Grandpa's gone. Grandpa's gone. Grandpa's gone.'

I said the words to myself like French verbs, letting them sink in.

Tears ran down my cheeks and wet the pillow. Had I neglected Grandpa those last few weeks? There had been no time to say goodbye. No last hug. 'Don't let things in life embitter you, let them enrich you.' That was Grandpa. I believe everyone is made up of a jumble of good and bad points. There are among us psychopaths and paedophiles, but few people are totally evil and few are totally good. I think my grandfather was one of the few totally good ones. He was my safety net, my comfort zone. I had grown dependent on his being there and now he was gone.

I cried and cried. I cried until my eyes were red and swollen. When I went to the funeral there were no tears left. I had cried myself out, and the tears I tried to force from me that bitter March morning a few months after my sixteenth birthday were false tears because that's what the occasion called for. I didn't grieve. I couldn't grieve.

We went back to Erdington with Grandma. Mother wore a black hat with a veil, carefully chosen. Father stood across the room in his black suit eating an egg and watercress sandwich. He looked like an undertaker. Clive was likewise in a dark suit and a university tie, very adult suddenly, very serious. He was studying law at university in Bristol and had chosen to go to the south-west 'to get as far away from my family as possible'.

Grandma had baked some apple envelopes, which I didn't touch. Even the smell made me feel queasy. I had a knot of pain in my stomach and I felt the nerve throbbing in my neck. I looked round the house and it seemed as if Grandpa had never been there, that he had never existed, that the man in the photographs on the shelf with Grandma was a stranger.

I thought back to those autumn days standing in the greenhouse sucking toffee and it felt like a false memory, something I had read in a book or just made up. And if I had made up memories of Grandpa, then what sometimes seemed to be memories of my father coming to my room and abusing me could just as easily have been fictitious. I desperately needed to know what to believe, to find something solid to hold on to.

One day, not long after Grandpa died, I went looking for clues.

Because I was finding it so hard to tell the difference between dreams and memories I had started to doubt the memory of my father giving me a tin of spaghetti hoops after arguing with my mother. Did he do that? Why would he do that?

I went into the Bird Cage and found scribbles on the wall and dents that could have been made by a child banging a tin on the plaster. I went downstairs to the kitchen, and returned with a tin of spaghetti hoops. The lip of the tin fitted in the curved dents exactly. I shut the door, sat in the corner and gazed up at the curved glass of the dome as if I might catch a glimpse of the past. Some of my old toys had been packed away in a box: puzzles, games, books, things that had lost their familiarity and could have belonged to someone else.

I spent too much time sifting through the past. I envied people who lived with the belief that there is only the present moment, that the past may never have existed and the future would be a construct of what you were thinking today, now, sitting there with these forlorn objects spread around me on the floor. I closed my eyes. I had a vague sense of waiting, for what I didn't know, perhaps to grow up, when I assumed everything would become clear. I put the toys and puzzles back in the box, closed the door behind me and never went back into the Bird Cage again.

My next piece of research took me to the shed outside. The garden was bleak and muddy. Mist clung to the holly trees where a pair of robins had built a nest. Every year I watched as they flew about with leaves and twigs making their home safe for the pale-blue eggs that appeared as if by magic in early spring. When I remembered, I put out bread-crumbs and water that would turn into an ice disc in the saucer when the weather was freezing.

My breath made a vapour trail as I ran up the path. The shed door was stiff and the hinges creaked as I dragged it open. It was a bitter day and seemed even colder inside the shed, the sort of cold that makes you shrink in on yourself like a tortoise into its shell. The air was static like air in a closed box. I had the feeling that no one had been in the shed for years. The windows were veiled in cobwebs. The woody aroma of sawdust I recalled from long-ago summers had been replaced by the acid smell of damp eating into the metal parts of the screwdrivers and chisels hanging on the wall. The nuts and bolts waiting to be called to some emergency job were turning to rust. I blew the dust from an empty jar with small holes drilled in the lid.

What possible purpose could those holes have filled except to allow insects to breathe? I knew by the shivery sensation in my bones that my father had sat me on the high wooden bench and tipped spiders on my belly. I remembered clenching my small fists. I remembered the feel of those tiny legs creeping over my bare flesh. I remembered trying not to cry out because that would ruin the game and make my daddy angry. Had it happened once? Or lots of times? If it was once, was it just a silly moment, nothing sinister?

I unscrewed the lid on the empty jam jar with holes in the top and peered inside. Nothing. No signs. No dots to connect. No shrivelled corpses of long dead insects. My memory of those summer days maybe ten or twelve years before was in fragments, the bits buried inside me like the ancient chips of pottery I had seen painstakingly pieced together at the museum in Knossos, the reconstructed urn or jug patterned with patches and cracks.

The door made a dull thud as I closed it behind me. It was like closing the lid on an airless box, like the door to the Bird Cage, like some part of my past submerged in deep water. I had proved nothing and yet my heart was pounding and my brow was clammy with cold sweat as I returned to my room. I shut the door, all the doors along the passage were always shut, and I had the peculiar feeling that I was returning to the scene of a crime but wasn't sure if I were the victim or the criminal.

The teddies were arranged as if for a group photograph on the pillow. I couldn't remember having put them there and wondered if they had made a secret pact to be brought back from exile on the shelf to their cosy place on the bed. If they had made a pact with someone, who, if not me? The house was empty.

The cuddly toys wore defiant grins and their glass eyes twinkled in the wintry light as if they knew something I didn't. The teddies, Mr Happy, the Snoopy dog and the rest of the gang were a comfort and sometimes a millstone, a reminder of my life in that bedroom growing up, an insinuation that at sixteen I needed to put childish pleasures behind me. You can get into a pattern of thought that spins in your head like plates on poles. I was sure that if you could break the pattern, you would leave that person with thoughts behind and step into another skin, another version of yourself with different thoughts.

I put the gang back on the shelf in two tiers, tallest in the centre. 'Don't you dare move,' I said.

I glanced at myself in the mirror. My eyes were black holes that had stopped reflecting the light. I had a pain in my stomach and felt dirty after rooting around in the garden shed.

After a mammoth session in the bathroom, I felt better and prepared a meal for Mum when she came home from work. In my contradictory way, I felt unusually confident striding through the kitchen cutting, stirring, rattling pots and pans, heart pounding, fingers tingling.

'I'm going to pack the teddies in a box and put them in the Bird Cage,' I said as she sat down to eat.

'About time,' she replied. 'You'll have a man sharing your bed soon enough.'

I dropped a plate and it broke.

'Mum!'

'You wait and see,' she said. 'You're sixteen, Alice. If you'd only put on a bit of weight you'd be quite pretty.'

'That's the last thing I want,' I told her.

'I was a girl once as well, don't forget. I know these things.'

'You don't know me,' I said.

'Of course I do.'

'Mum, you think you know me. *I* don't know me.'

She sighed and I left her to eat dinner alone. I would read

a lifetime later that the most important thing a family does is to eat together; in our family that almost never happened.

I retreated to the bedroom, trembling. Sex discussions in our house had always been taboo. That's why, when I found Mum and Stephen virtually in the act, it had been so upsetting. I didn't want to know what went on between men and women in the bedroom. The whole subject was disgusting, and when it came up at school – she's having it off with him; she's pregnant; he's gay – the things kids said made me feel so nauseous I clamped earphones over my head, slugged back a shot from the beaker and turned up the volume on the Walkman.

My body was a Pandora's box of aches and pains. When Grandpa died all the ailments came jumping out. I was forever twitching and shaking. I had a persistent sore throat and had difficulty swallowing except when I was taking nips from my illicit cocktail. I was constantly constipated, holding everything in – a disorder that had started when I was two years old. It burned when I passed urine, and my migraines were so severe it felt on occasions as if I were going blind.

When I was running, my route took me down a long straight avenue of denuded trees. The road became a tunnel that narrowed to a void and I ran faster and faster, wondering if I might one day reach the vanishing point.

It felt on these occasions as if I were one of the leaves that had fallen from the trees that winter. My thoughts were tossed about as if on the wind. Just as sometimes I wondered if Grandpa had ever existed, sometimes I wondered if I truly existed myself. As I was running, I could see myself from outside myself: a skinny girl with the flapping shorts and too-big a T-shirt, always watching the other girls at school, a girl in a pink bedroom sitting with a book propped on her knees, the words she was reading entering her mind, some sticking like glue, never to be forgotten, others disappearing instantly. I could remember everything and remember nothing. I would watch a movie and recall every scene as if I had written the script, then watch another movie another day and be unable to recall it at all.

My running shoes had serrated soles and white leather tops. I cleaned them every day. I used a special cream and polished them until they were as shiny as the refrigerator door. I cleaned them first with a brush, then with a yellow cloth, slipping them on, tying the laces with even loops, buffing the toecaps. When I went out, I pressed my jeans with a knife-edge crease that reminded me of the crease in my forgotten Grandpa's trousers. I arranged the teddies on the shelf according to height. When I came home from school, I locked myself in the bathroom, scrubbed myself clean in the bath, took a shower, then scrubbed myself again. Mum would stand outside on the landing, sighing. Father would arrive from work. Mother would tell him to make me come out and he'd knock tentatively on the door not knowing what to say, and knowing, it seemed to me, that it was best to say nothing at all.

When I was running, these obsessions were absorbed in the repetition of motion. I slipped from the silent house at dawn and listened to the sound of my trainers slapping a path along the road, the wintry smell of change in the air, the pounding of my feet in tune to the beat of my heart. My footprints on the damp pavement would fade as the sun rose like a sightless eye over the rooftops, shedding its light across the windows of houses with their secrets and discontent. Cars hissed by on the rain-slicked streets, percussion to the slap, slap, slap of my running shoes.

During this hour in the waking streets I felt at ease, at peace; my body, which I despised, operated like a machine. I was spaced out, the catchphrase my friends at school used to describe their first experiments with marijuana and booze. This buzzword perfectly described a picture in my mind of me, Alice, hovering just below the ceiling like a balloon and looking down at my own small bed where a big man lay heavily on a little girl I couldn't quite see or recognize. It wasn't me. I was spaced out on the ceiling.

I had that same spacey feeling when I cooked for my father, which I still did, though less often. I made omelettes, of course. I cracked a couple of eggs into a bowl, and as I reached for the butter dish, I always had an odd sensation in my hands and arms. My fingers prickled; it didn't feel like me but someone else cutting off a great chunk of greasy butter and putting it into the pan.

I'd add a large amount of salt – I knew what it did to your blood pressure, and I mumbled curses as I whisked the brew. When I poured the slop into the hot butter and shuffled the frying pan over the burner, it didn't look like my hand holding the frying-pan handle and I am sure it was someone else's eyes that watched the eggs bubble and brown. As I dropped two slices of wholemeal bread in the toaster, I would observe myself as if from across the room and, with tingling hands gripping the spatula, folded the omelette so it looked like an apple envelope. My alien hands would flip the omelette on to a plate and I'd spread the remainder of the butter on the toast when the two slices of bread leapt from the toaster.

'Delicious,' he'd say, commenting on the food before even trying it.

While he ate, he retreated into his aura of Brylcreem and aftershave behind the *Daily Mail* and I retreated to the annexe, where I scrubbed mud from the soles of my trainers, creamed the leather uppers, my hands prickling with pins and needles. I had that same prickly feeling when we did home economics at school and felt like a fraud whenever the teacher praised my cooking.

My obsession with larding my father's omelettes, pressing my jeans, eating two sweets but never one or three, my manic cleanliness and all those long showers began to worry Mum and finally she took me to see our GP. Dr Bradshaw explained that I was suffering from Obsessive Compulsive Disorder or OCD; one more ailment to add to the list.

It was useful to have this new label to pin on me, as if in the acronym OCD everything was explained. Next time Clive was home for the holidays he brought a new girlfriend, who made a big show of shrinking from me as she passed me in her mini-skirt. 'Keep away from me, you loony,' she hissed, and my brother just grinned. The girlfriend had a name like Lucy or Emma or Gemma, I can't recall, but I remember wide-spaced blue eyes, a neat little nose, a waterfall of lustrous blonde hair, perfect lips twisted as if seeing me was akin to sucking a lemon.

'Keep away from me, you loony.'

Pretty, confident girls don't know the effect they have on mere mortals, the pain their clever quips inflict. It was easy to dismiss Lucy or Emma or Gemma as a lightweight, but when people keep saying you're crazy, it's almost a self-fulfilling prophecy because you think about it so much it comes to pass. I would stare at myself in the mirror.

'What's wrong with you, Alice? What's wrong?'

I would close my eyes and shake my head, trying to shake out the memories, shuffle the chips in the kaleidoscope into a new pattern. Was I crazy? Was I delusional? I didn't feel I was. And yet why was I seeing this shaky, unclear image of a little girl who looked like me but, in my mind, wasn't me, lying in the pink bedroom with my father's penis in her mouth? It was like watching brief clips and flashbacks of a movie, real but implausible. My father couldn't have done those things. It was impossible. It was my own horrible imagination and I tried all the time to drive these thoughts out of my mind. I ran and starved and washed and studied, eternally trying to suppress the creepy things I couldn't put into words.

Mum and I had become closer since Grandpa died. Death makes you think about life. She was in mourning for her dad, but considering her own future and had let me know in her roundabout way that she was in love with Stephen and, at the appropriate time, planned to leave my father. She was also paying more attention to me.

If I wanted money for a cassette or new trainers, she would open her purse immediately. But I still didn't feel as if she understood me. If I was troubled by a bad dream, or if my hockey team lost a match, important when you are sixteen, she would try to jolly me out of my mood. Just get on with it, she'd say. Go and do your homework. Don't let things get you down. Mum tried to sound like Grandpa, but Grandpa had a contentment, an inner stillness that had not been passed down through his genes to her and most certainly not to me.

She circled my spindly wrists with the thumbs and first fingers of her two hands, she turned my gaunt cheeks to the light, and made the appointment for me to see Dr Bradshaw to try and get to the bottom of what was now being called 'my eating disorder' – a phrase that entered the house vocabulary after gossiping neighbours took note of how thin I had become. Dr Bradshaw recommended Mum made sure I ate regularly, even if I didn't eat much at each sitting. I didn't like the idea of being controlled in this way and reacted by becoming a health-food freak and a vegetarian.

At my next appointment, I met Dr Robinson, who had joined Dr Bradshaw's practice. I would come to call Dr Robinson Dr Bobby or just Bobby, although at that first meeting it was all very formal and I sat there with Mum detailing my eating habits, my obsessive running and washing compulsion. Dr Bobby was young and good-looking, and I was impressed because he had run the London Marathon to raise money for charity. He looked at me for a long while without saying a word and I'm sure I flushed before he finally spoke.

'Tell me, is anything worrying you, Alice?' he asked.

I shook my head.

'Is there anything you haven't told Dr Bradshaw?'

He stared at me with his big brown eyes. I shook my head again and stared down at the scuff on the toes of my trainers.

'You're sure, Alice?'

These words formed in my brain: I think that when I was a little girl my dad used to come to my room and put his willy in my mouth.

But I couldn't say those words. I wasn't sure I believed them. We sat there in silence, my thoughts like pennants waving in the breeze: Dad used to stick his willy in all my openings. Dad used to put spiders on my belly in the garden shed.

It sounded like a blatant lie; something a girl would say to draw attention to herself. The foul-tasting black feeling in my gut was a burning shame. It was as if what had happened to me was my fault. And if it had *not* happened, it was my fault that I had such noxious thoughts. At sixteen, everything is embarrassing. You don't talk about things, not those things. You look away. You giggle and shrug. There was no way I could tell anyone about anything. I sat there in the surgery wishing I were outside in the waiting room playing with the Lego.

Dr Robinson sat gazing at me, and I sat there wishing I were somewhere else. The silence stretched. Mum took my hand, which was nice. The doctor made an appointment for me to see a clinical psychologist the following week. I had already rejected this particular avenue of investigation once, but I didn't want to disappoint the bright young doctor and decided to give it another try.

The appointment was at the Naydon Clinic, where I had been before to see the tall, pale psychologist who had unwittingly turned on the light in the childhood bedroom of my ugly past.

I took the afternoon off school and sat upstairs on the bus eating an apple for lunch and doing breathing exercises. I wanted to present a calm, relaxed Alice to show there was nothing wrong with me. It's impossible to define normal but, whatever it is, that's what I wanted to be, that's the image I tried to show the world.

It had been raining most of the morning. But now the sun had come out. Spring was in the air. The robins were busy in the garden at home. Daffodils filled the grass verges. As I made my way towards the entrance to the clinic I watched a man ripping a parking ticket to shreds. 'Bloody people,' he grumbled, and I remembered Grandpa once saying it was a waste of effort getting angry over the past or the inevitable. I always thought it wasn't so easy to apply.

I entered the clinic through the blue side gate. I knew where to go and listened to the beat of my shoes on the stone corridor. It was a replay of my previous visit. But I didn't remember it in the normal way, more with a sense of déjà vu. Hospitals and the like have that effect on me. The smell of lemon and the whiff of sulphur I would come to associate with hell on earth. You imagine people dying and suffering. Everyone is rushing. You don't know where or why. I could hear the rustle of my school skirt, the echo of my shoes, and suddenly I couldn't decide if this scene belonged to the memory of my last visit, or came from a dream of that visit. It also occurred to me that I could be dreaming at that moment and might wake suddenly and find myself somewhere else.

This had happened to me a couple of times. I would remember sitting in my bedroom studying one moment, and then be walking through the shopping centre with music blasting in my ears the next. It seemed sometimes as if the two parts of my brain, the left and right, were connected by a door that swung open of its own accord between one side and the other.

I looked up left brain–right brain activity, and discovered that the two different hemispheres are responsible for different modes of thinking. The left brain is logical, sequential, analytical, objective, and focuses on the individual parts of things. The right brain is random, intuitive, synthesizing, subjective, and looks at the whole picture. Most people have an inclination towards one side or the other; some are equally at home in both hemispheres. Schools tend to favour left-brain logical thinking, analysis and accuracy, in preference to the right-brain focus on aesthetics, feeling and creativity.

It was difficult for me to work out in which hemisphere I dwelt. I lived totally in my left brain when I studied, but bolted the door behind me as I entered the right brain where I lost all sense of time and logic. My thoughts became irrational, preoccupied and haunted by that malevolent sense of déjà vu – the very sense that struck me like a hammer at three o'clock when I entered the clinician's room and the tall psychologist I'd seen before rose like a long thin shadow and waved me to a chair.

'Ah, Alice, you're here,' she said.

Am I? I wondered.

She introduced me to Dr Jane Purvis, a consultant child psychiatrist, a woman of fifty but girlish in a bright skirt and blouse. She was sitting to one side like a nurse during a gynaecological examination. That's how it felt, as though their questions were probes trying to get inside me. We chatted in the way my parents chatted when we sat down together at Christmas wanting to talk and having nothing to say. Deeply creepy scenes flashed through my head on a daily basis, but I couldn't describe them. I didn't want to try.

The psychologist may have been named Dr Flowers, but that may just be a memory of the flower prints on the wall and the flowers in the vase adding a bit of colour to the small melancholy office. The psychologist looked at her notes and we focused on my anorexia.

'Are you afraid of weight gain, Alice?'

'Not particularly.'

'Do you think you are fat?'

'No, I think I'm thin.'

'Do you weigh your food before you eat it?'

'No.'

'Do you count calories?'

'No.'

'Do you binge eat and then want to vomit?'

I paused. That's a big mistake, of course. You must never pause because that gives the quacks something to ponder, something to scribble on their narrow-lined pads. The truth is I did binge eat, but always with a sense that it wasn't actually me eating but someone or something else – that black thing in my gut – something connected to me but not me. It was that thing that kept me alive.

The questions went on like a game of table tennis – ping pong, ping pong – until the two women, the psychologist and the psychiatrist, decided that whatever it was that was wrong with me, apart from the obvious anorexia, I should see Dr Purvis from then on. I did this throughout the rest of the school year while I worked for my O levels, and through the following year until I was seventeen and no longer fell under her remit.

I begged Mum not to tell a soul I was seeing a psychiatrist. Everyone thought I was strange; I didn't want them to think I was a nutcase as well. In fact now I was undergoing treatment, the topic, in the time-honoured way, was swept under the carpet. Mum made sure I kept my appointments, but didn't ask what took place in Dr Purvis's consulting room.

Father didn't even know about the sessions. Mum didn't talk to him and I certainly didn't tell him. I cooked for him less and less and avoided him more and more. He had grown older, darker, thinner, a stick insect creeping through the house in the same ponderous way as the spiders had crept over my belly in the shed at the bottom of the garden. There was a question that rose into my mouth every time our paths crossed: Did you do bad things to me when I was little?

It was always there, stuck in my throat. I couldn't spit it out. I chewed at it, spun it round in my mouth and it died before it left my lips. We create patterns and repeat them. I do. I went once a week to see Dr Purvis and every week I put the same cassette in my Walkman: *Quadrophenia* by The Who. I'd have the volume on full, as if to say: I don't want to be here.

But I did. After all, I'd made the journey to the clinic. I had brought myself there as if the songs written by Pete Townshend contained the very words and messages I needed to convey to Dr Purvis. Could she see the real me? Who was I? I mean, who exactly? Inside my head lots of people seemed to be barging about. But I'd lost myself and was alone in the crowd trying to find me.

Only as I entered the consulting room did I turn off the

music. First we'd go through the ritual of the weigh-in – obsessively, compulsively, I always weighed exactly six stone. We'd then continue with the ritual chatting over things we had chatted about the previous week and would chat about again the following week.

I was sixteen. I knew I was fucked up. I tried to explain that I felt alone, but I didn't feel alone in the normal sense, in the way that lots of teenagers feel alone. I felt alone in the sense of being separated from the rest of the world, but not alone inside my head. Like the song 'Four Faces', there were other selves in there clawing at the thin veneer of my sanity trying to get out. I was struggling to find out who I was, and couldn't be sure if I was the person sitting opposite Dr Purvis or if I was one of the others at the point of making their first appearance.

CHAPTER 4
The Voices

The first time I heard voices was in my bedroom. Dire Straits was playing softly in the background while I was revising. That's when I heard it.

For your grandpa, to make him feel proud.

The voice erupted into the room. It was as though someone had shouted from close range. I almost jumped out of my skin. I looked round. The door was closed. There was no one there.

Without those, you're shit, girl.

There it was again. I turned off the music and stood beside the bed trembling. I knew exactly what the voice was referring to. It was about taking my O levels. I wanted to do well for a whole number of reasons.

What came next was petrifying.

You're not worthy of anything. You should die.

I switched Dire Straits back on. The song was 'Money For Nothing' and I turned it up to full volume. It made no difference. There were voices bombarding my brain, not one, but two or three, more, a little crowd that had gathered to mock me.

You'd better make your grandpa proud otherwise he'll stop loving you.

Grandpa's gone to heaven, so fat chance you have of seeing him again.

You're going to hell.

I slapped the side of my head and had a strange mental picture of myself as I did it. I looked like a mad person.

'Stop it. Stop it. Stop it. Leave me alone.'

The voices carried on talking to me, at me, about me. And what was terrifying was that the voices were so normal, not freaky or exaggerated, but dark and intimidating. Most of the voices belonged to men, but there were women too; some of the voices were loud, as if close by, others were distant, separate; they came together like a gang, or faded away as if they were talking to each other.

I grabbed an armful of teddies and buried myself under the pillow. The voices babbled on. I wasn't listening. I sang Mark Knopfler's lyrics to myself, competing with the voices until they grew silent. I was covered in sweat and totally exhausted. My head was pounding. I fell into a fitful sleep and saw in my dreams flickering shadows and small children.

It was still dark when I woke. I have never slept well without drugs throughout my life. I dressed in my jogging kit and laced my trainers in precise loops. The green numbers on the digital clock clicked to 5:00 as I crept down the stairs and set off running through the empty streets.

I sang as I ran the ten-mile route, listening for voices and feeling grateful they had gone.

It was the beginning of a lifetime of accommodation and negotiation with the voices. Over the coming months while I took my exams, the voices were intermittent, sometimes murmuring incoherently, sometimes shouting.

Was my brain tricking me into believing I was hearing voices that weren't really there?

No. The voices were real. They were there. I could distinguish one from another. The voices came from outside my head, not inside. When they first appeared I was sure that other people must hear them too, and became paranoid when I discovered they didn't.

Among the voices was the harsh, dominant tones of someone who became known as 'the Professor'. I didn't name him. He materialized with that name, perhaps because *he* thought he had superior knowledge and intellect. The Professor scolded me and encouraged me to work hard for Grandpa. Not that I needed to be told. No one was more aware than me that I had serious problems. Achievement was one way to prove that even if I was weird, I wasn't an idiot.

Dr Purvis would study me at our weekly meetings with her big girlish eyes and say, 'There is something else, Alice, something you're not telling me.'

I would avoid responding. I would be thinking: That was a well-phrased probe. You almost caught me there. I would examine her bright skirts and tops. I would gaze into her eyes. They were shiny behind big glasses that she was forever putting on and taking off, as if this action was a generator reviving a dead battery that would suddenly produce in me a burst of lost memory and confession.

The glasses went up and down, up and down, the reflection making stars of light that danced over the dim walls. She wore green tops with sunflower-patterned skirts, red tops with orange skirts, a pale-blue top the colour of her eyes with a navy-blue skirt like the sky just before it rains. I knew Jane Purvis's wardrobe as well as she did, but I never let her into my own. There was no room in there, not with all the skeletons.

I was so busy avoiding telling Dr Purvis that I heard voices that when one day she asked about my father, the session took a whole new course I had no control over.

'Tell me about your father, Alice.'

'My father?'

46

'Yes. You never talk about him.'

'Oh, he's frightfully important, at least that's what he thinks,' I said.

'He's a solicitor?' she asked

'And a golfer,' I replied.

'Do you get on well?'

'I rarely see him. He's a very busy man.'

'Did you get on well when you were a child?' she continued.

'Suppose so.'

'He loved you?'

'What? Yes, course . . .'

She leaned forward and lowered her glasses. 'Did he ever abuse you in any way, Alice?'

The question came right out of left field and I almost fell off the chair. I didn't answer. I didn't know what to say. Dr Purvis persisted.

'Did he abuse you?'

'No. No, he did not. I don't know why you're saying these things.'

I felt caught, tricked, trapped. I wanted to tell her about my dreams, the man coming night after night to my room, but the words stuck in my throat. If it were true, if that man, who could only have been my father, did come to my room, why couldn't I remember? And if it wasn't true, why did I have these things in my head? Was I a bad person? A promiscuous child? Was it all my fault?

All the things I should have discussed with Dr Purvis I kept inside me. I was too ashamed to talk about what may or may not have happened at night in my bedroom. I thought, too, if I told her or anyone about the voices, if I gave them too much attention, they would gain power and confidence. They would become the soundtrack to the visions that had been playing inside my head for as long as I could recall. I had dealt with the video footage in my own way. Now, I would do battle with the voices.

I would leave the consulting room, listen to my shoes drumming along the corridor and stand at the bus stop feeling alone and depressed. At sixteen, you want to be like everyone else. I felt different, separated, a freak. I was pretending, always pretending, that everything was all right when Mr Keating, my head of year, Dr Purvis, my friends and my mother knew otherwise. Not many people at sixteen except in American movies have a psychiatrist. It didn't make me feel privileged but alienated and despondent.

I concentrated on running, blending cocktails, reading until my retinas were on fire, filling my mind with the words and thoughts of authors. I never knew when the voices would come, what they would say, or how long they would remain chattering in my head. I felt like a doorman at a night club who had lost control and was no longer able to regulate who entered and who stayed in my brain. If I let down my guard, they would all come rushing in and start their bullshit.

You're worthless.

You think good grades will make it better.

It won't, you stupid bitch.

You may as well die.

Go on. Go on. I dare you. Do it now. Do it now. You want to die.

I remember in an exam, history probably, I paused for a moment to recall a date and the Professor piped up.

You think you're going to get it right. You'll never get it right.

I slapped the side of my head. 'Not now. Go away,' I hissed.

'Shush,' said the invigilating teacher.

The kids round me raised their eyebrows and shook their heads. It's only Alice! My classmates probably thought I was seeking attention and had no idea that was the last thing I wanted. It is a constant struggle to act as though everything is swimming along smoothly when it isn't. I was living a lie, to the world, to myself. At first glance I must have appeared to be the lucky girl with the nice family in the pretty house with robins in the garden. That was the image, not the truth. It was never the truth. We look at other people and imagine we know them. We don't know them. We can't know them. Everyone is a mystery. I was a mystery to myself.

Every day I felt like quitting my O levels, although it wasn't actually me feeling like that, the me that is me – Alice. It was another part of me, some demon hopping mischievously from my left brain to my right.

Give up. Give up. Do everyone a favour. Top yourself, Alice.

The Professor and his cohorts kept up the hubbub and I ignored them.

'Shut up. Shut up. Shut up. Go away. Leave me alone.'

I refused to listen. I ran, I binged, I starved and I carried on working with a crazed passion until Mum in a state of panic bribed me to calm down by booking a week's holiday for the two of us in Venice in July. I finished my nine O levels and walked out of the gate at Dane Hall on the last day of term with a spring in my step. I'd beaten them.

Mum was still upset by Grandpa's death and the plan was for us to spend some quality time together while she recovered, as she put it, her *joie de vivre*. What she was in fact doing was making final preparations to leave my father. She hesitantly broached the subject one morning as we sat down to breakfast overlooking the gondolas gliding by on the Grand Canal.

'I don't know if I can go on much longer in that house,' she said.

'You mean with Dad?'

She nodded.

'Nor do I,' I replied, and her lips puckered at the corners.

'We'll get a flat or something,' she continued. 'Things will be better, don't you think?'

'Mum, the day you leave will be the best day's work you've ever done.'

She looked relieved and her face glowed in the morning light. The anxiety had superimposed a mask on her features but now her true face appeared. My hands were tingling, trembling. It felt strange being so honest. It was a good feeling. Mum took a grip on my fingers across the white linen tablecloth and the Italian waiter smiled brightly as he poured coffee from a silver pot.

Venice was the perfect setting for this brief scene and the ideal choice for our holiday. It was the first time we had gone away, just the two of us, and I enjoyed showing off my knowledge as we toured the museums and galleries.

When I travelled, I felt as if I were a different person. *Really* a different person. The Alice at home was always fretting over something. The Alice overseas could open her lungs and breathe. The voices grew distant. Alice could read a book without having to finish exactly at the end of a chapter. Adventurer Alice forgot the meaning of words like insomina and nightmare. She strode through the shifting tide of grey pigeons on Piazza San Marco towards the Basilica where the bells were ringing in the *campanile*. With its palaces and art galleries, its bridges and silvery light, Venice for me and this self-confident Alice was the ideal size for a city – small enough to explore on foot and big enough that you might run into a surprise when you turned the next corner.

Soon after we returned from Italy, I went to visit the Timmins – relatives on my maternal side – who lived in Switzerland. For two weeks while I was their guest, I made a bold attempt at learning German and absorbed all the history and architectural peculiarities of Zurich. I also ate chocolate until I was sick and bought a cuckoo clock.

It was agreed that I had been 'spoilt rotten' by all these holidays and as soon as I came home from Switzerland I got a job at the greyhound track three nights a week collecting empty glasses and cleaning tables. I'd stop to watch the races, the dogs lining up in their coats of many colours before chasing without ever catching the electric hare, which reminded me of me chasing my shadow when I ran.

As a result of my running obsession I was now clocking up good times and was in training for the Brum Fun Run, the annual half-marathon organized by Birmingham City Council. Running fast for long distances creates a feeling of well-being. The release of endorphins works as a natural painkiller and the buzz gave me the nerve to extend my route down the secluded lane through woodland close to our house.

I was scared of this lane and had avoided it for years. Now I sprinted below the overhanging trees, testing my courage.

Images flashed into my brain, bright and clear. What I saw was a summer's day when my father's friend, the man who liked to show off his flash cars and who had touched my minute breasts when I was fourteen, had come to the house in a new Rolls-Royce Cabriolet. It was white and the open top was down.

Mother was upstairs in her room at the back of the house. In the drive playing there was a little girl in a skirt and a top who looked about seven. When the man asked if she wanted to go for a ride in his car, naturally she said yes and jumped in. The other man, my dad, closed the door and the man drove out of the drive, turned left and then directly right, and stopped in the secluded lane next to the woods.

He put his arm round the girl. 'Come on, give us a kiss,' he said.

He slipped his hand into her panties and wormed his finger up inside her. 'You like that, don't you?' he added, and pushed his tongue into her mouth.

She didn't stop him. She didn't struggle. She didn't object. This was normal. This man had done this to her before. She couldn't remember where or when, but had a foggy recollection of a big building that looked like a castle and a flight of steps going down into the dungeon where naked children and clothed adults moved among the shifting shadows.

'Lift your bottom,' he said and as I ran along the avenue I could see in my mind's eye that little girl lifting her bottom so he could pull down her panties.

'There, isn't that better?'

He eased her legs apart, wiggled his finger into her front botty and slid his tongue back into her mouth.

The car was parked in the shade of a tall tree, the light through the leaves making it look as if it was raining chips of glass. The man was strong. He had hairy arms and hair on the backs of his fingers. The little girl didn't know why the man had taken off her panties, but they always did that. She imagined that this was what mummies and daddies did. She didn't like it, but it made her feel special being with this important man in his big car.

'Does that feel nice?'

She nodded and smiled her smile. It didn't feel nice. It hurt. But she wanted it to feel nice. She wanted it to feel nice for Daddy's friend. She gazed up through the high branches of the tree and when she screwed up her eyes she could see fairies on transparent wings darting through the rays of sunshine.

The kissing and the wiggling stopped. She stood up on the seat and the man held her panties for her to step into. He pulled them up and she sat down again. He kissed his fingertip and touched it to her lips.

'You're a real smasher, Alice, you know that,' he said.

She grinned. He lowered his voice. 'It's our little secret.'

The engine boomed when the car started and it was like floating on air as they completed the circle and drove back to the house.

Mother stood on the drive, hands on hips. Father was in shadow in the porch.

'What the hell's going on?' she demanded.

'We just went for a ride, Jenny. Come and take a look at my new car,' the man replied.

Mum hauled the girl out of the front seat and whisked her into the house.

'Don't go near that man again,' she said. 'I don't like him.'

She was red-faced, her teeth clenched. She put the girl down roughly and she went scampering upstairs to hide in the Bird Cage.

The little girl didn't know what she had done to upset her mother, but whatever it was, she was sure it was her fault. She had made her angry. She didn't want to make it worse by making the man angry as well. That would infuriate Daddy. 'It's our secret,' the man had said. You have to keep secrets. If Daddy and other men wanted to touch and kiss that little girl it would make Mummy angry. She wasn't exactly sure why, but she knew Mummy must never know.

As I sprinted along below the trees, I had total recall of the scene in the white Rolls-Royce, the images crossing like a recording from the right brain to the left. The details were clear, but the incident seemed fantastical, like the memory of a bad dream or a television programme.

I found it difficult to identify with the little girl sitting in the leather seat in that car. I could visualize her. I could see what was happening through her eyes: the man telling her to lift her bottom so he could take off her panties; the sway of the branches above the open car, the shifting light of fairy glimmers. I was observing the little girl as if I were behind a screen watching secretly. The little girl was not an illusion, an apparition; she was not an imaginary friend. I would rather have enjoyed having an imaginary friend, but I never had one. The girl in that car was not imaginary. She was very real. I could see her, she looked like me, and yet I was certain that little girl *wasn't* me.

But if it wasn't me, who was it?

And why did I carry this revolting memory? I hated and despised thinking about sex, but it was everywhere. By the time I left school, most of the girls had acquired a boyfriend and talked incessantly about how they kissed and how far they intended to go, the topic making me turn pink with embarrassment.

Do you fancy . . . Mark or Gary or Greg?

No, I did not fancy . . . Mark or Gary or Greg. But I had to play the game in order to fit in with the crowd. My job at the dog track gave me some extra money, but it was more important as a way of getting out and doing normal things: wandering round the shops, talking about boy bands, going to the pub on a Friday night when I would meet my underage friends and drink a lager, which had about as much effect on me as a glass of milk.

My constant struggle was to be normal. Not that I had any idea what normal meant. A girl of sixteen from my class at school went to a party in a drop-dead sexy dress. She drank half a bottle of vodka and went to bed with two boys at the same time because she'd always fancied a threesome. Was that normal? Another girl left school after taking her O levels and moved in with a teacher twenty-five years older than her. Was that normal? A girl who lived close to us named Hasna went to visit her relations in Pakistan that summer and found herself married to the brother of her father. Was that normal?

If I was set an essay on Friday, I'd spend three hours on Saturday morning in the library. Was that normal?

I didn't know.

What I did know was that I felt less prone to depression and more normal walking through Venice or staring out over the lake in Zurich. At home I wrestled continually with my moods. The black thing inside me gnawed like a rat at my self-esteem and self-confidence. I felt there was a happy person inside me too, who wanted to enjoy life, to be normal, but my feelings of self-loathing and the deep distrust I had towards my father wouldn't allow that sunny person to come out.

When the black thing had an iron grip on me, I couldn't even look at my father: Did you do bad things to me when I was little?

Like a line from a song stuck in your brain, the words ran through my head and never once came out of my mouth. Not that I needed to say what was in my mind. I was sure Father could read my thoughts in my moods, in the blank, dead stare of my eyes.

It was hardly surprising that there was always an atmosphere of strain and awkwardness in the house, and the blame was always mine: Alice and her moods, Alice and her anorexia; Alice and her low self-esteem; Alice and her inescapable feelings of loss and emptiness.

I ran the Fun Run half-marathon that year in 1 hour 40 minutes, clipping twelve minutes off my best time, then carried on training, though for what I wasn't sure. I played my music loud enough to terrify the voices babbling away in my head. I studied everything: French, English literature, history, dates, facts, statistics, all that left-brain sensible stuff, busy, busy, busy, filling my time with action and activity.

But the black thing was always there: an unwavering sense of doom and foreboding, an all-consuming misery like a whirlpool sucking me into a vortex where everything was lost, pointless, hopeless. It felt as if I were in the midst of a fog. It clung to me like a shroud, bending my shoulders, weighing me down.

By the end of the summer, Mother had come through the worst of her grief over Grandpa and rediscovered her lost *joie de vivre*. I was still unable to grieve. Grandpa had given me a sense of balance. While he had been alive, I had been a child still – safe, protected, embraced. Accepting that he was gone was accepting that I had grown up, that I should sling Snoopy and Mr Happy in the bin bag for Oxfam and go out to parties half naked. Rather than mourn Grandpa, I stacked all my memories in a neat pile and filed them away on a high shelf in a dark corner of my brain. I was afraid that if I took that file down and looked at it too closely, I would slip so deeply into that depressive vortex I would never escape.

When the black thing was at its worst, when the illicit cocktails and the ten-mile runs stopped working, I would feel numb as if dead to the world. I moved unconsciously, with heavy limbs, like a zombie from a horror film. I felt a pain so fierce and persistent deep inside me, I was tempted to take the chopping knife in the kitchen and cut the black thing out. I would lie on my bed staring at the ceiling thinking about that knife and using all my limited powers of self-control to stop myself from going downstairs to get it.

When sleep came, I would dream bad dreams. Not the baby and the big man with a cigarette-lighter dream. Another dream. The castle dream.

A little girl of about six who looks like me, but isn't me, is happy as she steps out of the car with her daddy. They enter the castle and go down the steps to the dungeon where people move like shadows in the glow of burning candles. There are carpets and funny pictures on the walls. Some of the people wear hoods and robes. Sometimes they chant in droning voices that make the little girl afraid. There are other children, some of them without any clothes on. There is an altar like the altar in nearby St Mildred's Church. The children take turns lying on that altar so the people, mostly men, but a few women, can kiss and lick their private parts. The daddy holds the hand of the little girl tightly. She looks up at him and he smiles. The little girl likes going out with her daddy.

I did want to tell Dr Purvis these dreams but I didn't want her to think I was crazy, and so kept them to myself. The psychiatrist was wiser than I appreciated at the time; sixteen-year-olds imagine they are cleverer than they really are. Dr Purvis knew I had suffered psychological damage as a child, that's why she kept making a fresh appointment week after week. But I was unable to give her the tools and clues to find out exactly what had happened.

She attempted to introduce what she called a 'Freudian element.' In other words sex.

'Have you ever seen or imagined your parents having sex?'

'No.'

'Have you ever imagined replacing your mother in this act?'

My jaw dropped and I just stared.

'When you think back, what do you remember about your parents?'

'I remember sitting at the top of the stairs looking through the banisters while they shouted at each other.'

'What did they shout about?'

'I'm not sure, but I always thought it was about me, or it was my fault.'

'It was never your brother's fault?'

'No. Always my fault.'

'Had you been naughty?'

'I don't think I was ever naughty.'

'You wanted to be a good girl, Alice?'

No reply.

I'd be thinking, Ha ha, Jane, you almost tripped me up. It was a game. There were things Dr Purvis had to know if she were going to deal with my problem (whatever it might be), and as a teenager I played the game to win and told her as little as possible.

My reaction to the questions wasn't always the same. It depended on my mood, my mood not exactly describing how I felt, but what characteristic happened to be dominant at that moment. I could be the timid six-year-old going down those steps into the dungeon. I could be outgoing and confident, when I was cooking and at other times too: running on sunny days, meeting my friend Karen in the shopping centre and buying a new cassette, visiting Grandma and remembering Grandpa telling his marvellous stories. On those Sunday afternoons after Grandpa died, I didn't think of Grandpa as being dead, just not there.

My mood would be stable. Then, for no apparent reason, I would feel a change come over me and I didn't know why or what instigated the change. It was like a cloud passing over the sun, or a song on a cassette slipping from one track to another unexpectedly. I told Dr Purvis once that I felt like The Incredible Hulk from the TV show, popular at that time. It was the story of a man with a broken memory who metamorphoses under stress from a normal person into a big green monster. I turned from being a normal girl soon to start sixth-form college into a small child lying curled on the bed sobbing in a lake of tears.

'What's wrong, Alice?' asks Mum.

I don't answer. I don't know. I am not Alice.

Today I'm Alice

There is in my fractured memory the vague recollection of my once telling Dr Purvis that I had an identity crisis. She was wearing a fitted blue blouse with pink stripes. I remember that blouse. It was one of her favourites. She noted down what I had said and returned to her primal act fixation.

We talked about the girl from school who'd fancied a threesome; the girl living with the older man; the girl forced to marry her uncle. All psychological and psychiatric problems seemed to be grounded in the sexual. Sex was in the air like an overpowering scent and its whiff just made me feel miserable.

'You don't like talking about these things, do you, Alice?'

'No, I don't.'

'Why do you think that is?'

'You're the psychiatrist.'

'That doesn't answer my question.'

'What was the question?'

Ping pong. Ping pong.

With Dr Purvis I was usually defensive. I had grown up learning not to talk about personal things. Now I had the opportunity to start sorting out my problems, I let it slip away in a miasma of obscurity and half-truths.

I would sit upstairs on the bus going home from the clinic, look out of the window and feel disconnected from everyone and everything. The more time you spend on your own, the more isolated you feel, and the more difficult it becomes to reconnect. During this black period, you start chewing over all the things that are making you feel isolated and depressed. The more you feel isolated and depressed, the more isolated and depressed you become. You start imagining slights where they don't exist. When you feel bad, you look at other people and they seem nasty and uncaring. If you look for good things in people, as Grandpa always did, then you feel good about yourself. I knew this. I had read hundreds of books in the library. But when you feel depressed you look only at the dark side of everyone and everything. You just can't help it.

Depression is your own worst enemy. After a depressed, sleepless, alcohol-fuelled phase, I would get a C for a piece of homework. This would make me more depressed, and the depression stopped me going back to the assignment to revise for the next test. You think: Why? Why? Why? You take another slug of booze and do nothing. It's mind-numbing, and totally exhausting. Running gives you energy. Depression sucks it out of you. If time is the essence of life, I was squandering mine by feeling depressed.

CHAPTER 5
Tricks of Time

My O level results arrived in a stiff manila envelope at seven in the morning. When I saw it lying on the doormat my throat went dry and my hands turned clammy. I carried the envelope upstairs like a relic from an Egyptian tomb and placed it on the shelf with the teddies to see if they had any idea what was inside. Not a murmur. They were useless.

I took the envelope away from them, went back downstairs and out into the garden. It had rained overnight and the flowers looked sad and wounded. I sat under the holly trees and watched a line of ants marching along in file. I thought it must be quite nice being an ant and knowing what was expected of you and what to do to meet everyone's approval.

My dressing gown grew damp as I sat on the grass. I went to look at the shed, a ruin riddled with bad memories just as the door and window frames were riddled with rot. One of the windows had broken and through the gap in the glass I could see spiders' webs clinging to the ceiling and walls, a fragile scaffolding holding the shed together.

Going back through the annexe into the kitchen, I shook the envelope as I sometimes shook my head to rearrange the contents. I said a prayer, a bit cheeky as I wasn't sure if I was a believer. The grades were already cast in stone so it was too late to call upon Providence to change them. The row of knives on the magnetic rack were glinting like smiles. I reached for the big carver, slit open the envelope and tipped out two sheets of paper. I closed my eyes, held my breath and unfolded the sheets as I opened my eyes again.

I had passed my O levels, mainly with As and Bs, and got one of the best results in my year at Dane Hall. I showed Mum the list. She hugged me, which was rare, and said how proud she was, but for me the results were personal, a vindication of something, I wasn't sure what, but I had proved myself to myself.

I listened for the voices. The Professor and his gang were silent.

There, that showed you!

I grabbed my bike and as I cycled along the street I had the sensation that I was seeing everything for the first time: houses I didn't know; a yellow Lotus in a drive being cleaned by a woman in a bikini – a sight unseen in our neighbourhood. When I jogged I had tunnel vision, focusing on the road ahead, at that dot on the horizon. Now, I could see beyond myself. I could smell the trees, heavy with the weight of summer; I gazed up long drives at the houses in their havens of greenery.

In a few minutes, I passed St Mildred's, my junior school. Mum had taken me there by car when I was little but as soon as I was eight I could walk home on my own in safety. I remembered my uniforms, a checked blue and white dress with a straw hat in summer; a navy skirt and blazer with a badge that showed St Mildred in a circle of light in winter.

As I turned left away from my old primary school, I could see Dane Hall in the distance. It only occurred to me now that I would never enter that gate again. I was going to miss the routine, the familiarity, the sense of being one among many, like ants, in our matching uniforms. My teachers and classmates had been tolerant of my moods: happy Alice a friend to everyone, sulky Alice not speaking. No one ever knew who I was going to be. I didn't know. My moods could change like the flick of a switch from light to utter darkness.

The bicycle zipped along with its own mysterious objective and I found myself in that secluded track where my father's friend had taken that little girl in his Rolls-Royce.

The pedals turned faster and faster. I was trying to work up a sweat, get that endorphin rush, but once one bad vision entered my thoughts, it set off others, each separate but indivisible, an unending sequence of self-torture and torment that had the odd quality of seeming unreal and hyper real at the same time.

I was back suddenly in the garden on another summer's day when the inflatable paddling pool had been filled with the hose. I could see a little girl enjoying the feel of the sun on her bare skin and the contrasting sensations of jumping in and out of the cold water. Daddy scooped her up in his arms and took her into the shed where the blue plastic sheet that covered the blades on the lawn mower had been laid over the surface of the bench. He sat her down and reached for the jam jars with holes in the lids.

It was that game again. He liked this game, and that day there was a new twist. He lifted her up from under her arms, pulled at her knicker elastic and ran her panties down her legs.

'Look what you've done, you've made them all wet,' he said.

He was smiling. He was only playing. She was about four, a little naked girl who sat back down on that plastic sheet and watched as Daddy unscrewed the lid on one of the jars and poured the spiders over her belly. They crawled over her tummy, across her vagina, down the insides of her legs.

'Don't move.'

She didn't move. She screwed up her fingers. She was trembling.

Then she relaxed. The trembling stopped. Her fingers straightened.

Daddy smiled and the little girl sitting on the blue sheet of plastic smiled back.

I could recall this scene with complete clarity that day as I pedalled along the lane beneath the mature trees. The little girl sitting there with her legs apart allowing the three spiders to crawl over her belly, over her private parts, down her legs, over the plastic sheet. She was observing the spiders and I was observing her from a magic carpet hovering just below the ceiling. There used to be a TV show called *The Phoenix and the Magic Carpet*. I knew all about magic carpets, I was on one at that second with a sense of floating free in the warm air far removed from the little girl watching the spiders.

I could remember all the details – the colours, the smell of cut grass. The blue sheet had a dark-green stain across one corner. The jars on the shelf and the chisels and screwdrivers on the wall were shiny in the beam of light that came in through the open door. The little girl had muddy feet. Her pink panties were on the back of the bench next to the empty jam jar where the spiders lived. Her daddy was watching, a big dark man with greasy black hair and a bald spot.

When the spiders ran away to hide, he ran his fingers like spiders legs over her bare skin. He slipped the tip of his finger into the cleft of her front botty.

'Does that tickle?'

She smiles and nods her head up and down.

He looks through the open door into the empty garden. He lifts the little girl's bottom, bends his head to wet her vagina and worms his tongue inside her. I can see it all from my magic carpet: Daddy's head nodding like a giant bird, the little girl with her legs resting on his shoulders as she gazes up at the fairy dust dancing in the sunlight.

My memory of that scene was perfectly clear but disconnected from me. It had been the other little girl in the garden shed that day, so why was it me, Alice, as I rode along on my bike, who felt a chill run through my bones. My stomach turned with bile, and the sensation I had then, all those years ago, I have right now, at this second.

Then, as now, I was able to analyse these scenes with the detachment that appeared at times when I didn't feel like 'me', – the girl who heard voices – but another facet of myself, the 'me' who cooked and drank wine and sang along to the songs of The Who and Pink Floyd.

I concentrated on that air of detachment. I left the secluded lane behind me and, as I reached the open land beyond, I put the memories of what had happened to that other little girl out of my mind and focused on feeling the simple happiness of a sixteen-year-old with the future before her. I had passed nine O levels. Grandpa would be proud.

In September, I started my A levels at the sixth-form college, a new, six-storey building where you didn't have to wear a uniform. I climbed into a pair of jeans and didn't put on a skirt again for about five years. I stuck close to Lisa Wainwright from Dane Hall as we explored the long corridors and bewildering flights of stairs.

I decided to study psychology and sociology, as well as taking two more O levels, in human biology, and psychology and child development. I only chose these subjects because they seemed interesting. It didn't occur to me at the time that I was delving into the human mind and body in search of something more fundamental than a pure thirst for knowledge. The O levels had been the first real test of our academic potential and the results had given me a boost in confidence. I knew there would be ups and downs, days of euphoria and depression; I didn't know *me* that well, but I knew me well enough to feel, in the autumn of 1985, that I had wasted too much time being moody, and resolved to make an effort to fit in.

When I was five years old, Mum had asked me if she should leave Father. After a decade or so of indecision, circumstances arranged themselves so that she could finally walk out as the injured party.

My parents had, for as long as I could remember, always shouted at each other and slammed doors as they marched off in a huff. When I was little, I had assumed it was my fault. Now they rowed over money, and I felt free from blame and totally unmoved as their voices rose up the stairwell.

One day, Mum searched for a bank statement in Dad's room and in the sock drawer came across some used condoms and contact magazines in which prostitutes advertised their services, some of which had been circled with comments along the side. My father had clearly been to see these women but denied everything. In fact, he came to my room and pleaded with me to intercede with Mother – for my sake, for the sake of the family. He had done nothing wrong. It was all a misunderstanding. Tears trickled down his sunken cheeks and I couldn't help feeling a vague sense of triumph. A weight lifted from my bent shoulders and I discerned an exaggerated row of smiles forming across the faces of the teddies lined up on the shelf behind him.

Mum packed her bags and moved into an unassuming semi in a part of town where neighbours seldom said good morning and few posh cars stood on the driveways. With

Clive at uni, I went with Mum, leaving Dad behind like Dracula brooding in his castle.

Stephen had already left his wife and lived in a flat close by. He came every evening and changed into overalls. While my father drove by night after night in his car watching the house, Stephen helped Mum with the decorating. I got into the habit of preparing dinner, listening as Mum and Stephen giggled like a pair of kids. I liked Stephen. He made Mum happy. He made me happy.

When I was cooking I enjoyed a sense of being 'out' of myself. The action of dicing vegetables and warming oil made my hands tingle and my thoughts switch to a different hemisphere, right brain rather than left, or left rather than right. In my mind there were many rooms and, just as I still got lost in the labyrinth of corridors at college, I often found myself lost, with a sense of déjà vu, in some obscure part of my cerebral cortex, the part of the brain that plays a key role in perceptual awareness, attention and memory. Everything I had lived through or imagined or dreamed appeared to have been backed up on a video clip and then scattered among those alien rooms. I could stumble into any number of scenes, from the horrifically sexual, horror-movie sequences that were crude and painful, to visualizing Grandpa polishing his shoes.

Mum and Stephen always had wine with dinner. I would open a bottle, to allow it to breathe, and pour myself a glass. I tried to analyse myself as I did this. I didn't like the taste of wine and would never at other times have dreamed of drinking the stuff. I drank hard liquor when I was depressed, but I was never depressed cooking. I sipped the wine as I prepared the food with a feeling of self-assurance. I felt at ease, but I didn't exactly feel myself, me, Alice.

'Not drinking now, are you?' Stephen said the first time he saw me.

'No, Stephen, it's all in your mind.'

He laughed as he washed out his brushes.

'Not there, for heaven's sake, do it outside, I'm just about to serve dinner.'

I sounded like my mother.

We sat down to eat together. We even talked. The odd sensation I had while cooking would often last through the meal, then dissolve as I climbed the stairs. I would enter my room and discover the homework books I had left on the bed had disappeared into my backpack. I'd look inside my books and be shocked to find that the homework had been done. Sometimes it had been done well, at others it was slapdash, the writing careless, my own handwriting but scrawled across the page.

As I read the work through, I would get the creepy feeling that someone was watching me. I would turn quickly, trying to catch them out, but the door would be closed. There was never anyone there. Just me. My throat would turn dry. My shoulders would feel numb. The tic in my neck would start dancing as if an insect was burrowing beneath the surface of the skin. The symptoms would intensify into migraines that lasted for days and did not respond to treatment or drugs. The attack would come like a sudden storm, blow itself out of its own accord or unexpectedly vanish.

Objects repeatedly went missing: a favourite pen, a cassette, money. They usually turned up, although once the money had gone it had gone for ever and I would find in the chest of drawers a T-shirt I didn't remember buying, a Depeche Mode cassette I didn't like, a box of sketching pencils, some Lego.

At first, when things went missing I thought it was Stephen teasing me. But I quickly realized that it wasn't Stephen and decided to add the comings and goings of my property to the list of things I pushed to the back of my mind to avoid thinking about.

My bedroom in the new house was smaller than my old one. There was no room for all the things I had brought with me and the excess remained in bin liners stacked against the wall. One day, Mum noticed the bags had gone.

'You finally managed to get rid of all that old junk,' she said.

Had I?

I didn't remember, and thought it odd because Alice is a hoarder. I must have taken the bags to the charity shop, but had no recollection of doing so. I became skilled at covering my tracks, filling in the blanks. Sometimes the blanks were never filled. At other times, I would recall places where I had been or things I had done as if from a dream, which made the playback of my father and other men abusing me seem even less real, fantasies conjured up from my imagination not my memory. Perhaps somebody else's memory. I didn't think of myself as having mental-health problems. You don't at sixteen. I thought of myself as being special, highly strung, moody.

The depression I had suffered during my O levels had retreated. During those months it had often felt as if I were floating through life on that magic carpet, not living, just getting through it. It was better in the new house away from Father and, just as I accommodated the periodic interruption by the Professor & Co., I treated these blank spells and tricks of time as the quirks of the doppelganger Alice with the damaged infancy, a girl connected to me but not the me posing in new Levi's and a Che Guevara T-shirt before the mirror inside the wardrobe door.

I had a bizarre rapport with this mirror and spent a lot of time gazing into the glass to see who was there. Sometimes it looked like me. At other times, I could see someone similar but different in the reflection. A few times, I caught the switch in mid-stare, my expression re-forming like melting rubber, the creases and features of my face softening or hardening until the mutation was complete. Jekyll to Hyde, or Hyde to Jekyll. I felt my inner core change at the same time. I would feel more confident or less confident; mature or childlike; freezing cold or sticky hot, a state that would drive Mum mad as I escaped to the bathroom where I would remain for two hours scrubbing my skin until it was raw.

The change was triggered by different emotions: on hearing a particular piece of music; the sight of my father, the smell of his brand of aftershave. I would pick up a book with the certainty that I had not read it before and hear the words as I read them like an echo inside my head. Like Alice in the Lewis Carroll story, I slipped into the depths of the looking glass and couldn't be sure if it was me standing there or an impostor, a lookalike.

I felt fully awake most of the time, but sometimes while I was awake it felt as if I were dreaming. In this dream state I didn't feel like me, the real me. I felt numb. My fingers prickled. My eyes in the mirror's reflection were glazed like the eyes of a mannequin in a shop window, my colour, my shape, but without light or focus. These changes were described by Dr Purvis as mood swings and by Mother as moods, but I knew better. All teenagers are moody when it suits them. My switches could take place when I was alone, transforming me from a bright sixteen-year-old doing her homework into a sobbing child curled on the bed staring at the wall.

The weeping fit would pass and I would drag myself back to the mirror expecting to see a child version of myself. 'Who are you?' I'd ask. I could hear the words; it sounded like me but it wasn't me. I'd watch my lips moving and say it again, 'Who are you?'

Mercifully, the voices didn't use this as an excuse to pass an opinion. They remained quiet for the most part through the two years of my A levels. When the voices returned it was like a dog barking in a neighbour's house, audible but external. I paid more attention to the intonation than the words, although when they were clear they kept up their persecutory invective.

Kill yourself, Alice.

Nobody likes you.

Do the world a favour and top yourself.

The return of the voices would end in a migraine that made my whole body throb. I could do nothing except lie in a blacked-out room waiting for the voices to get infected by the pains in my head and clear off.

Knowing I was different with my OCD, anorexia and the voices that no one else seemed to hear made me feel isolated, disconnected. I took everything too seriously. I analysed things to death. I turned every word, and the intonation of every word over in my mind trying to decide exactly what it meant, whether there was a subtext or an implied criticism. I tried to recall the expressions on people's faces, how those expressions changed, what they meant, whether what they said and the look on their faces matched and were therefore genuine, or whether it was a sham, the kind word touched by irony or sarcasm, the smile that means pity.

When people looked at me closely could they see the little girl in my head, being abused in those pornographic clips projected behind my eyes?

That is what I would often be thinking and such thoughts ate away at the façade of self-confidence I was constantly raising and repairing. I needed to get As in essays. I needed to run like the wind to hold back the creeping tides of depression waiting to drown me in feelings of despair and self-hatred.

A bad day – seeing my father; a C for an essay; a cruel word from the voices – would send me into a downward spiral that could last for a week. These were lost days when I would retreat into the routine of starving, binging, reading into the wee hours, running until the streets jangled with the throb of my trainers. Ten miles was a breeze. I could do a half-marathon after college and still cook dinner before Stephen arrived with a fresh tin of paint. Next stop: 26 miles 385 yards, the distance the Greek soldier Pheidippides ran without stopping from Marathon to Athens to announce that the Persians had been defeated. He burst into the Senate and exclaimed, 'We have won!' Then he dropped down dead as a doornail.

Dr Purvis seemed impressed that I was training for the marathon and saw this as a good sign. I knew Dr Purvis liked me. I tended to like anyone who liked me, so I treated our weekly meeting at the Naydon Clinic as a sort of get-together with a mate rather than an appointment with a shrink.

On occasion I went into those appointments with a Zen-like tranquillity, and left for the long walk down the corridor feeling despairing and fatigued. I kept a diary, lots of diaries, most of them lost now, but I have some scraps of paper that have survived. As I read them it's like looking at old photographs that capture a one-dimensional memory of what you once were. These words are from something I wrote at seventeen:

It's hard to feel supported when you can't tell people everything. People haven't really got a clue what it's like. It's hard to trust anyone. It's hard to believe people won't let you down. I'm feeling like I want to cry. My body feels hollow. Empty. I don't feel like I'm 17. I feel young. I'm not sure how old, maybe about 10 yrs. It's hard to accept that I can't get all the support I need from one person. From any person. It's hard that no one can fully understand. It's hard for me to admit that inside I feel a really lonely person. What do I need to do to take care of myself right now? Well I need to cuddle my teddies – it sounds silly, but I need some comfort...

I was still cuddling teddies when I should have been cuddling boys. The sick imagery in my mind, rather than making me sexually active, had closed that door completely.

And my nightmares persisted. my feet on fire, the monster coming to my little bed, and another where I am in a room with other children, some naked, some dressed. A man in a white car is coming to take us away and we are tying each other to chairs so that he can't take us. In this dream I am frantic. My fingers are sticky and can't coordinate. I am not afraid of being abused. I am afraid that the man in the white car is going to kill me. I am overwhelmed with fear and wake disorientated in a cold sweat, voices murmuring in the background, unsure as I open my eyes if I am Alice at seventeen or Alice at seven.

Dr Purvis, in a pale-lemon top with red flowers and a bright-yellow skirt with matching heels, listened and made notes of this dream at one of our last meetings. I can't recall her analysis, just the sound of her pencil scratching on the lined pad, the flash of light from her glasses, the stripes of shadow made by the sun through the Venetian blinds.

My time was running out. At seventeen, I was too old for teddies and outside Dr Purvis's remit. I was an adult, on my own, and as the days got shorter and the nights grew darker I began to polish my running shoes with new fervour. I spent more and more time locked in the bathroom and ate so little I was vanishing inside my own clothes.

Alice Jamieson

It was hardly surprising at the end of my first year at sixth-form college that I got another row of As. I went back in the autumn with a feeling of running over the same old ground, that a cycle had come to an end and a new cycle had begun without the oil of joy and good memories that keeps the wheels in balance.

CHAPTER 6
First Love

The head of faculty at sixth-form college suggested to Mum that I apply to the University of Liverpool to do a degree in sociology and social policy. I did look at various other prospectuses, but finally took the advice and sat my exams with a feeling that fate was in charge of my future.

I had two months to wait for my results and decided to go to Israel to work on a kibbutz. Mum worried while we were making the arrangements and took the morning off work to drive me to the station. As the London train approached, she helped me strap myself into the gigantic backpack that held enough 'essentials' for an attempt on Everest. I had yet to learn that the first rule of travelling is travelling light. We had one last hug, and I listened to Mum's heels snap jauntily along the platform.

At Gatwick I joined a party of ten volunteers and we exchanged names while we waited for the flight. This was my first solo adventure and I had chosen Israel because I had a teacher at school who was Jewish and he had painted a picture of a biblical paradise, which it most certainly wasn't in July 1987. Israel and Lebanon had been at war and had just reached an uneasy peace that had left millions of Palestinians in refugee camps from which the Shiite militia Hezbollah had launched a campaign of guerrilla resistance.

We arrived at Tel Aviv's Ben-Gurion Airport at night and the first thing that struck me was that the air was warm and sultry as if it the weight of history moved in its ancient dust. We climbed into a blue bus and set off below a sky lit by so many stars I appreciated just how wise the Three Wise Men must have been to have followed the right one to Bethlehem.

We were on the road to Tiberias heading for Afula, a small town not far from the Sea of Galilee where the disciples had fished. On its shores, Jesus had instructed his followers to treat others as you wish to be treated, a teaching the people of the modern Holy Land were sadly unable to heed then and now, almost two milliennia later.

The Bible stories I had learned in infants school came back to my mind as I gazed out of the window at Arabs in long cloaks leading camels that moved like ships, rising and falling on invisible waves. I could see the silhouettes of palm trees that reminded me of Grandpa's drawing *The Waving Palms of Tropic Isles.* I had avoided thinking of Grandpa but I thought of him now, in that bus, and felt at peace.

We arrived at Kibbutz Neve Eitan at three in the morning and I was assigned to my quarters in a concrete shack. Like Goldilocks in the house of the Three Bears, I found three metal-framed beds. One of those beds had a feeling of being untenanted, and I fell exhausted on to the thin mattress. The other two beds, as well as an assortment of books and dirty laundry, belonged to two French girls. They were expected back shortly, but I didn't wait up for them. I fell into a deep untroubled sleep and woke with the sun as hot as an oven baking the concrete walls. The volunteer accommodation at Neve Eitan had no shutters, no glass in the windows, and the doors had handles without locks.

It was already 30°C by the time I joined the other volunteers. We toured the kibbutz with the volunteer leader, Delilah, a strong, bony woman with carved features who could have stepped straight from the pages of the Old Testament. We had breakfast together at a long table. The conversation was so lively and multilingual it wasn't hard to imagine the problems the masons must have had building the Tower of Babel. We tucked into bread, cheese, fresh fruit and yoghurt, healthy food all made on the kibbutz, and which I managed to eat with rare hunger after the long journey.

Our jobs had been posted. I joined the caterers and, for the next ten days, helped provide food for 150 people. Luckily, cooking was my *schtick*, and I was soon bustling through the kitchen with piles of dishes and uneaten fruit.

After worrying myself sick over the exams I was as thin as a shadow. But in the communal atmosphere of the kibbutz, I discovered that I did have an appetite after all. In fact, I had an unusually full stomach as I made my way back to my quarters that first morning and, as I walked along rubbing my tummy, I had that curious sense of time playing tricks with me.

I often lost time, but the sensation that day had a different texture, as if time had ceased to be hard blocks of inflexible data and had become pliable without sharp edges and invisible ties binding it together. I could remember the clip clop of Mum's heels retreating along the platform. I could remember collecting the uneaten fruit from the long table and placing it on the shelf in the cupboard. I knew exactly where I was, and I knew I must have been on a plane to get there. But the details were sketchy like an incomplete drawing.

When this happened, I was always afraid that I may have done something inappropriate or embarrassed myself in front of a stranger or, worse, a friend. Other people didn't know I lost time, so I couldn't ask anyone what had happened during that time. My mind would race through every conceivable scenario, I would start to get anxious and the panic attack would end in a migraine.

I had always thought that during the lost time I had lost bits of my life, of myself. But it occurred to me that day that the lost time wasn't lost at all. It was simply misplaced. While I was chasing after time that had gone, I was missing the present moment, that gift of time to stretch and savour. This might sound obvious, but when you have holes in your memory you instinctively want to paper over the cracks. It took the new environment of the kibbutz to show me that the past couldn't be changed or improved by collecting its random parts and sticking it together. It was important to remember but perhaps forgetting was even *more* important.

There was always a slightly tight feeling round my neck, and my throat was often constricted. The tightness had gone. I could breathe freely. I could taste the heavy air with its earthy odour wafting through the open window into my concrete shack. I unpacked my rucksack and wondered why I had thought I needed five pairs of shorts.

After our chores, I tagged along with three Irish girls who were spending the afternoon by the swimming pool. They had only been at the kibbutz for a short time and were considering the merits of the various boys as we slathered ourselves in Ambre Solaire and stretched out to sunbathe beneath a brilliant sun far too hot for that delicate Irish skin. In the coming days, while they grew pink and peeled, I turned a healthy shade of bronze, my eyes took on the same clear blue colour as the sky and freckles began to multiply across my nose. In the mirror, my adversary, the harbinger of surprises, I began to see a slender, eager, wide-eyed creature with hair turning golden and lips that smiled.

Now, who the hell's this?

I washed, chopped and cooked courgettes, carrots, onions, sweet potato, shiny aubergines the size of pineapples all served in big ceramic bowls with spicy roast chicken and rice. I slept without dreaming with a small teddy who had slipped unseen into my backpack and enjoyed having the room to myself. The two French girls had found two Israeli boys and, observing the kibbutzim philosophy, were saving on beds. I made my cell cosy by putting pictures on the wall. I turned a crate into a night table and even managed to acquire an electric fan.

I woke at dawn and the sun would be climbing into the sky by the time I began my work preparing food with Esther, a Polish woman who had survived Buna-Monowitz, the largest concentration camp in the Auschwitz complex. As a girl, the same age as I was that summer, Esther had worked twelve-hour days in the rubber factory a brisk march from the camp in the town of Monowitz. People worked until they died, or were too weak to work and were then sent to the gas chambers at Birkenau.

At Buna-Monowitz an orchestra made up of prisoners played as the workers set off in the morning and struck up lively pieces to hurry them back into camp at the end of their shift. The musicians were forced to play at the executions of prisoners caught trying to escape, and performed concerts for the SS officers and camp guards. It is remarkable to me that men who listened to Mozart and read Goethe could carry out the inhuman barbarisms of a slave camp, that their wives in the town had the capacity to accustom themselves to such suffering, that in people was the potential to torment, torture and inflict such evil on others.

It was the beauty of the music in this world of brutality that kept Esther alive for three years until she was liberated by the Russians in 1945. She found her way to Israel where she finally reached the conclusion that the world is marvellous and beautiful, and man is cruel and incomprehensible. She had lost her entire family. She had lost everything. She had nothing, she needed nothing, and the hatred she had felt, her sense of horror and loss, had slowly transmuted at

Kibbutz Neve Eitan into a form of forgiveness apparent in the mirrors of her cloudless eyes. Esther showed me the fading blue digits on her arm. She could forgive without ever being able to forget.

We were sitting outside the kitchen below an olive tree with roots bigger than the slender trunk. There are olives in the lush environs of Galilee planted almost a thousand years ago. Through their long lives they have seen floods and fires, they have been blighted by disease and frost. But the roots are so deep they spring up again, the perfect symbol for the eternity of all things.

I am not sure why, but it seemed appropriate to hear Esther's story in the shade of that tree. Tears washed over my cheeks and I had the feeling that Esther had allowed me into the soul of her suffering because it was something she believed I needed to hear. My tears that day were for Esther, for her loss, but also for my own, for my lost innocence, my tormented childhood, my inability at seventeen to respond to the boys as the other girls at the kibbutz were able to do.

Away from my father, not just a few streets but a continent away, he was out of my mind, out of my dreams. I was able to think about Grandpa. I had avoided missing him but I missed him now, his humour, his humanity, his ability to show his one true face in a world where people like my father and his friends had many faces and you never knew which one they were wearing.

When I ran into the garden at my grandparents' house it was like entering a make-believe world, a sanctuary away from the horrible dreams that haunted my childhood. With Grandpa particularly, and Grandma too, I was myself. At home, I often felt as if I were an actress playing myself. I was confused about my role, my character, my identity. The tattoo on Esther's thin arm was the ultimate loss of identity because the Nazis reduced the individuals condemned to the concentration camps to nothing more than a number.

Later that summer I visited the Holocaust Museum in Jerusalem, a cold, modern building where even the tramp of the tourists couldn't stir the chilling silence. Torture implements are displayed in glass cases alongside piles of dusty belongings, twisted spectacles, letters never posted, suitcases with names and addresses stencilled on the side, children's shoes and men's boots still caked in mud. These items personalized the methodical mass murder of the Holocaust. As you exit you cannot suddenly switch back to feel as comfortable in your own skin as you did before you entered.

While I was working with Esther, eating properly and sunning by the pool, my body was filling out and getting freckled, but these external changes were merely outward signs of a more profound transformation.

One morning, walking through the kibbutz to what was called the Baby House, I became aware that my head was upright.

This was strange. I could see the world before me and around me: palm trees still as statues, people to whom I said, 'Boker tov', and who replied with the same cheery 'good morning'. I was only used to seeing the world about my feet, the pavement or the gravel or the tiles on the kitchen floor. I had looked into Esther's eyes with greater concentration than I had looked into the eyes of my mother or brother. This sensation of holding my back straight and my head high was almost a spiritual experience. It was as if I faced my own soul and was content with what I saw.

There was something else too. I could hear birdsong. I liked birds. They ate spiders. I waited each spring for the robins to start building their nest. Blackbirds danced over the grass tricking worms into thinking it was raining and gobbled them up the moment they peeked out of their holes. The odd magpie would stand on the roof of the shed like a king surveying his kingdom. I put out crumbs for the birds. I watched the birds. Now, for the first time in my life, I could hear them chattering, squawking, humming.

One night I was woken by what sounded like a flock of fluttering birds. In the REM phase of waking, I thought I was having a strange new dream, but when I turned on the light, there were three very real chickens flapping about trying to find their way out of the window through which a couple of boys had thrown them. I didn't see the boys, but it was common knowledge who was getting up to these pranks. I was furious having to get the chickens back into the hen house, and then clean up the mess. But I understood I wasn't being picked on or singled out. It was just a bit of fun. It's what boys do, usually when they like you. In fact, the Irish girls had woken one night to find a donkey in their room.

There was a faint smile on my lips as I tried to get back to sleep. I didn't feel paranoid or depressed. This was another revelation. Depression for me was like a cloud that some-times engulfed me and sometimes hovered above my head. It was always there, lurking. Now it had gone. Just as I could look straight ahead, I could see behind me, from side to side, up at the sky. In just a few weeks my self-esteem and social skills had improved considerably. I didn't spend hours in the bathroom, there was always someone waiting behind you. I even forgot to polish my shoes!

The chicken incident made me take a closer look at the two perpetrators; or at least one of them. His name was Patrick O'Hay, he was from Dublin, and every time I saw him my palms grew damp. Patrick had an oval face, a mop of dark hair, dark arching eyebrows and soft blue eyes. We had never spoken. We looked at each other and looked away.

I lay under the thin sheet in my hot little shack and couldn't stop thinking about Patrick. I had cut myself off from boys and had never imagined there were intimacies I might want to share with one.

The rota was changed ten days after I arrived and I was allocated work in the cotton fields with a volunteer named Avi, and Rebekkah, a kibbutz member, who drove us around the maze of narrow tracks so that we could open and close the sluice gates and pumps on the irrigation system. We cleaned the filters and checked the pipes for several hours a day in temperatures peaking as high as 44°C. A week into the job I was so dehydrated I came down with sunstroke, ironic as I'd been busy ensuring the crops got enough water.

After a few days spent recovering, I was reassigned to the Baby House. I joined a couple of girls from the kibbutz and from seven in the morning, while their parents worked in the fields, we looked after eight babies aged from six weeks to twelve months old. We fed them, changed their nappies and placed them in giant wooden carts that served as prams, three or four to each cart. I wheeled the little ones round the kibbutz calling out '*Boker tov*', with my head held high. We played with the babies after lunch and drank iced coffee when they took their nap in the hot hours of the afternoon.

I had never spent any time with babies before and discovered that they are mirrors of your own moods. If you smile, they smile. If you're agitated, they get cross and cry. They are unconditionally trusting. How anyone could betray that trust and hurt a baby I cannot begin to imagine.

Over the weeks I went on several excursions. One with the Irish girls to Afula, the nearby town, where we ate falafel and corn on the cob sold by old Arabs with wizened faces and scruffy galabeyahs. I found myself talking about Patrick and burned red with embarrassment when the girls asked if I fancied him. I protested loudly that, on the contrary, I thought he was immature and I couldn't stand him.

In Nazareth I was surprised that there were no sewage pipes and waste flowed in clotted rivers along the side of the streets outside the houses and bazaars. After the long journey to Jericho on the West Bank, we took it in turns to have our photograph taken in the classic pose lying on the Dead Sea reading the *Jerusalem Post*. Delilah organized a coach trip to the River Jordan, which was fun as we rode the torrent downstream each sitting in a sturdy rubber tyre. On another occasion, on 21 July, we went to Tel Aviv Park to see Tina Turner live in concert. The night was humid and Tina slipped about the stage barefoot singing songs such as 'Private Dancer' and 'What's Love Got To Do With It?'

Later in the summer with my *Let's Go Israel and Egypt* in hand and the big rucksack discarded for a smaller one, I journeyed to Rosh Hanikra on the Lebanese border. I asked a tourist to take my photo standing in front of a wall between a sign that read on one side 'Jerusalem 205 Kilometres' and, on the other 'Beirut 120 Kilometres', just for the record that I'd been as close as I would ever get to entering Lebanon, unless I was to become the next BBC correspondent in the Middle East. Over the next two days, I travelled back south across Israel by bus and over the Egyptian border at Taba into the Sinai desert. I stayed in a Bedouin tent and smoked hashish prepared in a carved silver hookah. I caught the bus to Sharm el Sheikh, by the Red Sea, where I learned to scuba dive, an experience just as intoxicating as smoking dope.

I had stopped being a tourist and become a traveller, a distinction I thought justified when I returned to Israel and stayed at a youth hostel in the Arab quarter in Jerusalem and the building was raided by the Israeli military hunting Palestinian terrorists (or freedom fighters). I woke when a soldier burst into my room, pointed his gun at me and screamed commands I didn't understand. As a girl terrified of my dreams and memories, I wasn't afraid of this particular danger and felt oddly safe clutching the St Christopher medal that had belonged to Grandpa and which Mum had given me at the start of my travels. The young soldier carried on shouting and I held up my palms to show they were empty.

'It's OK, I'm English,' I said.

He thought about that for several seconds before answering.

'English,' he repeated. 'I need to practise my English,' and rushed off.

As I listened to the doors banging all through the building, I wondered why it was beyond the capacity of civilized people to sit down with a big map of the Middle East and draw a border that was fair to both sides. I had grown to like Israelis. They seemed liberal, free-spirited and generous, and I was sure it was the politicians on both sides and not the people who kept the divisions alive.

I returned to Neve Eitan with a heavy heart. The days were growing shorter and the sweet, overripe smell of mature crops was a reminder that summer was coming to an end. Each day volunteers packed their bags and said farewell with tears in their eyes and promises to stay in touch. I did consider abandoning everyone and everything to stay at the kibbutz, but the fantasy ended the moment Delilah handed me a letter from Mum with my exam results. As the head of faculty at college had predicted, I had passed them with four good As.

Liverpool, here I come.

On one of the last nights I was chatting with a girl named Antonia in the long communal dining room while we watched the sun going down through the window. Suddenly, two faces blocked the view: the chicken boys, Karl and Patrick O'Hay. Karl said I had 'come to bed eyes', and red flowers bloomed on my cheeks.

The following night, Patrick came to my room. He was leaving next day and wanted to give me his address. We went for a walk under the palms and I was surprised to learn that he was a runner like me and he liked reading; we had read many of the same books. We sat in the light of the moon and I listened to the melodic song of his soft Irish voice. Patrick was as shy as I was, that's why it had taken eight weeks of embarrassed glances for him to pluck up the courage to speak. He apologized for the chicken incident and when I said it didn't matter, we sat silently unable to think of anything else to say.

I knew nothing about boys except what the girls said at school and had anticipated that boys, all boys, would instantaneously make you submit to their expectations. I didn't know that my own expectations might play a part in this boy/girl thing. If there was a general rule, Patrick was the exception, and I felt instantly exhilarated and confused, a mass of swirling, changing sensations unbalancing my equilibrium as we walked together through the kibbutz menagerie.

That summer I had discovered that I could cope on my own. I had a new sense of self-worth and confidence, but suddenly, inexplicably, the person I had left behind in England was trying to climb back into my skin. I felt giddy sitting in the moonlight beside Patrick. The voices had been silent all these weeks. They didn't return now, but I caught myself listening for them.

We touched fingers as we walked back to my shack. At the entrance, we touched lips, faintly and briefly, like the touch of butterfly wings. He turned and walked quickly away, and I ran my tongue over my lips.

Today I'm Alice

Teddy was waiting for me and we cuddled under the sheet. No man had ever shared my pillow and I wondered if one ever would. I had a phobia about getting close to anyone. Closeness was the promise of suffering and pain. On my first day at Neve Eitan, I had experienced an attack of lost time due to the strangeness of my new situation. It had not happened again. It did not happen that night. But with Patrick's taste on my lips, I had the sense of not being myself.

CHAPTER 7
Liverpool

That new-found confidence from kibbutz life faded immediately I moved into the halls of residence at the University of Liverpool. The newly weds delivered me with my teddy bears and junk. We set the boxes down in the low-ceilinged room with its view of endless rooftops and had lunch at Pucci Pizza. My parents had divorced and Mum, after a lengthy courtship, had finally married Stephen. They were happy. I was happy for them.

They drove away from the pizzeria and I stood wondering where to go in this new city with its pattern of unfamiliar streets and the sky threatening rain. The Mersey was sluggish and grey as it meandered out to sea. The horn on the ferry as passengers disembarked made me feel lonely and melancholic. Like my suntan, my new-found self-esteem had gone.

Perhaps it was just end-of-summer blues, an outbreak of SAD, seasonal affective disorder, sun deficit in other words. After Israel, autumn in Liverpool was chilly and overcast. Perhaps I was more suited to opening sluice gates and carrying platters of chicken than the intellectual challenges of sociology and social policy. Better to live in your limbs than in your head. For some reason I didn't manage during freshers' week to sign on for the hockey team or the athletics squad, although I did resume my jogging regime, carving a path out of the city centre into the leafy lanes of the countryside.

My blue-eyed Irish boy with the sweet voice and floppy hair made good his promise and appeared one wet weekend. We left the city for the day travelling by bus to nearby Chester. We attempted our first proper kiss in the shelter of the monkey house at Chester Zoo watched by the gibbering astonished chimps. We got the bus back to Liverpool and went to my room with some unspoken plan to go all the way. I couldn't. I was overcome with feelings of despair and disgust, of sadness. Patrick was the perfect gentleman and blamed himself for my fear.

He returned to Dublin and I became a recluse, obsessively writing and rewriting assignments in an attempt to find the essence of my thoughts. In an essay, there is a point at which the analysis of the views of others ends and the creative rush of personal speculations begins. This rush is like the endorphin buzz reached when running long distances. I began to seek this release inside my head.

The assignments received admiration as well as As. Tutors photocopied them as paradigms of a well-judged essay and this encouraged me to open myself up to the other students. I made friends with two of the girls on my course: Debs, with blonde curls and a boyfriend who could hardly keep his hands off her; and Sarah, an English rose with a false leg as the result of a car accident and the nervous smile of someone who constantly tries to please others. Sarah did everything in her power to keep up with the demands of studying and student life, which I duly took note of.

We three became close to another student named Elaine, who had unconventional ideas and advocated alternative medicines. She was also said to have psychic powers. So, one night after a meal at Sarah's house, we sat cross-legged in a circle on the floor while she predicted our degree results.

Her eyes closed, she asked us to give her all the names of the students in the sociology and social policy group. After each name there was a pause, then she'd say in a sure voice, 'a 2:2' or 'a 2:1'. When it came to my turn, she predicted a first.

Was Elaine making fun of me? I remembered the chickens being tossed into my room at the kibbutz. After thinking it through and looking at it from every possible viewpoint and angle, I decided it was just a bit of fun and the predictions didn't matter.

The forecast that I would get a first secured my reputation as an intellectual. Students who had avoided me because I was strange started coming to me for advice, an ego-boost with weird side effects. Sometimes when I was speaking I had the feeling there wasn't a solitary person listening, but a small gathering just outside my range of vision. These others mumbled incoherently behind the left/right brain divide in my head. When this whispering campaign became unbearable, I resorted to the bottle. Gin was my tipple. A good binge would shut up the voices and as I drank alone, unlike most students, this enhanced my reputation for being eccentric as well as brainy.

The voices had returned, but in a different mode. They became watchful and made me self-conscious. For example, in a lecture when I knew the right answer to a question and no one else appeared to do so, I felt obliged to negotiate with the murmuring others before speaking. They were observing, so be careful. Don't show off. Don't trip up. Don't make yourself appear foolish. Sometimes the tutor, assuming that I knew the answer, would glance in my direction, so would the students, and I would sit there speechless listening to the racket made by the invisible 'others'.

At these times, when the tutor and students looked at me, I experienced myself being looked at as a disengaged third party. I looked at myself with a vacant expression just as the other students were looking at me, in the way you would at someone naked, or someone in fancy dress, or at someone or something that's not quite right. The tic in my neck would do its little dance. I would sit wondering if the people in the lecture hall could hear the chatter I was hearing. It was so loud, so real, I couldn't believe others were unable to hear anything.

I was a hostage to the voices. A prisoner. I didn't want to draw attention to myself, upset the voices, provoke their wrath. I was unable to connect with people. There was a dialogue in my head and it excluded everyone else, my friends, even Patrick. In love we are validated by the person who loves us. I loved Patrick but couldn't show it. He was gentle, kind, patient, my hope of normality.

He returned again to Liverpool. He went to the barber to have his hair cut and stepped out of the shop with flushed cheeks and a packet of condoms. I had no idea that the hairdresser was the place to buy condoms or why. The thing with being clever is that so many simple things remain a mystery. We went to a boarding house in the country for a night of romance – dinner with sparkling wine and candles, holding hands as we climbed the squeaky stairs, kissing behind the locked door. This was my first time. Patrick's first time. We undressed in the dark and five minutes after climbing between the sheets in the big double bed, I got up and went to catch the last train back to Liverpool's Lime Street station. I was useless.

Patrick, for reasons I never completely understood, moved from Dublin to Swansea and we tried again when I went to visit him there. Once more, we got as far as the bed, but that night I got up and crept into the sleeping bag I was carrying in case of an emergency. I loved Patrick, but there was no way for me to connect the dots between love and sex. I was desperate for love but I couldn't bear to be touched. I couldn't imagine someone, anyone, entering my body.

I had physically escaped from my father, from the sound of his short-wave radio, his steps climbing the stairs, his ghostly voice at the bathroom door whispering, 'Your mother says you've been in there long enough,' while I remained concealed in the steam scrubbing bad dreams from my gaunt frame with ribs and hipbones pushing through the flesh, the deep shadowy wells below my collarbones, my flat fleshless bottom, which I pictured him balancing in his two big hands while his fat tongue pierced my innocent little-girl body. But he was omnipresent in my dreams at night. The nightmares haunted me so I woke breathing air that, for a moment, held the tainted tang of Brylcreem and aftershave.

My vulnerability encouraged the voices.

No one loves you. You're nothing. Come on, kill yourself, Alice. You know you want to. Do it. Try it. Do it now.

If the voices were trying to cut me off from human communication, that's what they achieved. I would make plans to see Debs or Sarah or Elaine, then cancel or not turn up. They would be upset, naturally, and the voices would pipe up.

See, even your friends don't like you now.

It wasn't long before the chorus of unfamiliar voices drifted into the background and the habitual tones of the Professor and his cronies rose up with their spiteful commentary.

You think you're so clever but you're not. You'll never get anywhere. You'll never achieve anything. A first? Don't make me laugh!

The voices accompanying the Professor chimed in with things like *Hear, hear. Jolly good. That'll show her. Who does she think she is?*

Today I'm Alice

It wasn't easy trying to behave normally with the persistent nightmares, and the voices telling me I was a waste of space. The persecutory narrative had for the most part remained at bay in Israel but now it was back in full flow. The voices made me feel cut off, separated like a balloon released from the fingers of a child. The combination of the voices and nightmares were washing away the last grains of self-confidence I had packed in my big rucksack and brought home with me from Kibbutz Neve Eitan.

As my confidence faded the weather started to show its darker side. Snow fell that winter. It clung to the trees and lay in cloaks over the roofs. The din in my head was as loud as the sound of a party in a neighbouring apartment, a bioacoustic clamour that interfered with my normal routines and, once again, I started to lose time.

I would find myself in a lecture hall with a mass of notes in my folder and be unable to remember taking notes or what the lecture had been about. I would be hurrying through Liverpool's Chinatown and forget where I was going, why I was in a hurry, who I was supposed to be meeting. I would look at the time and forget it instantly, lifting my watch mechanically back into view and immediately forgetting again. Sometimes it was comical. The hands on my watch seemed to stop or spin or go backwards, changing time from a continuum to a conundrum: 'What is *the* time?' becoming 'What *is* time?'

Time was irrational and so was space and geography.

I would set off jogging, the city streets stretching to infinity, the buildings growing taller, closer. The Liver Building with its four giant clocks would loom up like a prison, like the castle in my worst nightmare. As I turned and turned again, I would feel trapped in a maze, like an Escher print, a bewildering world without beginning or end, the streets all the same, the Liver Building revolving as if on an axis, following me, observing me, the tight feeling in my throat making me gasp for breath.

By luck, or karma, as Elaine would say, I would find myself beyond the city perimeter and dash over the bridge that led to open fields. The trees were bare, silvered with frost, and I got the creepy feeling that I was running along the lanes close to my old home. The beat of my trainers set off a cycle of memories, as the touch of a stranger's hand could send me plunging into a pit of depression where the only release was to rush home and take a slug from the bottle under the bed.

Elaine was a touchy-feely person. She wore wooden beads and big skirts. She hugged me every time we met, her large breasts crushing my skeleton. I'd close my eyes and say to myself: It's all right. Hold on, Alice. Don't pull away. She's your friend. If the voices weren't talking to me, I was talking to myself.

My lifeline was Patrick's occasional calls and letters. But Patrick made me think about sex and sex made me think about my nightmares. I was driven to work hard at my degree by a mixture of ambition and a lack of self-worth through those three years at uni. And all that time I struggled with the dreams and I struggled with the voices.

Kill yourself, kill yourself. Cut your arms, cut your throat. You're nothing, you're useless, you're scum. Nobody likes you, nobody wants you. Do the world a favour, Alice, and take a bottle of sleeping pills, take them down with a bottle of gin. Give up. You know you can't do it. You're going to fail, so just stop trying. Nobody likes you. Nobody wants you. Go on, have another slug from that bottle. Take another pill.

I did think about seeking medical help, but I had already tried that with Dr Purvis. I had liked Jane Purvis. Jane had tried to help me. But all that chitchat about Freud and the sexual act seemed banal and pointless. I often left her consulting room, with the sunken chairs and Venetian blinds, more depressed than when I had gone in. I took a leaf out of Sarah's book and tried to learn to live with my particular ailment and wondered what was worse, as I jogged along on healthy limbs, a broken body or a broken mind. You are born with all the brain cells you will ever have. You become who you are depending on what happens to you and what choices you make. What happens in those first formative years affect later choices, and altering or influencing what you turn into is practically impossible. The murderer and the paedophile were always there.

I clung to the illusion that I was a normal girl with a boyfriend and plans to go back to Israel for the summer. All year I had been looking forward to returning to Neve Eitan, but at the last minute I changed my mind. I didn't want to sully the memories and went instead to a different part of Israel to work picking fruit at Moshav Bene Atarot where at least the long days of sunshine had a palliative effect.

Sarah joined me in Tel Aviv two weeks before the end of my trip and we went to Egypt to see the pyramids and the sphinx. We were unable to make the bone-shaking bus rides and hikes I would have made travelling alone. I had to remember that Sarah had a physical disability and was making a super-human effort to keep up. I in turn made an effort to do what was best for Sarah and what was best for Sarah turned out to be best for me too. The voices those two weeks in Egypt left me in peace.

I am not entirely sure where that second year at university went. It is a blur of late nights beneath a bare light bulb listening to the chitchat with one side of my brain and writing notes for essays with the other, a balancing act keeping the two hemispheres functioning, a reflection of my relationship with Patrick, together yet apart. The Professor was my constant companion in my new digs at the YWCA, where I had bars on the window, a bed, one chair and a table. I was studying politics and the history of social policy, both of which I found difficult, as well as sociology, which I was familiar with from my A levels.

The YWCA was three miles along the banks of the river from uni. I bought a mountain bike from my savings to make the daily journey there and back, via the same streets like a bus following the same route past the old potteries and copper works, St Michael's Church, Sefton Park, the rhythm unchanging. In routine I was able to function. I was maintaining the illusion of being normal, while in my head there were subtle shifts like cracks in ice, my conscious mind battling with my unconscious mind.

My relationship with remembering and forgetting became more unreliable. I was able to recall pages of text but I forget to eat, appointments, promises. If lecture times changed it would throw me into a spin. I would stand outside a closed lecture room at ten staring at the schedule and not know if I had known the lecture started at eleven and forgotten, or if it had been changed from ten to eleven, and I'd forgotten that. In reverse, I would arrive an hour late, look at my watch, forget the time and look again. Is it Tuesday or Wednesday? Politics or social policy?

Am I Alice?

Who's Alice?

The memory is like a woven rope with three strands that function by an arrangement of encoding – the processing and combining of information; storage – a system for filing the encoded information; and retrieval – the process of recalling that information. We have a billion neurons in our brain that communicate by chemical and electrical synapses in a process called synaptic transmission. It's hardly surprising the wires get crossed, in fact it's surprising they don't get crossed more often. I suffer, in memory terms, a combination of amnesia, just plain forgetting, with a depressing trace of hyperthymesia, the opposite. This is when you can remember small personal details with uncanny recall; useful when you apply the ability to the learning process, soul-destroying when you delve into the past. My past.

Patrick came to stay and we had one last hopeless attempt at making love. It didn't work, and it set off a cycle of nightmares when he went back to Swansea. Night after night like episodes in some dreadful soap I saw myself or someone who looked like me at age six getting into Daddy's car and stepping out at a tall building that looked like the Liver Building, but in my dream had become a castle. We held hands as we went down a flight of stairs to a door and entered the dungeon where lots of people were chanting, the children were naked and candles made shadows on the walls.

I would wake disorientated to the distressed sound of a child's voice and imagine the child was there in my tiny room. I would turn on the light, look under the bed. The child wasn't there. The child was *inside* me, but also external to me like the shadows flickering over the dungeon walls. The child was afraid of what had happened to her on past visits to the castle and was afraid of what was going to happen to her again. I say 'her', but the little person who cried out at night was neutral and I had a distinct feeling it was more male than female.

Someone or something was growing inside me like a foetus. Could my sad attempts at making love with Patrick have left me with a phantom pregnancy? I could feel something forming, evolving, kicking, but I didn't feel happy in the way pregnant women feel happy and contented. My thing was a monster and it filled me with shame and self-loathing. I couldn't explain my fear to Patrick and finally wrote to tell him I was unable to continue any sort of relationship. It broke my heart, and I think it broke his too.

I spent the summer at home with Mum and Stephen. In the last few weeks I collected an application for the Birmingham Centenary Marathon (1889–1989). I had pushed my limit up to 15 miles and that had nearly killed me. Could I do over 26 miles, almost twice as far?

Don't try, Alice. You can't do it. You'll never be able to do it. You're not good enough. You're not good enough for anything. You'll always be good for nothing.

The Professor was back in my brain.

'Oh, for heaven's sake, *shut* up.'

'Is that you, Alice, talking to yourself again?' Mum called from the kitchen.

'Yes, Mum, that's me, talking to myself again.'

I wanted to tell her about the voices, the nightmares where I saw the bedroom door opening in the dark and my father entering my room. I had been trying to tell her since I was five years old. Now I was twenty and a woman but I still couldn't do it. Each time I tried the words withered into a migraine.

I sighed and plonked the form down on the table.

'Sign on the dotted line,' I said.

The idea was to collect money for charity from sponsors. I stuck a pen in her hand while she glanced over the form.

'You're not serious?' she said.

'Never been more serious in my life.'

'It'll kill you, Alice.'

'Then you won't have to worry about me any more,' I said.

She tut-tut-tutted and signed her name.

'Well, who's it in aid of then?' she asked.

I hadn't thought about that but answered instinctively, 'The NSPCC.'

Mum put herself down for £2 a mile. Stephen took his guide from her, as in all things. I called Clive to try and persuade him to enter with me, which gave him a good laugh, but at least he added another £2 per mile to my tally. I contacted friends, some lecturers at Liverpool, and by the weekend I was wearing in a new pair of Nike Airs.

Marathon running is a question of mind over matter. As I set off each day, I listened to my body and knew if it was going to be a short run or whether I was going to push up the distance as I headed into the great unknown. I began with a low-intensity programme, developing aerobic fitness and endurance, before hotting up with the Swedish fartlek method, a modified form of continuous training involving regular changes of pace. I often went to Sutton Park, jogged a few times round the perimeter at a slow pace, then put in some sprints before walking to recover. I also went to the athletics track and did some 100-metre runs before jogging, building up a tolerance to the lactic acid that gives you the burning sensation in your muscles when they are beginning to fatigue.

One day at lunch with Mum's friends John and Penny, John spoke of his time as a long-distance cyclist. John was 'comfortable' and 'knew a thing or two'. He didn't think I had done enough preparation for the marathon but he sponsored me anyway.

The event took place on a clear, cloudless, Indian summer's day on the last Sunday in September. Thousands of runners gathered at the start line at The Alexander Stadium, a pistol fired, the crowd roared and we set off, a river of psyched-up humanity. The Birmingham run was a trial for the Commonwealth Games, not that I got a glimpse of the elite athletes from my position way back behind the starting line. I had estimated on my application a finishing time of between 4 and 4½ hours, but had quietly moved up to the next zone as if, by autosuggestion, I might break the magical 4 hours.

As I settled into a rhythm all I could see was an ocean of bobbing heads, all the same, all with the same purpose. I thought the similarities between us were greater than the differences. Male and female, young and old, tall and short, we all wanted the same thing: to complete the course, succeed against the odds, feel proud and hope to be loved and respected a little more.

The field quickly thinned. I was one of a pack of a dozen runners with our numbers flapping on our backs, our breath pumping, our trainers beating like drums. I didn't want to dehydrate and grabbed a bottle of water each time we passed a milestone. When we crossed Centenary Square – the halfway point – I checked my watch and felt a buzz of excitement. I was within reach of my target.

The course took us through the Birmingham university campus and up a steep hill towards Edgbaston. In my obsessive/compulsive way, and with the memory of what had once happened to me in Israel, I had been so anxious not to dehydrate I had taken on too much water. At 17 miles, the furthest I had ever run, we were passing through a residential area and I asked some people standing outside their house applauding if I could use their toilet; this short break was the only point in the race when I actually stopped running.

Back on track, I raced to catch up with my group as the course turned into Kings Heath Park. People in the crowd were eating ice cream, shouting, urging us on, but the extra effort took its toll and in the shade of the tall elms I 'hit the wall'. I could barely put one leg before the other. My quads were dead. I'd never make the 4 hours. I just wanted to finish. I pleaded with the young guy running at my side to talk me through the pain barrier, but he just groaned and stumbled on. The marathon is only a race for professionals. Everyone else is running against themselves. You are alone and must persevere alone.

We left the park at a snail's pace and ran down Cartland Road, an extremely steep hill. At the bottom I got my second wind and started passing people struggling along Pershore Road. We turned into Cannon Hill Park, where I drew on the last of my renewed energy to sprint over the finish line with the time overhead displaying 3 hours 46 minutes 14 seconds.

Mum, Stephen, John and Penny were waiting at the finishing line to see if I completed the course. Oh, ye of little faith! I had known when I set out that I would do it. It was breaking the 4 hours that mattered. I received my medal and a foil blanket to keep warm, although the temperature at 12.45 that day was 32°C – Israeli weather.

John got a photo of me crossing the finishing line and immediately gave me a cheque for £26.00. I drank about a gallon of water and was still feeling high as we drove home, a feeling that transformed to lead in my legs next morning when I had to come down the stairs on my bum because my thighs and calves were killing me. I went swimming to prevent my muscles from seizing up completely.

When I collected all my sponsorship money, I had raised more than £500, which I sent to the NSPCC. It has remained my charity of choice ever since.

Things were changing inside my head. I could feel it. Hear it. It was like mice running on a treadmill, their little legs turning the wheel, all those elastic synapses like silicone chips changing, re-forming, preparing me for the inevitable. Long-buried memories were climbing out of storage and shaking off the dust. Mental disorders are like rust. They never sleep.

They creep up on you. They get worse. I needed help. I needed to get through my last year at uni before the volcano exploded.

Mum and Stephen drove me back to Liverpool at the start of the autumn term and we had the traditional lunch at Pucci Pizza. Mum said work hard, do well, as if I needed telling, and Stephen stuck £100 in my hand when she went to the loo. It was depressing having such a nice stepfather.

I rushed back to the YWCA and spent the afternoon in the kitchen full of cookery confidence making apple envelopes and catching up with Sarah and Debs. Debs was intense and opinionated with a frenzied dash about her. She had broken up with the latest in her string of boyfriends after going to his flat to surprise him and being surprised to find him in bed with her best friend. She said she would never speak to either of them again and we didn't doubt it. Sarah and I were jealous of Debs but found vicarious pleasure in the soap opera of her love life. We knew it wouldn't be long before another Mark or Gavin or Jason came along to give us a thrilling new instalment.

In my final year, I specialized in political issues in social policy and community health between the broad social groupings of social class, age, gender and race. I had to write two dissertations and chose domestic violence as the theme for one, the other a comparison of the health-related behaviour of employed and unemployed men using a questionnaire I created myself.

It didn't occur to me when I chose men's health as a topic that, living as I did in the inaccessible world of my head, I had little understanding of the day-to-day pressures of people in general and men in particular. It wasn't obvious to me that my survey would reach the obvious conclusions. Unemployed men tended to drink more, smoke more, avoided exercise and were more disposed than working men to mental and physical ailments.

Bottom line, men, if you want to get healthy, get a job.

The dissertation was carefully structured and went through many drafts, but the paper threw up no new data and achieved a disappointing 68 per cent, two crucial points off my target if I was going to get a first.

My study on violence against women had more scope and was something I did know about, even if I didn't know how I knew. For many women 'home' is a contradiction, a paradox. We think of the home as being a comfort zone, a place of security, but it can also be a battlefield of unremitting violence. This setting where human companionship and human brutality coexist, got my mind buzzing and my Olivetti portable clacking away all through the night, to the annoyance of my neighbours in the adjoining cells at the YWCA.

Feminist writers explain domestic violence as the most explicit form of men's power, which to me was overly simplistic. I came to see violence as the denial of a woman's liberty. Once a woman is imprisoned by fear, she has lost the freedom to be herself. If violence enters a relationship, the shattering of the taboo takes on an aura of allure and fascination. Once a violent man has tasted the forbidden fruit, like a heroin addict he can't wait for another hit.

The man who hits a woman or abuses a child and gets away with it will grow obsessed with his sense of power and will often come to the disturbing belief that he is above the laws and norms of society. This attitude damages his victim, but also robs them of their freedom. Of all animals, only humans are gratuitously violent, and violence often has a sexual component. I argued in the dissertation that freedom is something that each of us values beyond all other things, and attempted to show how violence is the negation of that freedom.

For my research, I arranged to visit a women's aid refuge to interview women who had endured such levels of brutality they had finally fled to social services for help. One woman had been attacked with an axe and felt lucky to have escaped with no more than a fractured skull. Another had been tied by a leash in a dog's kennel and fed scraps from her husband's plate. Another had been repeatedly raped and beaten. These women spoke honestly and openly. They were so damaged and broken they didn't even ask why a twenty-year-old student was questioning them.

'Why didn't you try to reason with him?'

'He didn't know how to be reasonable.'

'Why didn't you call the police?'

'I couldn't. I was afraid to.'

'What about when he was at work?'

'He never worked.'

It was the same pattern – all life, it seems, is about patterns – and once the pattern of violence begins, it is repeated again and again. Men with low self-esteem, frequently the result of disappointment and unemployment, usually fuelled by drink and drugs, often want to harm themselves but are afraid to do so. Instead, they harm the one person within reach, their wives or partners. If they see themselves as nothing, she is less than nothing, and it must be her fault when they lose their rag.

A lot of husbands and partners, I discovered, believe it is a wife's duty to love, honour and obey. Their duty is to punish their wives if they fail to do so. These men will tell you that they never set out to hurt their women. They only wanted to help them be a better person. They strike them as an act of kindness. Of love. It hurts them, they tell their beaten women, more than it hurts the beaten woman.

Respect is the key element. If the woman has done something wrong, he believes she will not respect him if he doesn't punish her. It would be easier for him to let her get away with the infringement – not cooking the meal she should have known he was going to want, failing to get another six-pack from the off-licence, failing to be a good housekeeper when she explains there was no money to go to the off-licence. He doesn't *want* to punish her, but it's a matter of respect. He craves respect because he does not respect himself.

What the women at the refuge told me was that they had put up with the violence because they believed deep down their partners loved them. They had become possessions and, as possessions, the men brutalized them out of fear of losing what they owned. The women, in turn, put up with the abuse and stayed under the same roof as proof that they had no intention of leaving and that they loved their partners in return.

It was all very twisted, but I understood. Men have a chronic need to believe they play some essential role in this life, that they are more than just a wave on the sea lost among other waves. When men feel ineffectual, their loss of dignity becomes the self-hatred that erupts in violence they then inflict on their wives, sometimes their children, often both. Boys who have been brutalized become brutes. Girls who have been brutalized are drawn to brutal men. There is a pattern, and social services often can't see it.

With my ability to compartmentalize different parts of my life, I was able to make notes on these terrifying experiences without being unduly affected by them. Like completing the marathon, the dissertation I was writing was so crucial to my self-esteem, I shut down all right-brain sensitivity and turned the dial to left-brain analysis. My own experiences, real or imagined, informed my thinking on domestic violence, but I was able to put them to one side and write the paper objectively.

The dissertation scored 80 per cent, the best in my group. I now had finals in political issues in social policy and community health. I'd been lucky to have excellent tutors at Liverpool; they were confident that I would do well, and I went into the exams chanting a little prayer: 'Don't say a word. Don't say a word. Don't say a word.'

The voices were quiet. They were biding their time. The intense work, late nights revising and a snifter before bedtime was a cure for insomnia, as codeine and a can of coke was a useful medication for hangovers and headaches. If the Professor's gang did feel inclined to scream their vitriol as I left for uni in the morning, I'd pedal faster and their voices would disappear in the wind rush. I felt like the legendary little Dutch boy who'd stuck his finger in the dyke. There was a whole fistful of fingers holding those billion neurons in place and I could feel the pressure building in my brain.

Elaine once said that if I ever got married I would go down the aisle in a pair of jeans. I stood looking in the mirror for a long time, looking for me, the real me, and then went out and bought a dress to wear to the Graduation Ball. I didn't care what any of them said.

The end-of-course knees-up took place at a hotel in the city centre where we sat in groups at long tables like in a refectory. We pretended to listen to the speeches, drank wine and then hit the dance floor. It was the first time in three years that I truly behaved like a student. Boys who had always ignored me were suddenly buying me drinks. I remember Sarah saying that without Debs and me supporting her she would never have got through the course. It made me cry. I got drunk. I was sick in the loo and fell over before going back to the flat of one of the boys on my course named Rob, where we smoked a spliff, giggled and ate chocolate biscuits.

A few days later, our results were pinned on a board in the Eleanor Rathbone Building at uni. There were crowds of people pushing forward and I found myself switching into the cookery-mode persona to force my way through.

'Excuse me.'

'Excuse me,' I replied.

'There she is,' one of the boys said.

I grinned and metaphorically punched the air.

Yes. Yes. Yes.

I stayed in Liverpool until graduation. I'd had almost no contact with my father. I didn't invite him to the ceremony, and asked Stephen in his place. After receiving my diploma at the Philharmonic Hall in Hope Street, we went to Pucci Pizza for the last time to celebrate.

In spite of losing time, lapses in memory, the nightmares and the voices, I climbed up on stage that year to collect a first-class honours degree. The predictions made by Elaine almost three years before had been right in every case. Very spooky.

CHAPTER 8
Rape

With my *Let's Go Italy* stored in the pocket of a lightweight pack, I travelled the roads and railways of Italy from Milan to Naples for two weeks before starting my first job as a research assistant in a Welsh health promotion department.

I rented a bedsit with a flimsy partition between the bedroom and kitchen where I had a table, the daily choice of two chairs, and Weetabix with Radio 4 for breakfast. It was like living on a set for a Ken Loach film: the washed-out light wan and misty through the narrow window, a swirl-patterned carpet on the bedroom floor, the flowers embossed on the wallpaper making the small space appear smaller. It was all I could afford and I was determined to make my own way without help from my family. I worked on the fourth floor of a modern building where I had my own desk in a shared office.

This was the real world, cramped, oppressive, encapsulated by routine and poorly paid. I was perfectly happy.

My two colleagues were good at their jobs, helpful to me, the newcomer, and we found lots of things to laugh about during our breaks. I'd landed on my feet. In our office Louise Lloyd-Jones took charge; a former nurse in her early forties, she was a gentle, perceptive woman, always elegantly dressed, with a soft Welsh accent and a friendly ear willing to listen to everyone's problems. Rosaleen Sharpless was a blonde bombshell, tall, slender, elegant, in her late twenties. She had got a first in sociology at Durham and was working on a health-promotion project targeted at homelessness. Rosaleen bubbled with the confidence I would so loved to have had, and I tried with little success to imitate her manner and dress sense.

It was 1990 and a European study had revealed the surprising news that smoking in the workplace was bad for your health. My job was to study the data and write reports that went up the chain of command as far as the Welsh Office. Hammering away on a computer at my corner desk with the wall beside me covered in maps and piecharts, I was reaching inside the Cabinet to the very heart of government. Alice's Warning: SMOKING CAN KILL.

Most weekends, I travelled home so I could run through my ideas on health promotion with Mum and Stephen. Since the separation of my parents, Clive had never once visited my father. I didn't know what that said about their relationship. I still don't, but I've always wondered if they too had skeletons in the cupboard.

It had been left to me to tell my father that Mum had remarried and I may, of course, have volunteered in order to see his reaction. There was some ill-defined bond between me and my father. He was the one who had pulled me on to his lap when I was little. My father was a source of love, and when you are a child bad love is better than no love at all.

During the three years I had been at Liverpool, I had rarely seen him. I decided to pay him a visit, which I rationalized as a sense of duty. I can now see it was a mixture of my need for approval and the chance to flaunt my growing status. Against the odds, I had survived. I was paying my own way. I was playing a part in the campaign to save lives by changing the law on smoking. I wanted to show him I mattered.

My father's new house was a white stucco villa set in a

garden with a neatly clipped lawn. There was an impressive porch with a pair of plaster lions guarding the black and white tiles and a two-tone chiming bell that made me wonder for a moment if a butler was going to answer the door.

I felt nervous for a moment, but then the door opened and my father was standing there in a dark suit and tie, his Rotary Club badge in the lapel of his jacket like a little gold sun. He led me through to the back of the house where the kitchen gave on to a sitting room filled with miniature palms and plants in pots. There were prints on the wall, a big TV, some family photos, which I found odd for some reason, and a posh set of golf clubs leaning against the wall.

He made tea and put some biscuits on a plate, which I didn't touch. He sat gravely listening in his wing-backed chair as I talked. He appeared harmless and smaller than I recalled. He had been a giant in my child's eyes. Now he was middle-aged, disappointed, alone. He asked questions about my job, about my student years in Liverpool. I was pleased to let him know that I had done better than Clive and got a first. I realized, even as I spoke, that I sounded resentful and boastful. The breezy self-confidence Clive took from his childhood was something I would never have, no matter how hard I worked or what I achieved.

Why did I go to visit my father? It is hard to analyse our reasons for doing the things we do, and we do those things for a whole variety of reasons. I was playing dare. Touching my tongue to poison. My father with his plummy voice knew how to say all the right things. He showed interest. He said he was proud of me, that he had always known I would do well. He ran his palm over his hair, still glinting with Brylcreem. As we talked it didn't seem as though I was chatting with my father but with someone I barely knew, an old teacher from primary school, a distant aunt, a forgotten acquaintance met by chance.

When it was time to go, he stood at the door and we looked at each other like two wary cats. He didn't kiss me. I didn't want him to. As I made my way to the station I had creepy feelings and decided never to go and see him again.

The train back to Wales was delayed. I stood alone on the long platform at New Street looking at the rails vanishing into the horizon and remembered running along the avenue of trees trying to reach infinity. The train when it came rumbled lethargically through the muddle of unknown towns and closed-down factories, slag heaps left from abandoned coal mines, windy high streets with dim yellow lights around pub doorways. When we stopped at stations along the way the people waiting looked like phantoms in the watery light. It was hard to imagine why they were there and where they were going, why anyone was going anywhere. The sky was black and I was soaked by the steady drizzle that accompanied me on the long walk home.

That night I couldn't sleep for many hours but, when I did sleep, I was woken by the sound of a child's voice crying out, a long pain-filled wail that startled me awake. I was unable to get back to sleep again and got up at dawn. I jogged through the wet streets where dustmen were emptying bins and the sun was ice white when it rose over the grey buildings. I went to work and tried to put the dream out of my mind, but it returned again that night and every night, the cry of the child followed by a nightmare that varied in detail and began always with an air of suspense.

This is my dream:

I am lying in bed staring at the ceiling where the mobile makes shifting patterns as it turns in circles above me. The shadows move faster as the door opens and a dark man softly enters. He takes my teddies and drops them on the floor. He removes my pyjamas. He kisses me on the lips. He pushes his willy in my vagina, my bottom, my mouth. I recall the taste of the stale milk that shoots out of his willy and the taste remains in my mouth all next day.

This nightmare was the same one that had been haunting me since I was a teenager, since puberty, but with a subtle difference. The other little girl observing those scenes wasn't there. The man in the dreams was very clearly my father and the little girl was me.

This was horrifying. Without the emotional distance the other little girl provided, I came face to face with the alarming possibility that these were not dreams at all, but memories of something that had happened and I had somehow managed to bury them in the deepest depths of my subconscious.

Even during the day, I would sometimes pause while composing anti-smoking statistics on the computer, drinking a cappuccino, running the bath, and my head would spin like in a movie. I would see some vivid and terrifying scene from the past: me at three and seven and fourteen, me all through my childhood lying in my bedroom at night feeling numb as I waited for the door to open, the mobile on the ceiling to race faster and that man, my father, to appear with his spider fingers and stale breath. That little girl, that young woman, that person who seemed to be me went into a daze and was only reminded of what had happened in the night when she woke with a sour taste in her mouth, a pain in her bottom or her vagina, or both. She bathed, she showered, she scrubbed herself clean and thought she was really quite mad to have these dreadful thoughts in her head.

Now, suddenly, these hazy nightmares and memories were growing more vivid, more connected, more in focus. I felt dirty, sullied, separate. As an adult I could now see that if the memories were true, I was a damaged human being who had been abused all through my childhood. Or, and this is what's so terrible, if they were not true I had a warped, pornographic mind that could invent depraved scenes more realistic than any writer had ever put into words or any filmmaker had turned into celluloid.

The new friendships developing with Rosaleen and Louise disintegrated. I became a recluse. I worked hugging the wall all day and rushed home through the winter to write reports in my flower-infested bedsit at night, drinking gin, staring at my reflection in the fly-flecked mirror while politicians on Radio 4 nattered on about the Iraqi invasion of Kuwait. I wanted to be involved, interested, concerned. I had been to Egypt and Israel. But the Persian Gulf and the looming war were far away and the sense of horror in my own mind was near and present.

Weekends would come and, like an addict, or Pavlov's most regressive dog, I started to visit my father again. We would sit in his living room with the insipid light falling through the windows talking about the likelihood of war, the commercialization of Christmas, the health of unemployed men. It was like putting your hand in scalding water, then putting it in the fire to see just how bad the burn was. I was a masochist, and I wasn't surprised to learn that even masochism has sexual undertones.

If my memories were real then I had been violated incestuously to a state of insanity by my own father. Not once. Not twice. But hundreds of times. Not some strange little girl from my obscene memory. It was me. Me. The girl sitting in the shadows drinking tea. The girl in the mirror. The girl who heard voices. The girl with stranger's hands combing her hair, holding the pencil that made editing marks down the left column of her reports. The girl who peers at her reflection in the bus window on her way home from the station, the big engine straining up the hill, the vehicle shuddering. There is something sorrowful about the sound of buses in winter.

Christmas passed in a flurry of forgotten good will and in the New Year I would be twenty-one years old. I was painfully thin, drinking a bottle of gin every two days, swallowing pills for headaches, stomach aches, back aches, brain aches. The teddies looked grim. Mr Happy had fallen from the shelf and landed upside down. Would he ever be happy again?

Decisions for me are like a coil of rope and I have to get compulsively to the end before the decisions get made.

Finish the gin. Kill yourself. Cut your arms. Slit your throat. No one likes you. No one wants you. No one cares.

What are you doing all alone with your blue-eyed Irish boy only a few miles away? Why haven't you called him? Was it too late to go back? Is it always too late? When you saw the job advertised in the *Guardian* didn't it jump off the page because it was close to him? Was some part of your brain working independently from the part you call Alice? It felt like that. I felt sometimes that I wasn't in charge of my destiny, but its victim, its slave.

I had done the worst thing that a girl can do to a young man. I had let Patrick love me. I had let him take me to his bed and shrank from his touch, his hand on my flesh making my skin crawl. I was ashamed.

I flicked through my address book and stopped at Sarah's number. Brave, determined Sarah. I stared at the digits until my eyes blurred. I looked at my watch: 10 o'clock. I looked again: 11 o'clock. I thought about calling Elaine but couldn't face going out in the dark on my own to the phone box. I'd call her tomorrow. I could hear the wail of fire engines and ambulances and didn't know if they were outside in the street or inside my head.

Elaine had said she would always be there for me. She said you couldn't change the world, only yourself, and I was changing, breaking down, unravelling. I could feel the tectonic plates below the surface of my brain shifting, the left/right hemispheres drifting further apart, a sound like tearing plastic screeching through my head, the voices barking.

Kill yourself. Kill yourself. Cut your throat. Do it now. Do it, Alice. Do it, you bitch.

The voices. Always the voices.

My head was exploding. I covered my ears and looked round the room with the flowers on the walls growing bigger, the white swirls on the carpet turning like fat maggots, the light bulb flickering. The cacophony in my head was like an orchestra moving towards the edge of a cliff, the instruments going out of tune, the cellos and oboes and cymbals clanging, crashing, tumbling into the abyss.

I have what's called a highly reactive temperament. I was wired at birth to startle easily. Perhaps that's why Mother said I was a difficult child. I didn't sleep. I couldn't sleep. I lay there with my eyes open as she shut the door leaving me in the dim glow of the night light. Primates have a fear reflex that increases in darkness. Yet we send infants to sleep alone in the dark believing it's good for them. Then we wonder why children cry for attention, why families break down, why almost everyone is neurotic, anxious, stressed, uncertain, afraid. It starts in the cradle.

I lay in bed waiting. I was two and three and four and five and six. I was waiting for my daddy. This is what daddies do with little girls when their mummies go to bed. They come to your room. They are careless with the teddies. They tickle you. They kiss your lips. They take off your clothes and it hurts when they put their big willy inside you. It hurts, but that's what daddies do and you love your daddy.

My skin had turned yellow. My eyes were hollow and dead. I was at the end of my rope.

I needed to challenge my father once and for all, look into his eyes and see the truth. Cure myself or kill myself, as the Professor kept suggesting. I caught a train to Birmingham and then a connection to home. I called my father from the red-brick Victorian station and told him I was there by chance. Why I needed this subterfuge, this lie, seems silly and pointless, but I was bracing myself for the confrontation. He would be, he said, happy to see me, and I walked from the station thinking over what I was going to say.

It was the middle of the afternoon, icy cold. I felt sick and anxious as I walked along the row of houses with their dying balloons and dead paperchains. I paused in the wide porch before ringing the bell. There was still time to leave. I'd call from the station and apologize, escape back to my work.

This is silly, I thought. I was acting like a child. I felt like a child standing there with my finger hovering over the bell until suddenly, as if against my will, I pressed down long and hard.

He opened the door and I followed him through to the back room. 'I'll put the kettle on,' he said. The room was unlit, the winter light pale through the half-closed curtains. I remained standing in the centre of the room and came straight out with the words that had been running through my head since I was a teenager.

'You abused me when I was a child.'

There. I'd said it.

Finally, after so many years, it had come out of me.

He stopped what he was doing. His hands were shaking.

'What?' he replied. 'Don't be absurd. Are you crazy? You don't know what you're talking about.'

'You did, you did. That's what you did,' I said.

I could hear my voice getting higher. I felt small and he suddenly seemed like a giant with big arms and a big dark face looming over me, an expression I remembered from long ago.

'Why don't you sit down, Alice? Control yourself,' he said.

I took a step back.

'You're a dirty bastard. I hate you,' I yelled.

As the words left my mouth, he crossed the room to the kitchen and I watched as he picked up a kitchen knife from the counter. Everything moved really fast, as though a flashback was happening and I could see all the fragments of the film at the same time.

'Just stand still,' my father said, threatening me with the knife.

I was frozen to the spot. He moved away quickly. He closed the curtains, shutting out the light. I stood immobile, trembling inside, terrified. All the years of those malicious voices, all those memories I had thought were false abruptly made sense.

My mouth had gone dry with fear. Tears glazed my eyes. I felt my heart pumping in my chest as I snapped out of my daze and raced for the door. I had done what I had come for. Now I wanted to escape.

I got to the door handle, but as I pulled the door open he slammed it shut and slapped me across the face. He grabbed my arm and dragged me back to the centre of the room, the knife in his free hand, the blade glinting in the dim light. He hit me again and again, his open palm slapping my face. He dragged at my shoulder to force me down on to the floor and fell on top of me, straddling me, holding the knife to my throat. He hit me again. Much harder.

'Don't move,' he said.

He touched the tip of the knife to my throat as he lifted his leg off me. I was lying flat on the floor. He unclasped the metal button on my waistband and, as he pulled down the zip on my jeans, I remembered wearing all-in-one pyjamas as a baby with a long zip and the sound of that zip being lowered in the night. He dragged my jeans down over my hips and I lay there numb and terrified as he pulled off my shoes. He shuffled my jeans and knickers down my legs and over my feet at the same time. He then held the knife to my vagina.

'Don't you dare move,' he said again.

I was looking at him across the length of my half-naked body. I knew he wasn't going to cut me with the knife. He was holding it there to make me submissive. It worked. I was submissive. I lay there like a child.

He undid his trousers. He forced my legs apart and pushed his penis up inside me. He jerked up and down with a rolling motion and I could smell his fetid breath as he gasped for air. He pulled out suddenly, sat up on his knees and ejaculated over my face.

He stood and looked down at me lying on the floor.

'Now get up, you slag,' he said. 'Put your jeans on and clear out.'

I could barely breathe.

I did as I was told, pulling on my jeans, my pants, my shoes, my hands moving mechanically, my brain and body disconnected.

'Learn one lesson; don't tell anyone because they're not going to believe you,' he said, and for years and years nobody did.

It was five in the afternoon, the light failing as he hurried me out of the door and across the wet lawn to his car parked on the drive.

'Get in,' he said.

I did as I was told. I liked going in the car with my daddy.

He drove me back to the station. He didn't speak. Neither did I. I sat there, childlike, his mess drying on my face, and I remember thinking: This isn't me sitting here. I don't know who it is – and I don't care that much. I'm just glad it isn't me.

He stopped at New Street station. Not a word was said. I stepped out on the pavement and his car pulled away. I had to think for a moment where I was, where I was going, how I had come to be in my father's car. It was like a puzzle with tricky pieces of information that took time to work out. I touched my fingertips to the left side of my face where it really hurt.

People dressed in dark clothes moved with a sense of purpose through the brightly lit passages and tunnels, their breath leaving vapour trails. The concourse was crowded. Noisy. Everyone pushing. The train announcements and people begging for change were disorientating, a verbal blur, and my eyes, like the apertures on binoculars, took a long time to focus on the departure times and platforms.

The train took me back to Wales, the pulse of the metal wheels on the tracks like a heartbeat. I sat in a dark corner with the hood of my anorak covering my face.

I didn't wait for the bus. I walked the two miles from the station in the chilly dark night and couldn't feel my legs moving me along a step at a time. They didn't feel heavy or weightless, they seemed cut off from my body. My limbs and body parts must have atomized and the only link was some detached part of me, like a brain wave directing this mass slowly through the dead city.

At the bedsit, I turned on the light and sat on the bed where I remained all night in a trance counting the bobbles on my green and red fleece.

By morning, the bruises from the beating had swollen and my face in the mirror was a composite of all the faces of the women I had interviewed for my study on domestic violence. Was that me who wrote that dissertation? Was I the girl who got a first-class honours degree? The marathon girl?

That girl, it occurred to me, had gone, died, faded away. I was the girl in the mirror and I didn't have to doubt my memory any more. The bruises were the final proof. My father had raped me on his living-room floor as he had raped me from the time I was a small baby, throughout childhood and into my teenage years.

For many years, for as long as I could recall, I had been holding back the tide of truth, pretending it didn't happen, imagining it had happened to some other little girl, this doppelganger girl that I saw from outside myself. The dyke had broken. It was all true: the spiders, the man in the white car, the dungeon where people chanted and children were laid on an altar before being abused. I always remembered watching. Now I remembered being laid on the altar naked and vulnerable like a doll.

My father had raped me yesterday. It was his semen cracked in patches on my cheeks. He hadn't only abused me, he had threatened me at knifepoint and humiliated me, aiming his old-man sperm over my face.

It was unbelievable but true, and a relief to know it was true.

There was a lump in my stomach the size of a football. Bile rose acidly into my throat and I was sick in the loo, retching over and over again, my eyes closed, an icy feeling gripping my spine. I thought this is what hell must be like. I washed my face, I washed my body, I washed my hair and I went out to the phone box on the corner to call the office and explain I was too sick to go into work.

Why didn't I go to the police?

You just don't.

Why didn't I call my mother or Elaine or Patrick?

Today I'm Alice

My father had said no one would believe me and I believed him.

Like the women I'd met at the refuge, I felt ashamed. They didn't want to tell anyone. I didn't want to tell anyone. Your mind gets twisted when your face is battered and bruised, when you can barely see through your puffy eyes. You look in the mirror and you don't even look like you. You imagine that you must have done something wrong. You are in some way to blame. You get what you deserve. Being a victim, you take on a victim mentality.

You can't change the past or the inevitable. That's what Grandpa had said and, fatalistically, I put on my Nike Airs and went for a run. The thing with running is, you don't think. You don't go anywhere. You put one dead leg in front of the other, you propel yourself along, and the act of running is an end in itself.

When I got back to my room I sat back down on the bed crippled with shock, hugging a teddy, in a state of denial, aching all over and worrying suddenly and obsessively about my work. New material was coming in all the time. I didn't want to get behind. I decided to go to the office when everyone had left at six to collect some papers to study at home. I showered, dressed and put on a woolly hat.

I left the bedsit like a thief and stood in the hallway with cold air rising up the stairwell like hands reaching for my throat. The banister was damp and the bamboo pattern on the wallpaper looked like bars in the murky light. My legs were shaky. I had no sense of balance. As I walked down the stairs and along the empty street it felt as if I were on one of those rope bridges suspended over a gorge, the paving stones were swaying and slicked silver with rain. The world was unstable and, as I gasped for air, it felt as if I were swallowing bitter crystals from the gathering night. I was unfamiliar with who I had become. I had always felt alien inside my own skin, the chrysalis that should have been a butterfly, an egg fallen from the nest, a salamander caught in the wrong colour. A gust of wind blew the misty drizzle into my eyes. I closed my lids to see how far I could walk without losing the path and running into something.

The office building was in darkness except for a couple of yellow lights behind dirty windows. I crept up to our floor at about 6.15 and was surprised that Rosaleen and Louise were still in the office. I mumbled a hello, gathered some papers and hurried through to the kitchen area to get a glass of water.

Louise followed and, in the bright light, could see that I was bruised and swollen.

'Oh my God, Alice, what's happened?'

'Nothing.'

'It doesn't look like nothing to me.'

'I, I . . .'

'You poor thing.'

A tear welled into my eye and I shrunk into myself as Louise put her arms around me. I closed my eyes, gritted my teeth, and instantly pulled away.

Louise shook her head. 'Leave those papers, they're not important. I'm going to take you home and let Bernard have a look at you.'

Bernard Lloyd-Jones, her husband, was a doctor, a jolly, plump man fond of blazers and striped ties. He examined my bruises at their house. When he shone a light in my eyes I wondered if he could see a video clip of what had happened on the floor in my father's house. Louise made baked potatoes with baked beans, which I barely touched, and then drove me to Swansea A&E, initials that would figure large in my life in the coming years.

Louise waited while I was directed to a cubicle where I sat on the bed with the curtain drawn checking the bobbles on the fleece I was still wearing. Everything seemed unreal, or surreal, the bright lights, the smell of antiseptic, a baby crying, the voices murmuring incoherently as if they were shocked by this new turn of events and weren't sure of their present role. For three years at uni the auditory hallucinations had goaded me and I'd fought them. We were at a new stage neither I nor they were accustomed to. I felt abandoned.

A black lady doctor examined me. She noted the bruising on my face and the rows of small bruises on each of my upper arms where my father had left his fingerprints tattooed on my flesh. She asked me what had happened. I told her I had been attacked and that I didn't know who by. It was too shameful, too personal. After hiding the truth from myself for so many years, I couldn't just blurt it out now.

'You are absolutely certain you don't know who it was?' she asked.

This was my chance. Perhaps the last chance.

I shook my head. 'No, I don't know,' I said.

We remained silent for a few moments. But there was nothing she could do unless I told her the truth and let her help me. I stared down at my shoes and just wanted to be anywhere but in A&E. I didn't want to be alive. I didn't want to be dead. I wanted to be someone else, some other happier version of myself like that girl who had once spent the summer at Kibbutz Neve Eitan.

I stayed the night with Louise and Bernard. Next morning, when we were on our way to work in Louise's car, she suggested we stop to see her GP to get the morning-after pill in case I was pregnant. I was stunned when she said this. It would never have occurred to me, and I didn't know how Louise knew I had been raped and that I could possibly be pregnant. The fact that my father had withdrawn and ejaculated over my face was too horrible and vulgar even to contemplate.

It seemed as if I was no longer in charge of my life, that events now carried me along to the surgery of Dr Graham Sutton, who prescribed the appropriate pill and Nitrazepam, a sleeping tablet. He also suggested I return the following day for a chat. He was bright-eyed, ambitious, self-assured and kind. I didn't tell him at first that I had been raped and, when I did, I never said by whom.

I didn't go into work that day. Louise took me back to her house. I took the two pills and slept until the early evening in the spare bedroom. Bernard made scrambled eggs when I got up, and I went back to bed with another sleeping pill.

When I awoke at about 10.30 the following morning the wailing sirens and exploding bombs were for once not coming from inside my head. I went downstairs to find Louise glued to the television. It was January 1991. After Saddam Hussein's invasion of Kuwait, the war that would drive him out of that country had started with the American bombardment of Baghdad. What went through my mind as I watched the buildings disintegrating in clouds of dust was that just as my life was collapsing around me so too was the world.

After three days staying with Louise and Bernard, I returned to my bedsit for a change of clothes and Louise took me to the office. It was good for me to get back into the ritual of work, but I couldn't concentrate. As I read the words of reports it was as though the ink was still wet and the words ran into a watery mess. I soldiered on, reading, re-reading, retaining nothing. I attended the Friday meeting when we reported on the progress of our projects to the rest of the department. This was a productive exercise, a time for pooling ideas and deciding on the best way forward. The gathering was informal and it made me feel normal being there, even though I had nothing useful to add.

I continued to see Dr Sutton on a regular basis. His

surgery was close to the office, so I was able to pop in during my lunch hour. Graham Sutton was one of those doctors who welcomed you with a friendly touch on the arm and each time he did it I shrank away as if from fire. He was set on me seeing a community psychiatric nurse, which I resisted. I was a psychiatric agnostic. Shrinks always appeared to have their own psychological problems and, as I wasn't ready to talk about what had happened with my father, I couldn't see how it would be anything but a painful waste of effort.

The rest of my routine remained the same: rising exhausted after nightmare nights; news of the steady destruction of Baghdad by bombers flying over a city with no anti-aircraft guns; collating statistics of nicotine-related health costs from Brussels and Amsterdam; walking home in the winter chill to my spooky bedsit with the two-ring electric stove, chipped mugs and *The Waving Palms of Tropic Isles* dwarfed by the big blue flowers blooming like damp on the walls. A glass of gin, a broken night, a weekend run, words in journals all lost along the way.

I worked. I ate chocolate and drank gin. I gazed at my reflection. The bruises healed and the girl who appeared in the mirror was a different person. She still had voices telling her to top herself but she didn't have doubts any more.

My work became impossible. I couldn't concentrate. Smokers would have to get by without me. I talked about this with Louise. I hadn't been home to see my mother since being raped and Louise had become my surrogate mother. We discussed my 'post-traumatic stress'. Doctors' wives imagine they are doctors by proxy, and finally Louise persuaded me to take Dr Sutton's advice and see a psychiatrist.

Analysis is a slippery path and, against my own better judgment, I was on it. Dr Sutton made the appointment and a week later I made my way to the hospital, where the psychiatric unit looked like a chapel and was set apart in the hospital grounds. My appointment was with Dr Simpson, severe in tight skirts and well-cut jackets, another woman.

This was my new routine. I left work early every Monday for my session with Dr Simpson and we talked. What we talked about I cannot remember, but I do know I never mentioned the voices. She prescribed Lofepramine, an anti-depressant, which didn't agree with me, and then I was put on Prozac, which I take to this day.

Prozac puts a new slant on life. Now, I got up after a bad dream and, while I ate half a Weetabix, the radio reports of deaths and disaster in Iraq seemed like some eccentric piece of theatre unrelated to my existence. As long as people didn't kill themselves smoking, how they killed themselves didn't matter to me.

The daily anti-depressants kept me going for another week until I lay in a semi-hypnotic state on a black couch – just like you see in the movies – and Dr Simpson set about unlocking my childhood memories. She's good, actually. But I fight her. My skeletons belong to me and they're not ready to come waltzing out of the closet.

The sessions went on for weeks and months. I'm not sure what I told her, what she asked me or what she scratched on her pad in pencil. What I do recall was that on one occasion when she was able to make me regress to a childlike state, the session ran over time. She was in a hurry and we left the building at the same time.

'Goodbye, Alice.'

'Goodbye,' I replied in a small voice.

It was pouring with rain. I watched Dr Simpson pull away in a new car as I sat cross-legged on the tarmac in the pouring rain with tears streaming down my face, unable to unlock the chain on my bicycle.

CHAPTER 9
Where Can I Go?

Alice is strange. She looks like everyone else. But she isn't. She's got creepy things in her head. When Alice was a little girl her daddy did things that he shouldn't have done. He came to her cot. He came to her bed. He took off her night clothes. He pushed his willy in her botty, her front botty, her mouth. He liked to do wee wee on her face. It was sticky and felt funny. Alice made herself think it was normal when she was little and made herself forget until she was old enough to remember. Alice is clever. That's what people say. That was why she could separate what happened to Alice in the night and who Alice was when she went to school in the morning.

Who am I?
Where am I?
What am I doing here?
My brain is on fire.

It rains a lot in Wales. The sky has a shade of grey like old people's skin. The green hills aren't green. They are grey. Black Mountain is called Black Mountain because it's black. Mist hangs over the valleys like ash. The damp eats the calcium from your bones.

Life was grey and work at the health promotion department was a flicker of colour.

Spanish men are the heaviest smokers in Europe. They prefer that really heavy black tarry tobacco that rots teeth. Nothing will make them stop. It occurred to me that the best way to prevent people smoking was to ban it altogether, but governments need the tax revenue from smokers to pay for the heart and lung facilities in hospitals. It all makes sense if you look at things the right way.

I had no friends. Going to work's not like being at university. I was a recluse, jogging, writing in journals that I would lose like brain cells, remembering and forgetting. The Professor grumbled because I wasn't listening. Why should I? I had my own grumbles. My bedsit for one thing was shrinking. My bedroom was a cage. The blue flowers turned grey as they wound round trellises, the roots and stems growing thicker, hemming me in. The monkeys at Chester Zoo have more space. You couldn't see my cage but I knew it was there. It was a force field, like the electronic beams that protect precious objects and set off alarms when the beams are broken. The force field invisibly encased my head, and it took all my willpower to get through the wet days and cold nights.

Actually, it took Prozac and Valium, the keys to the cage. Skeleton keys. I have grown to know them well.

Valium belongs to a group of drugs called benzodiazepines. It deadens the senses. It is used for the management of anxiety disorders and affects those chemicals in the brain that are prone to lose balance and cause anxiety. Valium is prescribed for agitation, shakiness, to relieve certain types of muscle pain, handy after a ten-mile run, and hallucinations during alcohol withdrawal. But, then, why withdraw?

Prozac is a psychotropic drug, a form of fluoxetine hydrochloride. It is effective against panic attacks, depression, anxiety, nervousness, bulimia nervosa and insomnia. It can cause suicidal tendencies, as well as impair judgement and motor skills. Prozac stretches your mind into new shapes and, once stretched, it never returns to the original dimensions. Heroin does that too, and LSD. Not that I knew that yet.

I rarely took the train back home. I was on the verge of erupting and all those magma toxins would have suffocated my mother. I thought about Esther and how strong she must have been to have survived Buna-Monowitz.

One weekend it rained for 48 hours without stopping. The rain beat like bony fingers against the window panes. Tap. Tap. Tap. Tap. Tap. Tap. Fungus was growing on the walls. I polished off a bottle of gin sitting huddled over the two-bar electric fire and wrote a poem, one of the few that has lasted through the moves and the years. It is called 'Where Can I Go?'

If this is not the place where tears are understood where
    do I go to cry?
If this is not the place where my spirits can take wing
    where do I go to fly?
If this is not the place where my feelings can be heard
    where do I go to speak?
If this is not the place where you'll accept me as I am
    where can I go to be me?
If this is not the place where I can try and learn and grow
    where can I go to laugh and cry?

It was time to move on. Louise Lloyd-Jones brought the thought into focus when she showed me an ad in one of the national newspapers for a research assistant at the University of Huddersfield. It was associated with a PhD programme on the topic of community health groups and came with a

£5,000 bursary, which would mean a severe cut in my income. I was flattered that after acting like a child around Louise and Bernard they thought I was up to it and persuaded me to apply.

I went for the interview and was offered the position. On the train back to Wales it stopped raining. Six months had gone by since that day my father raped me. I wasn't healed. I would never heal. I was a cracked egg, cracking more, but slowly. I served out a month's notice and my colleagues, as a going-away present, gave me a cuddly Welsh dragon. It terrified the teddies until they got used to its devilish grin and scarlet coat.

To find digs in Huddersfield I started by calling the number on an ad tacked to the university notice board. I spoke to a woman named Kathy Higgins, who arranged to meet me at the railway station in order to take me to see the room in person. I understood why when we arrived.

The house was at the top of a steep hill and further from the university than most students wanted to be. Kathy showed me into a large, bright, airy room with a view over fields turning golden in the lowering sun. She said I would share the bathroom and have the run of the house. I met Kathy's partner Jim, a roll-your-own sort of man, and decided to take the room and not mention that smoking is bad for your health.

Before I went up to Huddersfield I had a few weeks' holiday. I was up at dawn to get the early train and by nightfall I was back in my beloved Israel. It was late in the season and I went straight to Eilat, which is close to the Jordanian border and hot all year round. I got a job in a beach bar – yes, me, Alice – and shared a shack with a man I'd only known for five minutes. Samir was a Druze from Lebanon. We made an odd couple, me filled with darkness and shadows, Samir austere with enlightened eyes and a gentle manner.

The Druze are a mystical Islamic sect founded in Persia. It is unique with its incorporation of early Christian Gnostic philosophy and monotheistic, just like Muslims, Christians and Jews, which made all the labels to me seem merely divisive and utterly ridiculous. I told Samir my thoughts and he said, 'Ah.'

'Ah?' I repeated.

'Ah,' he said.

'Well, aren't I right?'

'You are neither right nor wrong. You have merely expressed an opinion.'

'What do you think, Samir? Wouldn't the world be better without religions?'

'When you are ready to know the answer to that question someone will appear to tell you,' he said.

He was frustrating and adorable. He reminded me of Patrick. He worked nights, I worked days, and when we crossed he was more embarrassed than I was to be sharing our free accommodation.

When I wasn't working, I spent my time on the beach with novels whose titles have escaped my memory, although sometimes I pick up a book and have that déjà vu feeling of having read it before. I swam with a snorkel and flippers and went often to the Coral World Underwater Observatory where, wrapped in the still green light, I would try to imagine what it was like being a fish.

When I had a few days off, I crossed into Jordan to visit the Red City of Petra. I stepped out of the dusty bus; the roof was piled high with hessian sacks and chickens in baskets. Men in burnooses chewed hemp, women in black toted suitcases on their heads. I watched a picture-book Arab playing a reed pipe while a browbeaten cobra rose sluggishly from a basket. The sun on my face was like standing before an open oven. There was the intermingled smells of spices, smoke and sweat. People jostled me as I studied the map I'd picked up in Eilat.

The bus driver stepped down and lit what I calculated was his two hundredth fag of the day. He looked at me standing there with my eyes filled with wonder.

'You, come, come,' he said. He pointed at the colonnade beyond the bus station

'Where?'

'You come.'

He crooked his fingers and I followed him into the shadows where metal tables and chairs were set out under the arches. It was like the catacombs below a cathedral and surprisingly cool. Old men with beards and serene faces smoked hubble-bubble pipes, their stained lips drawing on the long tubes, the water bubbling like indigestion. We sat at a table and a waiter in a soiled white coat brought a pot of mint tea, two glasses and a little bowl of sugar cubes that instantly attracted a swarm of flies. My companion waved his cigarette about.

'Ahmed,' he said, introducing himself with an old-fashioned bow.

'Alice. I'm pleased to meet you.'

'Pleased to meet you. Thank you very much.'

The driver was Palestinian and spoke a few words of English, which must have come from a basic course that every man who climbs out of his galabeyah into trousers and a shirt is required to learn: Where are you from? Are you married? Do you have any children? I said I did medical research. He nodded wisely.

'A doctor?'

'A student.'

'A student doctor?' he asked.

I went along with the fantasy. People believe what they want to believe.

Ahmed had a son and three daughters, he told me. He held up three fingers and the downturn of his lips seemed to ask why he should have been condemned to such a fate. We settled into an amiable silence and drank our tea. Once you become acquainted there is no need for gratuitous gossip in Arab countries, and I wondered if perhaps we talked too much about the wrong things in order to avoid talking about the things that matter.

I tried to pay for the tea and Ahmed looked offended.

'No. No. No. It is me.'

'*Shukran,*' I said.

He smiled again. '*Assalamu alaikum.*' God be with you.

While I had been sitting in the shadows, the sun had stoked up its fires, but I was anxious to keep to my schedule and spent the next three hours exploring the Red City. The sky was a blue sheet, the light making the edges of things well defined. Petra is an archaeological ruby and as I wandered the narrow streets I was moved to a hypnotic state by the shimmering palette of reds in the ancient stones, by the sense of the eternal captured in every grain of sand.

Petra is on the edge of the Wadi Araba desert surrounded by soaring hills of rust-coloured sandstone, a natural protection from invaders. Building at Petra began in the sixth century BC when Arab nomads planted the first date orchards and abandoned their camel saddles to farm and trade. Herod the Great tried to bring the Arabs under his control, but the Red City remained independent until the Romans took over in AD 100. The fort constructed by the Crusaders in the twelfth century turns in the sun from yellow to pink to the same shade of brilliant red as the Welsh dragon at home with the teddies. The early Arabs carved temples and tombs into the soft rock that crumbles easily back into sand, a lesson to me that all things are fragile and fleeting.

From the ruins of the Crusader castle I gazed at the severe existential beauty of the desert. I remembered Samir when I asked if the world might be a better place without religion and he had answered enigmatically that when I was ready to know the answer someone would appear. I felt ready at that moment, but there was no one there in the sun but me.

I could travel alone through macho Italy and into the unpredictable perils of the Middle East without fear. I stayed in villages where every woman was veiled except me. I slept in youth hostels and pensions. I ate street food from stalls and in dim cafés suggested by guide books or, best of all, discovered alone and by chance. While I was travelling I was a different part of me, an international, more cosmopolitan, more receptive Alice. I quickly picked up essential phrases and found that a few words in another man's tongue was enough to build lasting bridges: please, thank you, goodbye – *min fadlik, shukran, ma'assalama.*

The cosmopolitan Alice disappeared the moment the white cliffs of Dover came metaphorically into view. That person closed down and I could feel the switch as I put my foot on English soil. I shrank an inch as my shoulders sagged. My hair lost its bounce. The tic in my neck arose from slumber and began to dance. Ah, home again, let's get nervous. I was a born expatriate and, just as nutty people become psychiatrists, and bullies, I would discover, were born for careers on the wards of psychiatric hospitals, I was destined ironically to live in middle England with my middle-class job, values and anxieties.

Did I think about my father during the time I was away? Yes I did. Every day. The picture in my mind of him holding a knife to my vagina and hissing 'Don't you dare move' was like a scene from some sickening film of the sort I never finished watching. Such things live with you all the time. They grow like a cancer, a black lump that throbs in your gut and sometimes you stand naked in front of the mirror wondering if the black thing is about to break through your skin.

Like a terrible burn, you are scarred for life, but the scar is on the inside, on your memory. No one can see it and you don't quite believe things you can't see with your own eyes are true. Even *I* found it hard to believe that what had happened had happened. I would forget for a moment and become a free spirit. I would lose myself watching a girl of about four washing clothes with her mother, both in the same pale-blue galabeyahs, heads covered, the little girl with a smaller version of her mother's bowl. The water in those bowls was sandy red and you had to wonder if the clothes were any cleaner after washing than before.

On my journey, I wasn't abandoned by the voices, by slips in time, by memory lapses, but the sense of otherness takes you out of yourself. You are not free from the past but abroad there was at least distance.

I returned from Petra and the last few days I stayed in Nahariyya, one of my favourite places, a town of 50,000 people settled mainly by German Jews in the 1930s. It is just south of the Lebanese border and stretches out behind the line of beaches along the Mediterranean. There is a narrow river dividing the town with bridges at regular intervals. Everyone is out on the street at night when the air is cool and the shops and street stalls are busy. The night smells of patchouli oil and roast corn on the cob. I ate sticky baklava packed with honey and pistachios and remembered eating those same sweet pastries on my school trip across the Aegean in the SS *Bolivia* all those years ago when Grandpa was still alive.

On my last evening in Nahariyya, I sat on the beach watching the sun go down. The sky was a pale shade of pink against the sea. I was at peace, something I had not felt for nearly a year.

Before leaving the country, I caught the bus back to Tel Aviv and hitched a ride in an old farm truck to Moshav Bene Atarot. I had stayed there picking fruit one summer for the Zimmer family and everything looked the same as I remembered: the simple unadorned buildings, the neat fields, the orchards laid out in lines. I entered the main door, it was never locked.

'*Shalom*,' I called.

Ruth, the mother of the family I had worked for, appeared on the top landing.

'Alice.' She came running down the stairs. 'I don't believe it.'

She welcomed me like the prodigal daughter. It had been more than two years since we had last seen each other but it felt as if only a day had passed. I felt strange, because I felt like me, that it was me, Alice, standing there unafraid to be hugged and hugging Ruth back.

That night, with Ruth's husband and grown children, we had dinner and talked about the Gulf War. Iraqi Scud missiles had landed on Tel Aviv when Saddam Hussein realized that the war was lost and decided to go down in a blaze of glory striking Israel.

I had listened every day to the news reports on Radio 4 but remembered nothing. Nothing. I just remembered the rain, the damp bedsit, the data from Brussels and watching Dr Simpson shifting adroitly through the gears as she shot off in her car from the hospital car park.

CHAPTER 10
Splitting

It was three miles to the centre of Huddersfield and I felt my suntan being sucked from my cheeks as I freewheeled down the long hill. It was cold and bleak. The streetlights were still on at ten in the morning.

Alice Jamieson PhD.

Dr Alice Jamieson.

It sounded silly. I felt about seven years old.

I had already been to check out where I was supposed to be going but I still got lost and cycled in circles round the one-way system. Huddersfield huddles at the bottom of a crater, but the wind finds its way through the gaps in the surrounding hills and blows in your face no matter which way you are going. The city was rich during the Industrial Revolution but the textile mills had nearly all closed and the people looked poor and ravaged, scurrying by with their hair tossed about and their collars turned up.

When the Methodist preacher John Wesley arrived in the city during his evangelical tour in 1757 he wrote in his diary: 'I rode over the mountains to Huddersfield. A wilder people I never saw in England. The men and women filled the streets. They seemed ready to devour us.'

Luckily there wasn't much meat on me and at Iceland you could buy fifty sausages for 99p. There were lots of second-hand shops. Sale signs were pasted on the windows though Christmas was upon us with fairy lights and paperchains and memories of the journey from New Street Station to the door guarded by white lions at my father's home.

When I passed the original college for the third time, I realized it looked like a birthday cake with its bunched towers and balconies like bulges of cream. Cramped terraces with slate roofs line the grey streets, but then you can turn the corner and come upon modern colleges like new-age temples with curving glass walls totally alien to the local architecture. The Harold Wilson Building reminded me of my sixth-form college.

Everything at that time reminded me of something else. There were 10,000 students in Huddersfield and I was reminded that not one of them would invite me to sit and share a pot of mint tea. I was reminded of how it was easy for me to travel alone without getting lost in the Middle East while here I was riding illegally the wrong way down a one-way street still searching for the university building where I'd be working. Kathy and Jim, my hosts, had strong Yorkshire accents and fiery tempers. They sometimes shouted abuse at each other up the stairs and I would remember Mum and Dad fighting and me listening until my father locked me in the Bird Cage.

What did that mean? Why did he do that? Was my father proving that even if he had no power over my mother, he had power over me, locking me up, coming to my bed, taking me to the dungeon? Was I being punished for being a bad girl, provocative, sexually precocious? Did I talk too much? Was I too clever by half, as Mum would say?

I knew I was none of these things but kept questioning myself, blaming myself. No matter how much I tried, I couldn't prevent my thoughts going back to my childhood, that melancholic tapestry I was forever trying to unpick in order to weave a different picture. The past looks better if you can lie to yourself.

I was twenty minutes late as I sprinted up the stairs to the third floor where I would be sharing an office with Gerald Brennan, my director of studies, and another lecturer who shall remain nameless because I've forgotten his name.

Gerald didn't seem to notice I was late. He lived in his head and didn't notice very much at all. I liked him immediately. We avoided looking into each other's eyes as we shook hands. Gerald said, 'You don't have to be mad to work here but it helps,' which made me feel at home. If Gerald with his round John Lennon glasses and straggly hair was breaking the ice with humour, his next comment was a real hoot. In two days, we had to deliver a paper on the relevance of Operational Research to Community Health Groups at the Young Operational Researchers Conference in Edinburgh. Operational Research was a completely new area of study to me and he asked me to cram up on two books on the subject in the next forty-eight hours.

'In two days?'

'I bet you can do it,' said Gerald.

'You must be a gambler,' I said, and his brow furrowed.

'No, no. Not really.'

In fact, Gerald was a Boys' Brigade leader concerned with the welfare of children, but I would come to see that he was unable to communicate his enthusiasms in a practical way. He showed me to my desk behind the door. We cleared the clutter and he gave me a book on operational research the size of the Oxford Dictionary. He wandered off polishing his glasses and I inhaled a mouthful of dust as I opened the pages. This was my kind of task. Big book. Head down. Left-brain logic without right-brain unpredictability. I was something of a speed-reader back then, but seemed to be retaining nothing and decided to return to OR later and focus for now on community health groups, my area of expertise.

For two days I read and made notes and, come the conference, I was almost wetting myself with nerves. In my daily life I spoke to almost no one. Me speaking to an audience was as rare as sun in Wales. Luckily Gerald was an incredibly dull speaker, which gave me confidence. He gave his spiel on OR and glanced at me.

'. . . and, finally, Alice Jamieson is here to fill us in on current strategies for community health groups.'

You can do it. You can do it. You can do it.

Nails in palms, knees shaking, I stood, stared without focusing and mumbled a few sentences rehearsed the night before in front of the mirror in Kathy's bathroom. There was a half-hearted round of applause, the chairs in the hall scraped back and the students raced off to light fags and act cool, the real point of student life. Grunge was in and I envied those confident girls with their multicoloured bovver boots and dreadlocks.

The paper we delivered outlined a project designed by Gerald, which I would later reshape. In my first few months at the university I was obliged to come up with a research proposal initially for a MPhil with a view to gaining a PhD. Gerald was more than willing to help, but living as he did in his own strange space, he was unable to explain the subject rationally and sometimes I wondered if he was madder than me.

Fortunately, there was a supervisor above Gerald. Colin Ince was tall and thin with stooped shoulders and a healthy measure of emotional intelligence underpinning his sharp mind. His was busy writing a book, which meant we rarely met, although when we did he challenged my ideas and introduced a fresh perspective without changing the basis of my research. He helped me shape my proposal round how I thought OR, as a research strategy, could be used to enable community health groups to become more involved in the decision-making process, and the implementation of initiatives that concerned people at grass-roots level. This required me identifying various community health groups and working with them, as well as with those responsible for making strategic decisions within the locality, including Kirklees Metropolitan Borough Council and Huddersfield and Dewsbury Health Authorities.

This was my life. I was happy. All the theories and research had an end product. I discovered that many people when they fall sick feel they are in some way at fault, they are malingering, exaggerating, that the hospital isn't there for them, but for the doctors and clinicians with their white coats and hurried sense of purpose. Doctors have a habit of chatting about you across the bed as if you're not there, which makes patients feel detached and vaguely ashamed. Cancer? Heart tremors? Overdose? Don't make a fuss, go home and make a nice cup of tea.

My research was designed to develop systems to help people with health issues overcome these innate doubts and feel more connected to the healing process, with the secondary objective of making clinicians more aware of the patients' need to be informed and involved in their own treatment.

One person who was to be a source of inspiration to me was Rebecca Wallington, a manager for the health authority. We met for the first time in her office. She made coffee, we sat down and she looked gravely across her desk.

'By the way, Alice, I'm a lesbian,' she said.

'Oh . . .'

Naturally I was surprised by this sudden announcement. People's sexuality was of no interest to me, although I believe adults should be free to be and do whatever they want as long as it doesn't harm or hurt or touch the lives of children. I told her so.

'I agree entirely, two hundred per cent,' she said, and smiled warmly.

Rebecca had long, silver-grey hair worn in a French pleat, strong features in a face with only a trace of make-up and a direct manner I appreciated. She must have sensed that I was needy and always went out of her way to help me with my project.

Christmas came and went. Huddersfield in winter was like Wales in winter, a solid sheet of grey, the wind rattling the windows in my room, the hill back to Kathy's house growing steeper.

I'd often find Jim sitting in the kitchen with a pot of tea, rolling a fag. He did this with great skill, always plucking the same amount of tobacco from his pouch of Golden Virginia, spreading it across a green Rizla and winding it into a perfect tube. His big tongue would pop out to lick the gum and he'd seal it with an air of a job well done. Smoking was a ritual as much as an addiction and I thought I ought to write to the Welsh Office to make that point.

Kathy would cook and Jim would sit at the table gripping his knife and fork ready to tackle her meat pies and meat puddings, stew with dumplings, roast beef with Yorkshire pud on Sunday, fish and chips on Friday, apple pie with custard, rhubarb crumble, plum duff, rock cakes. Kath was a whiz in the kitchen. When I helped we made a great team, and when we sat down together like a family I felt as if I were their child and they were my mum and dad. They talked about politics and money, TV programmes and football. They had arguments and swiftly made up, they hugged and said, 'Bye, love,' when they went out, and, 'I'm home, love,' when they came in. I learned to speak like them and wanted them to adopt me.

We didn't eat together every day, and there were days when I didn't eat at all. I stocked up like a camel and when I got obsessed by some community health issue, I'd forget about food and make do with a few nips of gin. Gin, Prozac, Valium and work were my four best friends. They were like the four elements, earth, air, fire and water, the essential combination to maintain life.

Like smoking, taking drugs is a ritual. There's an exquisitely sensual feeling in pressing the lozenge-shaped pills from bubble packs, tapping out the daily dose from a bottle into your cupped palm. You count how many pills you've taken and how many remain. It becomes part of you. Then it becomes you. Drugs make reality pleasurable. Pain disappears. For a while. But the thing about drugs is that they are false friends that soon turn nasty. You need more and more to do the same job, then you need still more to modify the pain of being and make reality merely tolerable.

I kept my pills in the drawer in the bedside table and was glad the colour coding made it hard to get them mixed up. Prozac was elegant in a half-green and half-cream capsule, one 20mg tablet a day, the lowest dose. Valium was a sunny yellow, three 5mg pills a day, morning and night, one to slow down, a couple to sleep .... The alarm with its green numbers magnified and distorted through the bottle of Evian beside the bed, the winter sun slipping through the bedroom curtains, the song of the wind as I freewheeled downhill to uni, Gerald talking to himself in a foreign language.

Sometimes I would get the shakes for no reason and remember I had forgotten to take my pills. I then had to rush home to my room, which by this time I had turned into a menagerie of stuffed beasts, the teddies, Mr Happy and the red dragon staring misty-eyed from the shelf. I would enter the compound saying to myself, 'Take your Valium. Take your Valium. Take your Valium', just to make sure I didn't forget why I had returned home.

If there was no water I would swallow the pills with a nip and abandon the office for the rest of the day. I would watch my hand trembling like a leaf on a tree in the wind and wait for the wind to go down. A relaxed feeling like diving into warm water would come over me and I'd work sitting on the bed with my books spread about me, or sit on the floor with my back against the radiator. I could start reading at two in the afternoon and if Kathy didn't call me I'd still be there at midnight.

I was living the life of a nun in the Middle Ages locked in my cell studying the gospels of community health and operational research, my mind straying on odd moments back to the sandy lanes of Kibbutz Neve Eitan, the taste of Patrick briefly on my lips. I had no sexual desires but I did have emotional ones. I felt isolated, cut off, alone, belonging nowhere and to no one. My work gave me a sense of purpose, but all work and no play was making Alice a dull grey mournful little girl.

Spring appeared like a nervous bird in the back garden. Daffodils popped up to face the arctic winds. Sometimes doubt stole over my feelings of well-being and on down days I felt of no value to anyone. I was studying for a PhD to prove myself to myself and my detractors, the voices who kept telling me my destiny was to fail at everything except killing myself.

Top yourself. Top yourself. You know you want to.

Suicide remained in my mind like a choice on the night's TV schedule: Channel 4 news, *EastEnders*, a documentary about Operation Desert Storm, save up the Valium, drink a bottle of gin and say, 'goodbye cruel world it's over.' Only Pink Floyd will do for a suicide funeral. It would be outdoors.

A big hole and a polished coffin with brass whatnots. They're standing there in black: Mother with a veil à la Audrey Hepburn in *Breakfast at Tiffany's*; Father like Dracula, grim and toothy; Clive with some model in a mini-skirt. They are staring dry-eyed at the black earth on a rain-washed day and thinking about the words in my suicide note. I had a notebook once with dozens of versions, gone now, but saying in essence that my father abused me in my cradle and there was no one there to save me.

When my father raped me on the floor of his house that day I lost the charade of my carefully constructed false past. I lost the flimsy tissue of trust I had in my mother. I lost any sense that with my brother Clive we were still a family. The days since that day had been confusing, overlapping, as if it had been one long day and I had been interminably awake sifting over scenes and memories to try and make sense of them and put them in some sort of order.

I was lonely, and looked forward to my meetings with Rebecca with her discreetly lipsticked lips and strong coffee.

Things had been steadily cracking and it was in her small room when something broke finally and for ever.

It was cold outside and warm in the office. Condensation ran down the window. Rebecca had concentrated dark-green eyes and sometimes I felt engulfed in her gaze. Her desk was ornamented with an oddly phallic cactus in a red pot and a photo of a woman with short hair and baggy dungarees with a bib and straps over her shoulders.

Rebecca suggested that day that it would be a good idea for Gerald to attend one of our meetings. As she spoke, her voice began to blur into a slow monotone. Then it faded. Her lips kept moving and what I heard was: *She's looking at you and she wants you to die.*

It wasn't Rebecca's voice but a stranger's voice from

outside my head. I have no idea how I reacted, but Rebecca sensed something was wrong. As she was shuffling the papers on her desk she kept saying, 'Are you OK, Alice?' and repeating the question about the meeting.

I managed to say, 'Yes, I think that's a good idea.'

I was on my feet and ready to go. I could hear movement inside my skull. It was as if a flock of birds were fluttering their wings. I dug my nails into my palm. Keep it together, Alice. Keep it together. I tried to see myself as others saw me. I was never natural. I was always watching myself. I was always acting Alice. Acting normal and feeling totally weird.

Rebecca suggested a couple of dates for the following week and I rushed out of her office and pedalled through Huddersfield as if the devil were chasing me. I kept it together long enough to speak to Gerald. He didn't notice anything was wrong, consulted his diary, and we arranged the meeting for the following Wednesday at two.

That evening at home, I was watching *EastEnders* on TV with Kathy, when all of a sudden one of the characters started to talk to me.

See her – Kathy ... she's your enemy.

It was an actress with lots of hair. She was looking out of the screen directly at me and she said the same thing again, *Yes, Alice, her. Kathy ... She hates you. She's your enemy.*

I didn't follow *EastEnders* and I didn't know this woman, but she was definitely speaking to me and she got louder and louder, more compelling, not a strange voice, but her own voice, the actress's voice.

She hates you. She hates you. She hates you.

I jumped up off the sofa and as I rushed from the room I bumped into Jim as he opened the kitchen door.

'Whoa. Where are you off to in such a hurry?' he said innocently.

Today I'm Alice

'I'm meant to be meeting a friend for a drink and I'm running late.'

Which friend? I didn't have any friends except Kathy and Jim, and now I wasn't sure about them. Adopt me? They wanted to kill me. They had lured me to this house in the middle of nowhere. My bedroom was at the top of a narrow flight of stairs that grew steeper and narrower as you climbed, the stairs shuddering like teeth on an escalator. My hands were shaking. The lights were flickering. The walls were clammy like damp rubber. I fell into my room and grabbed some money.

I inched my way out of the house and down the hill to town. The voice of the woman from *EastEnders* was still calling, *Get ready, Alice. Get ready to kill yourself.*

At the off-licence I asked for a bottle of gin and heard the shopkeeper say, *You may seek salvation in the drink, but eventually it'll happen. We will soon see the end of you. You will kill yourself.*

Swigging from the bottle, I walked for miles. I drank myself into a stupor. It was a miracle I found my way back to the house in the early hours, my breath icy, my fingers prickling with cold. The voices were chattering away, the Professor, the actress from *EastEnders*, a sad little boy, probably the child who had woken me crying out in my dreams those weeks immediately before I confronted my father and he raped me. I felt the little boy growing inside me like a chick in an egg about to crack through the shell.

My head was spinning with alcohol, splitting, the left hemisphere untying its knots with the right. I imagined two bubbles of the sort children blow through metal rings, first together, then separating and floating off, oily blue, into the universe.

I must have slept because I woke fully dressed with my

head buried under the pillow. Kathy and Jim had gone to work. I hurried to the drinks cabinet. My hands were shaking so much as I opened the door that one of the ornaments leapt into the abyss and landed on the carpet. The figure was from the cherished collection of what Kathy called Capodi-monte, a coy Victorian girl with golden locks holding a large pink hat. Things were breaking but they weren't all broken yet.

I put the figure back in its place, took a slug of brandy from the bottle, had a shower and put on some clean clothes. As I was my own person at the university it didn't matter what time I got in, if I got in at all. I swallowed two Valium and walked down the hill. I was afraid to cycle. The voices started shouting. They came from around corners and from behind closed windows, from the external world, but hidden.

You can't hide from us, Alice. You can run away, but we'll find you.

I stopped to cross the road. My eyes were fuzzy. I slapped the side of my head. Focus. Concentrate. As the green crossing man lit up, I had the feeling that I was that green man running across the road.

Wherever you are, we will be there too. We're the best friends you have, Alice. Don't you know by now? How much more will it take for you to realize that your destiny is to fail at everything except killing yourself?

The voices had always been intermittent. Now they were constant; a radio stuck between stations. I tried to study in the university library as I thought the stillness would make the voices calm down. I was wrong.

You're a fraud. All these books and journals surrounding you don't make you clever. Stop trying to be Einstein. You're just pathetic little Alice, pathetic little Alice, pathetic little Alice.

I left everything except my pencil case on the desk. I'd had enough. I had £10 in my pocket. I made my way into town and at the off-licence I bought a bottle of gin.

When I woke I was in a strange bed with misty lights that smelled of dust flashing as if in code on the ceiling. My first thought was that I had been abducted by aliens.

In fact I was in the recovery room at Huddersfield A&E.

I just stared. I didn't know who I was. Where I was. My arms were pinned down by the tightly tucked sheet. I felt like a child and the body lying in the bed belonged to someone else. Prozac made me feel like me. Without it, who was I?

I wriggled out of the sheets and as I sat up I was instantly sick. I was shocked to discover that my arms were heavily bandaged from my wrists to my upper arms. A nurse was sitting beside the bed keeping vigil. She cleared up the sick. She was gentle and efficient.

'There, there, best to bring it all up,' she said.

My memory was in shreds. Imagine a photograph cut into narrow strips then jumbled up. Everything is there, but you can't see the whole picture and even the strips have no bearing on reality. I did know I had consumed a large amount of alcohol. But I must have done something crazier than just being found drunk to have a nurse sitting by my bed.

I thought it would be a good idea to say something and planned it for several seconds.

'She's all right,' I said.

'Who is?' asked the nurse.

'Alice. I'm all right now.'

As I spoke I wondered if I had said something wrong. It didn't sound like me. There were so many voices muttering in the background it was hard to tell. I thought this was probably the voice of my subconscious, and I had a sudden, foggy recollection of blood running in streams like the condensation running down Rebecca's office window.

'We're waiting for the psychiatrist to come and see you,' the nice nurse said.

Something snapped, or something that had snapped fixed itself.

A psychiatrist.

'A psychiatrist?'

'Yes, she won't be long.'

I wasn't having any of that. I was afraid that I'd be transferred to a psychiatric unit: I'd seen them during research trips and they were filled with nutters.

I didn't shout or kick up a fuss. Not clever Alice. I quietly explained that I did not have a medical condition. I was an overworked PhD student, I said, and that they couldn't hold me against my will.

'You are only here for your own safety,' the nurse said.

'I know that, and I really do feel better.'

The nurse decided to go off and see if the psychiatrist had arrived and I made my escape. By a stroke of luck – we all get them sometimes – my clothes were in the bedside locker. I dressed and slipped like a shadow down the long corridor passing signs with yellow and black symbols – Radiography, Outpatients, Pharmacy – out through the double doors that made a sucking sound and into a new day smelling of spring.

Not having anywhere else to go, I made my way home, suspicious that Kathy and Jim were not my friends but secret enemies. I retreated to my bedroom, took my Prozac and Valium and must have gone to sleep. I woke at five with the voice of doom booming inside the room.

You must die.

Other voices joined in.

You must die. You must die.

At first I didn't know where I was. Was I at home? Was I asleep? Was I awake?

The booming voices continued: *You must die. You must die.*

I grabbed Mr Happy.

'Can you hear that?'

He just grinned and I grinned back at him. I tried singing along with the voices. *You must die. You must die. You must die.* Like a football chant. I'm not sure how long we kept this up, but eventually I snapped into reality.

I was in my bed. Arms bandaged. I didn't know why and didn't want to find out. I thought about Kathy and Jim. Were they plotting to get me? Jim had evil red eyes and Kathy had the same face as that woman in *EastEnders*.

Why had Kathy wanted to meet me at the train station and take me in person to her house? She must have put that advertisement up on the notice board in secret, then taken it down as soon as I called. No one knew I was in this house of horrors at the top of a hill. I was trapped. Alone. They were going to kill me. Hide me under the floorboards. I was sure of it. I had to get away from them. They were behind the voices.

You must die, they chanted. *You will die.*

Where do I go? What do I do? It had turned black outside. The voices were echoing round the room. Kathy and Jim were plotting downstairs.

I couldn't think what to do.

I had to clear my head. Finally, I changed into my jogging clothes. I grabbed my keys and sneaked out of the house. I ran. My head was full of wild, strange thoughts. I was sure people were plotting to get me and kept thinking: It's just not fair, I haven't done anything. It's not my fault. Are they going to lock me in the Bird Cage with a tin of spaghetti hoops? I had to get away. If I could run fast enough, I'd be able to outrun the voices. Cheat time.

I ran and ran, still hearing the voices ringing in my ears.

You will die, Alice. You will die.

Shut up. Shut up. Shut up.

We'll soon see the end of you. Kill yourself. Kill yourself. Do it now. Do it today.

I ran with tears streaming down my face. I ran until the sun began to peek through the clouds. I ran until I was out of breath and exhausted. And still the voices continued pounding into my head as my feet pounded the ground.

When I arrived back at the house it was gone ten. I had been running for almost four hours. I had completed another marathon and, with a flash of sanity, regretted that I hadn't raised another £500 for the NSPCC.

Listen to the children, I thought. Listen to the children.

Kathy and Jim had gone to work. I was alone. I stripped off my clothes in the bathroom and stared again with surprise and disbelief at the bandages round my arms. I snipped through the bindings just above my elbow and as I peeled away the dressing I felt sick at the sight that met my eyes. On the soft inner flesh of my left arm from my wrist to the crook was a series of red, almost parallel welts and lacerations, some stitched and coated in yellow betadine antiseptic. My right arm was also cut, but less so. The cuts were clean, slightly jagged, as if made with a serrated knife, already healing, and I wondered who the hell had done this to me.

You did it.

No, I didn't.

Yes, you did, Alice. You.

I didn't.

You want to kill yourself. But you're afraid.

Shut up!

I showered for about an hour. I knew in a hazy, detached way that I had harmed myself. But had no memory of having done so and no idea why I would do such a thing. I can't have been in my right mind. I had been drinking for sure. I had a recollection of a pain like a thousand migraines, a pain so sharp it was as though the blade of a knife was actually slicing through the membranes and muscles and synapses of my brain, cutting out the memories.

You did it.

I didn't. I didn't. I didn't.

You did.

I was conversing with the voices, but it wasn't my voice responding. Or rather, it *was* my voice but it didn't sound like me. I dried myself on a towel and stared into my eyes in the mirror. Someone else was in there.

There are two schools of thought when it comes to open wounds: the first that it is best to allow them to heal in the fresh air; the second that it is best to keep them covered. I subscribe to the second, so I wrapped the bandages up to my elbows.

I slept for a few hours and returned to the university as if nothing had happened.

CHAPTER 11
The Children

There's a gun in my backpack. There's also a monkey on a key chain with no keys. A tube of Smarties. A copy of *The Magus* by John Fowles, with a bookmark at the beginning of chapter 5. On the first page written in pencil is the name Rebecca Wallington.

Did she give it to me? Lend it to me? Did I steal it? Have I read the first four chapters? Because if I have I'll have to read them again to see what the hell they're about.

The gun is made of plastic and fires caps that explode like Christmas crackers. I tried it. Twice.

Bang. Bang.

I am sitting on the bed with this stuff spread out on the duvet cover. The sunlight dances with dust as it slips through the window and shines the eyes of the teddy gang. I am in Kathy and Jim's house. It's quiet now. Empty. I'm listening like a cat.

If Kathy and Jim are out to get me, they haven't got me yet.

I spend a lot of time gazing at my arms. The cuts are healing in jagged scars. I run the pads of my fingertips over the welts, sometimes the tip of my tongue. If there were lines going the other way we'd be able to play noughts and crosses with a biro.

Today I'm Alice

Every day I stick to my regime of taking 20mg of Prozac. But these days I eat Valium like Smarties. There is a pain in my liver. Perhaps it's cirrhosis. My savings have nearly all gone from the post office. I must have been dipping into the money, my safety net, but have no recollection of doing so. I live from week to week. From day to day. From moment to moment.

I pretend to be a PhD student. I am not entirely sure who or what I am. One thing I know for sure is that I'm not me. I stroll down the hill, wander into the university, climb the stairs to the second floor and watch Gerald pecking at his keyboard like a pigeon pecking at litter.

'Morning.'

'Morning.'

'How's that proposal coming along?' he asks.

'Like a dream.'

'That's my girl.'

Gerald's glasses glint like two silver coins. He smiles.

I look for the other bloke who appears periodically. Perhaps he has faded into the stained walls behind the reminder Post-its and the calendar showing scenes from the Yorkshire moors and dales. Perhaps he only exists as a construct of my imagination, a bearded, silent, prematurely balding man in grey jeans and a T-shirt with a picture from the Spanish Civil War.

Ah, now I remember.

The Trotskyite.

That man who had remained nameless since the day Gerald introduced us when I started at the university.

One evening when we were working late he asked if I wanted to go for a drink.

'Yes, please,' I said, racking my brain. 'I'm terrible with names . . .'

'Brian,' he replied as he shut down his computer.

Alice Jamieson

We stood in a pub with smoke hanging from the low ceiling while this pleasant, normally silent man named Brian spoke for an hour and a half about his brother who made a fortune as a financial analyst. 'The thing is, he's crap at maths. He'd wanted to be an architect. Now he's raking it in hand over fist ... holidays in Florida, a flat with a balcony like a ship's prow on the Thames. The bastard wears those shirts with a polo player on them.'

During the occasional pause, Brian's brow crinkled. He'd say, 'Er, Er ...' and I knew by the way he was looking at me, the way people look at the small print on a medicine bottle, that he couldn't remember my name and didn't want to ask.

He drank two pints of Fosters. I drank two halves. It had gone nine by the time we left and as I trudged back up the hill I remembered reading in a microbiology paper that there was no such things as mind, only matter. The me that I think I am doesn't exist. Alice is just a mass of exploding and dividing cells. The body goes through a daily big bang and emerges renewed, changed. The child I was does not exist within my matter, only my mind, my memory; it is a false me, a dead me, a me that was and is no more, and the problem with two halves of lager is it leaves you thirsting for a drink.

I work on what's called a multimedia personal computer (MPC) developed by Microsoft and Tandy. They say one day there won't be a need for libraries or universities. All knowledge will be stored in a giant electronic brain. You will just send a question to the nerve centre and it will have all the answers. It sounds like one of those marvellous ideas, like people one day will all be flying their own personal helicopter, and I'll believe it when I see it.

I press the 'on' button, the MPC hums like a short-wave radio and the screen flickers to life. My notes are stored in cyber files and appear in pulsing green letters like insects marching across the page. If you make a mistake, you don't have to white it out with Tippex. You highlight the text you don't want in order to write fresh text over the top. If we had a backspace key in our cerebral cortex we would be able to do the same with memories, just go back and turn them into black holes. This is exactly what they are at birth, at least according to some psychologists who see the initial infant's mind before it receives the impressions gained from experience as a *tabula rasa*.

Alice, the child abused by her father, has gone, the cells scattered. Alice from moment to moment malfunctions on the premise that there is a direct line from that little girl to me. If there is a line, it is drawn with invisible ink. We can't see it, taste it, smell it. It is a mirage where Alice continues by convention more than desire to hold memories that may belong to someone else and have the power to do her harm.

Memories are, by their nature, false, in as much as they construct pictures and narratives of that person that once was, with those cells that once were, but are no more. Those cells have mutated and turned into something else. Everything that is always has been and always will be. The dust in the light shaft beaming through my window carries the dead cells of dinosaurs and the ashes of Grandpa.

The MPC has false memories; a mind of its own. It's careless. It loses things. I keep handwritten notes in a blue-covered exercise book and only share them with the computer as a back-up.

One day, they say, computers will talk to each other. That's something I do understand.

I conjure the file from the ether; glance at my watch. Ten past nine. I look again. Ten past nine.

My main responsibility is creating a research proposal for submission to the university board, as well as producing an interview schedule for the work I'm doing with Rebecca on community participation in a new health initiative. Various agencies were in the process of implementing the initiative at a local level within Kirklees Metropolitan Borough Council and Huddersfield and Dewsbury Health Authorities.

I read through what I had written.

Mmm, not bad.

I was having a mental breakdown and working on health programmes for the community.

Absurd, right?

One day I was stopped taking a transistor radio from a shop without paying. A big man chased me. He wore a beard and a pink turban. He looked really angry and I burst into tears. I was so distraught, he stopped being angry and became apologetic. He still took the radio away from me though. I went to the off-licence and only realized once I entered that I didn't have any money.

My bike wasn't outside. I looked for it. I couldn't remember if I had come on my bike or not. It's dangerous cycling. I don't like men in cars. I don't know why. I just don't. I feel like shooting them and do so with my fingers.

Bang. Bang. You're dead.

There are lots of ugly buildings in this place they call Huddersfield. I don't like it here and I don't like the ugly buildings. The people are cannibals. They want to eat you. I shoot as many as I can.

Bang. Bang.

I blow up the buildings with Molotov cocktails. I like the combination of these two words, the way they slide from your tongue, 'Molotov cocktail', as the bombs glide flaming from your hand and explode in showers of molten glass.

*

Today I'm Alice

My name is Billy. I am five. It's me who shoots men in cars. Bang. Bang. It's my gun in Alice's bag. She bought it for me. She bought me the Smarties and the monkey on a chain. She didn't pay for it though. She just took it. Bang. Bang. You're dead. That's another one.

My face in the mirror is blank. It's like a film clip frozen on a television screen, like the computer screen in save mode. The power revs up and my expression becomes me. Alice. The same Alice with a new set of cells and a new set of voices pressing out the old ones.

The old voices are still there. But it's different now. The furniture in my head has been rearranged. The Professor, that woman from *EastEnders* and the rest, the sycophants, they seem to belong in the *external* world. The children, on the other hand, are *in* my head, talking, crying, kicking up a fuss.

Billy is always cheerful. It may have been Billy who cried on those nights in my bedsit in Swansea after you-know-what happened. But I don't think so.

It was probably Samuel.

Samuel is six. He cries all the time. Non-stop. Sometimes he curls up in a ball, leans against the wall and just cries and cries.

Baby Alice cries, too, but she's only six months old. She doesn't know what's happening.

The children just appeared. They happened. Like seeds growing underground and rising up through the earth. They just grew. They were concealed in all that 'matter' and popped out fully formed with names, ages, mannerisms. Butterflies bursting from cocoons. I didn't name them. They made me aware of their names, but I seemed to know their names automatically, and I soon got to know who was who by their different voices.

Billy likes his gun. He likes Smarties. I don't know what Samuel and Baby Alice like. They just keep crying, which is a nuisance because while they're crying I can't get on with what I'm supposed to be doing.

There's an angry boy named Kato. He's sixteen, and he's so angry and in such torment he doesn't know what to do. I feel him teetering on the edge of violence, his face burning red. I worry sometimes he might explode.

Then there's Shirley. She's fourteen. God knows why she's called Shirley. I don't even like the name. Where did it come from? Shirley is in league with Kato. She eggs him on. She makes him do things he might not do if she wasn't there.

Then there's Eliza. The Devil's Child. She's coming, she says, but she's not here yet. She's not 'out' yet. Like me, Eliza enjoys playing with dolls and she feels a bit outnumbered among all the little boys who prefer teddies.

There were loads of other kids straining to find their voices, but they remained in the background, fighting for space and time.

Gerald calls from the doorway.

'Fancy a cuppa?'

I have to think about this. Has Gerald asked me if I fancy a cup of tea? Or has one of the voices migrated inside his skull and is working his lips like a ventriloquist? Perhaps Gerald is a cipher, a dummy? Perhaps I am?

'Well?'

'Yes, please, Gerald.'

'How's it coming?

'Great. John Fowles better watch his back.'

'You're reading *The Magus*?'

Today I'm Alice

'Am I?'

He grins. He thinks I'm a real wit. Maybe I am. One Prozac, two Valium, a couple of codeine and nip of mother's ruin for breakfast. It does the trick. I feel . . . what's the word? That's it: happy. Well, perhaps not happy. I don't feel unhappy.

The voices are exasperating. But they can be fun too. I peek in my backpack: the gun, the monkey on a chain, the tube of Smarties I share with Gerald when he returns with two mugs of tea, bacteria breeding in the cracks. Maybe that's why the English are all mad. All that tea and bacteria.

When time stops operating in the normal way, when there are gaps in the normal stream of things, days cease to have any meaning. You lose time and you miss appointments. You take too many pills and, if Shirley gets her way, you drink.

When Shirley takes over, anything might happen. You 'come back' suddenly, there's a shudder as though you're waking, and you might find yourself sitting in the gutter with blood running down your arms, or lying flat out in hospital wrapped in bandages

Shirley is self-confident. It dawned on me that it is Shirley who likes cooking. She has always been there, operating the kitchen knives, persuading the broken glass from a smashed bottle into Kato's hesitant fingers.

It came to me in a flashback, a fleeting image that raced through my mind the moment I opened my eyes in A&E.

It was Shirley, not me but Shirley, who had drunk a bottle of gin, broken the empty bottle and convinced Kato to cut my arms.

Why did Kato do that?

He did it because he was so befuddled, so anguished, so stressed, the physical pain was a relief from the mental agony.

He did it, too, because the sight of red blood running over white arms has an aesthetic quality, a bright beauty in dull grey Huddersfield.

Weird? Absurd? That's how it seemed to me. I had these forces, these compunctions, these alternative personalities inside me, driving me. It was like being a jack-in-the-box and I was unsure which personality was going to jump out next: Billy, who thought of himself as a cowboy or a terrorist; Kato the cutter; anorexic Shirley, whose only self-indulgence was binge drinking and the occasional salad sandwich. I didn't dislike Shirley. I was afraid of her. Shirley knew things I didn't.

I knew it was Wednesday when I woke up, then forgot.

I had woken in a sweat, certain my feet were on fire and had seen myself in my childhood bedroom. I was four. Cute as a button. I was in the little bed that had replaced the cot. I was wearing yellow terrycloth pyjamas with ducks across the front and I was staring at the mobile on the ceiling.

He came in quietly. He put his finger to his lips and smiled. He tickled me under the chin.

'Who's Daddy's girl?' he whispered.

'I am.'

I smiled. He kissed me on the cheek. He pulled back the bedclothes and the teddies fell on the floor. He slid his hand under me. I pushed down with my feet and arched my back so he could pull down my pyjama bottoms.

'There. What a pretty girl.'

He wet his finger and it snaked its way into my front botty.

'There. There. That's nice, isn't it?'

He was wearing pyjamas and his willy poked through the gap at the front.

'Look who's here,' he said.

He put his willy in my mouth to make it wet, then carefully, so he didn't hurt too much, he pushed the head of his willy into my front botty. In a short time he did his wee inside me. He had a handkerchief in the top pocket of his pyjamas. He wiped the mess away. He put my pyjama bottoms back on and pulled the sheet and blanket back over me. He bent and kissed me on the lips.

'That's lovely,' he said.

He left the room and I got up to get my teddies. They didn't like it on the floor.

That was me in the little bed.

Alice.

The recall of this memory was so vile, so degrading, so painful, I swallowed all my pills at once. I took a swig of brandy from the cabinet in Kathy's lounge and went back upstairs to search for some money.

I ran down the hill to the off-licence, faster and faster . . .

The next thing I remembered was the dull dusty lights fizzing above my head, the half-closed curtains, the familiar smell.

I was in A&E again.

Rebecca was sitting beside the bed. She took my hand and gazed at me with her hazel-brown eyes. I thought, Oh my God, she's a lesbian. And then I thought, What do lesbians do? I thought about the girl at college who had fancied a threesome. I had thought about it for years. What is a threesome?

I had been raped incestuously, constantly, over and over again and knew nothing about sex, love, relationships. Tears washed over my cheeks. I could taste the salt. Rebecca squeezed my hand. I sobbed. She squeezed harder. I sobbed even more.

I thought: Why is this woman touching me? It's nice this woman touching me.

There was all this wet stuff over my face but my throat was as parched as the Red City of Petra. Those pink stones in the setting sun must have been a mirage, a false memory, they belonged to a bunch of cells gone for ever.

I had a pain down my left side, a graze on my cheek. At least Kato hadn't cut me.

I emptied the jug on the bedside table, drinking glass after glass of water. Rebecca went to find the sister in charge and returned with a Scottish woman who looked like a nun in a starched navy-blue uniform and an upside-down watch. It was hard to understand what she was saying.

'Let this be a warning ta you, lassie. I donae wanna see you in here agin,' she said. 'You cannae go collapsing in a heap due to tae much aethe drink.'

I had no recollection of falling. I could only guess that Shirley had drunk herself into a stupor and I had been injured as a result.

Rebecca knew the sister and convinced her to discharge me into her care. I dressed, and limped along the corridor past the black and yellow signs about the dangers of radiation and out into the car park. The hospital doors made a sucking sound and the car doors snapped open as if the car was anxious to be on its way. We clunked into our seatbelts and Rebecca put her hand on mine. It was weird, all this personal stuff, and I looked down at her hand nursing my fingers.

'My place?' she said, and I nodded dubiously.

'OK.'

What did I have to lose?

It was nice sitting in the car, a VW I think it was, a big toy zipping along, the city vanishing behind us as we climbed out of the crater through winding country lanes. I realized with shame that the closest I'd got to the moors was the calendar from the tourist board on the office wall.

'I thought something must be wrong when you didn't turn up for our meeting,' she said.

It dawned on me that it was Wednesday. It was the day planned for that tête-à-tête with Gerald at Rebecca's office.

'I'm so sorry,' I said.

'Alice, I was worried about *you*, not the meeting.'

I wondered how she had found me at A&E but didn't ask. Fresh tears welled into my eyes. Rebecca's concern was overwhelming. I didn't cry often. Samuel and Baby Alice do the crying. Not me. Although a good cry helps sometimes.

The sky was turning red, orange, pale green. Rocks like missiles thrown by giants littered the landscape that rose into hills turning shadowy on the horizon. My intuition is not something I can trust but I had an intuition that Rebecca really did care and I could do nothing except hope for the best. She had, from the beginning, encouraged me with my project and must have known I was isolated.

Kathy and Jim thought I was out boozing all the time with mates from uni. The opposite was true. I boozed on my own walking the streets, and on nights when I didn't make it back up the hill I slept in shop doorways, or I'd walk for miles along the Manchester Road and climb the rubble in a derelict mill in the pitch-black, cutting my hands, or I sang away the hours swinging as high as I could go on the park swings. As Shirley or Kato, even as Alice, when the memories turned to torture, I had no sense of vulnerability and was only afraid on those vagrant nights of being picked up by the police.

Rebecca lived in a stone cottage with roses climbing over the entrance, and scrubbed-pine furniture in the kitchen and sitting room. There were big, bright-coloured cushions, Indian rugs on the floor and books in tiers on the bookshelves. Rebecca opened all the windows and hurried through to the kitchen to make a nice cup of tea.

On the table there was a photo of the same woman I had seen in the frame on Rebecca's desk in her office.

'That's Zoë, my partner,' she said. 'She's working in Newcastle at the moment.'

Rebecca settled a tray on the coffee table.

'You must miss her.' I said.

'All the time. Even though we live apart anyway and have our different interests.'

I thought how nice it must be to have a partner yet not live in each other's pockets. I remembered feeling contented in Liverpool knowing that Patrick was going to visit; just having him there, even if he wasn't there, kept me in balance. I still had his address and decided to write to him and explain why I had been afraid.

Thinking about Patrick made tears well up in my eyes again. With the children chattering away in my head, the flashbacks, the drugs, the booze, time those last few weeks had become spherical, without beginning or end. Past, present and future had merged, melted into one ball. That ball of time was passing. Before a new ball began to grow there would be a moment of hollowness and clarity. I was often 'away' but I was 'back'. I was me. That's why I kept crying.

'You can tell me if you want to, Alice,' Rebecca said.

I stared back at her. Rebecca's silver-grey hair looked like a halo with the light behind her. Had she read my mind? Had she seen the letter I planned to write to Patrick?

I looked down at the cups of tea she'd poured.

'Do you have anything to drink?' I asked.

She smiled. 'What a bloody good idea.'

She removed the tray and produced a bottle of wine, some cheese and salty biscuits. I could feel unspoken things welling up inside me, finding shape as words, dead memories rising like Lazarus. If I was going to talk, I needed to be outside, in the air, under the great dome of the sky. We polished off the wine and pulled on anoraks.

We walked over the moors on winding stone paths. The shadows were turning into night and in the cover of darkness I told Rebecca my story. A version of it. The voices I kept to myself. I had yet to grasp the connection between the voices and the abuse. It was the abuse that saw the light that night: how I'd been molested continually as a baby in my cot right up to being a teenager. I told her my father had raped me at knifepoint on the floor of his house. And I told her that I had never told anyone these things before.

Rebecca was pale. The wind was blowing.

'But why? Why?' she demanded.

It was the obvious question. But there is no simple answer. The women at the refuge I'd interviewed in Liverpool all had different answers: shame, love, fear that no one would believe them; fear that no one could do anything to prevent the abuse even if they did believe them; fear of being alone – a fear I knew all too well.

'You just don't,' I said.

'Poor Alice. Poor, poor thing.'

We huddled together as we raced down the hill to the cottage. We made hot soup and Rebecca showed me that by coating stale bread with water and baking it in the oven it comes out fresh again. Even if you've been raped at knifepoint, even when you tell your story to a sympathetic listener, life goes on. It has to. I worked continually, daily, hourly, moment by moment to split myself from that little girl with her dad's cock in her mouth from the woman who had stood on the crenellated battlements of the crusader castle in Petra and was now working towards her PhD.

Rebecca found a bottle of gin, thank God. We sat drinking late into the night while I told her about my father's nocturnal visits, the spiders, the dungeon where people chanted and children were abused, the man in the white Rolls-Royce.

I remembered the day my mother was standing outside the house when the white car came to a halt.

'What the hell's going on?' she yelled.

'We just went for a ride, Jenny, come and take a look at my new Roller,' the man replied.

She dragged me out of the car and then leaned back through the door, raising her voice: 'You go near my daughter and you'll regret it,' she said, slammed the door and whisked me into the house. 'Don't go near that man again. I don't like him.'

After the day my mother threw a fit, my father stopped coming to my room for some time – weeks, months, I'm not sure. But then he started again. He was addicted. He couldn't stop. He didn't stop until I finally moved out from under his roof.

Why did I allow the abuse to continue? Even as a teenager? I didn't.

Something that had been plaguing me for years now made sense. It was like the answer to a terrible secret. The thing is, it wasn't me in my bed, it was Shirley who lay there wondering if that man was going to come to her room, pull back the cover and push his penis into her waiting mouth. It was Shirley. I remembered watching her, a skinny little thing with no breasts and a dark resentful expression. She was angry. She didn't want this man in her room doing the things he did, but she didn't know how to stop it. He didn't beat her, he didn't threaten her. He just looked at her with black hypnotic eyes and she lay back with her legs apart thinking about nothing at all.

And where was I? I stood to one side, or hovered overhead just below the ceiling, or rode on a magic carpet. I held my breath and watched my father pushing up and down inside Shirley's skinny little body.

As I was talking to Rebecca another memory flew like an eagle out of the past. I remembered during puberty, through the anorexic mists of intermittent menstrual cycles, that man, my father, lifting Shirley's nightdress over her head and asking her in his mocking way to choose what colour condom she wanted.

'Red or yellow?'

Which did she choose?

I can't remember. Perhaps she alternated. Perhaps there were other colours. It didn't happen once. It happened again and again. I had no power to stop it. That man, my father, had some control over me. I was drugged by the black silence in that big house, the vile whiff of aftershave, the crushing torment of inevitability. My father fucked Shirley using red or yellow condoms and it was those condoms that brought it all to an end.

It was my last realization of the day; any more would have been too much to contemplate.

That time when my mother had found used condoms in my father's bedroom, he had admitted, after a pointless burst of denial, that he had been going to prostitutes. That was no doubt true, but I can't imagine clients take used condoms away with them; prostitutes would surely get rid of the things. No. My father kept those used condoms as a prize. He was fucking his fourteen-year-old-daughter. He was proud of it.

Rebecca welled up with tears.

Poor thing, she kept saying. Poor thing. I told her I'd never had a proper relationship, that I'd loved a boy named Patrick and had broken his heart. She cried. I found myself putting my arms round her and I thought what a weird thing it was to be human. I felt cleansed. The black thing inside my gut was smaller.

It was hard to get to sleep that night. The voices were still and the silence was eerie. I opened *The Magus* but couldn't concentrate and lay on the futon in the guest room with the moon and stars crossing the uncurtained window.

Next day after eating muesli and drinking about twelve cups of tea, Rebecca asked if I could do her a favour. Her sister was in hospital having treatment for cancer and every Thursday after work Rebecca went to Coventry to spend the long weekend helping her brother-in-law look after their two small children. Would I look after the cottage for her?

She gave me the spare keys and as I clipped them on the monkey keyring I realized that someone somewhere must have known it was going to come in handy. As I strolled down the path following Rebecca to the car I saw myself as Cathy in *Wuthering Heights* striding over the moors. I had a bolt-hole for a few days, in a setting where my spirits could take wing. A place where I could go to cry. Somewhere I could just be me.

I went in to university to explain to Gerald why I had missed the appointment with Rebecca the previous day. I decided to tell him the truth. I said I had some personal issues, and he just got angry for some reason.

'If you want to be preoccupied and stare at a wall all day, that's your decision,' he said.

I thought: You clearly don't live in the real world, Gerald, and, what's even sadder, you don't even realize it. I tried a smile.

'Would you like a cuppa?' I asked.

'No I would not.'

I turned on the MPC, listened to the hum, and opened the

file for my proposal. I needed to do some revising in preparation for the academic paper I was slated to deliver at the
annual conference of the Operational Research Society,
which was due to take place in two weeks' time at Birmingham's International Convention Centre, not that far from my
father's house.

Everything, it seems, is both connected and disconnected.
Like the terraced houses lining the streets of Huddersfield,
touching yet apart. It occurred to me how we all live in our
own world. How Gerald worked with me but didn't understand me; how Brian, at his desk across the room, had never
asked me anything about myself, even my name, how my
father's clients had no idea that the avuncular man who drew
up wills and advised on house sales had abused his daughter
all through her childhood. The Indian man in the pink turban
had no way of knowing that it wasn't *me* who stole the radio
from his shop. It was Shirley or, if not, Kato at Shirley's
urging. You see a woman hit her child or a couple arguing in
the supermarket and imagine you have some insight into
their situation but you have none whatsoever.

It was hard to focus on my work. The hours slipped by as
hours do. Hours are like the sea, always shifting, appearing
to go somewhere but going nowhere at all. I caught the bus
back to Rebecca's cottage and walked for miles over the
moors, making up for lost time. Pun intended. The children
seemed content but the Professor popped in for a visit.

*Get ready to die, Alice. You are blind if you see safety in this
place.*

Oh, do shut up.

He tutted theatrically and fell silent.

I was thinking with clarity. Now that I had brought the
abuse out into the open, I felt more able to face the fact that
I needed help. When Rebecca arrived back that Sunday from
Coventry, I told her I was going to seek counselling, and

found myself crying again when she said she would support me in every way she could.

It's not easy to admit you have mental health problems, but after waking early and going into the city next day, I went to the University Counselling Service. I told the secretary that it was pretty urgent that I see someone. She made a couple of phone calls and at four the following afternoon I saw a university counsellor, a serious, middle-aged woman with glasses hanging on a thin silver chain and a short, no-nonsense haircut.

Eyes closed, fists clenched, I managed to tell her that I had been abused as a child and was now suffering depression, anxiety and other effects as a result. I didn't need to spell out what those other effects were. She knew immediately that I needed help and made an appointment for the following Wednesday for me to see a woman by the name of Roberta Stoppa, who was based 16 miles away in Leeds city centre.

CHAPTER 12
Opening the Closet

Brian was enraged that wealth, as he saw it, unfairly provided power, prestige and all the things that money can buy. At the same time, he envied his brother in London 'raking it in hand over fist'. He retreated from this dichotomy behind the logos on his T-shirts, his Workers Revolutionary Party leaflets and in his assertion that he wanted to 'shape a better future'.

The future is a mystery; we can survive an unspeakable present *because* the future is unknown – I thought of Esther in Buna-Monowitz. The more I got to know Brian, the more it seemed to me that what he wanted to reshape wasn't the future but the past, that time when he chose the poorly funded sinecure of the university and his brother chose the electric world of finance.

Having studied psychology, it wasn't difficult for me to see the faults in others, but it was through Rebecca's generosity that I became more aware of my own. Mental-health issues are intrinsically selfish, and the struggle to be normal has to be accompanied by the struggle to pay attention to the needs and cares of others. I was trying but receiving unwelcome help from Shirley.

I was always coming across things in my backpack acquired with Rebecca in mind: a tin of mint tea, a box of After Eight mints (why all this mint?), a carved giraffe to go with her collection on the bureau in the cottage. Where did these things come from? I had my suspicions and couldn't help feeling guilty when I gave the gifts to Rebecca.

It was certainly a relief to have a friend. Perhaps that's the cure for most problems: someone to share a bottle of wine with and follow over the moors. The two of us became three when Zoë appeared. I observed them together – loving, giving, selfless – nothing like the immature pictures I had drawn in my head that day when Rebecca leaned across the desk and said, 'By the way, Alice, I'm a lesbian.' Zoë was older than Rebecca and it felt on our blustery walks full of chatter and gossip as if I had two mums, a hand to hold on each side.

I had convinced myself that I found it easier to connect with men than women: Patrick, Samir, Grandpa. But when I looked back it had always been women who had been there through my various crises; and now Rebecca, who spent every spare minute caring for her sister and her sister's children in Coventry, yet still found time to drive me to Leeds the following week for my first appointment with Roberta Stoppa.

It was a bright morning, the sun sweeping away any lingering traces of SAD and putting a glow on the marble columns of Leeds town hall, a Greek acropolis that could have been transported through time from ancient Athens. The Victorians, who had built it, had eccentric ideas on architecture but it all seemed to work somehow. The counselling department was along the road from the temple in a red-brick building with people swarming round the entrance.

Rebecca dropped me outside, did a nifty U-turn, and set off back to Huddersfield.

On the third floor, I gave my name to a receptionist and sat in the waiting area flicking through the *Guardian* and resisting an urge to take a closer look at the cupboard filled with toys and games. My fingers were tingling and I had a sense that someone was whispering to me through cupped hands. Billy probably, perhaps Samuel, who had spotted a rather scruffy pink teddy bear.

The *Guardian* and the teddy. It was left brain/right brain interchange and these days the link between them had become a revolving door.

I glanced at my watch: nine o'clock. I glanced again. Ten past. The world was in order.

'Alice Jamieson.'

That's me, I thought, and took a deep breath.

I entered a large sunny room where we introduced ourselves with first names. Roberta was a senior counsellor for a project offering one-to-one counselling as well as a telephone helpline for adults who had been abused as children. She was forty-something with a calm, almost languid demeanour and wispy blonde hair like threads of gold in the bright light.

After shaking hands, we sat in post-modern grey chairs with steel legs and wooden arms, like strangers when a train stops unexpectedly and you remain unsure whether or not to start a conversation. Roberta wore a black and white checked suit with black nylons that made little ripples of sound as she crossed and uncrossed her legs.

I had decided on the way to Leeds not to mention the voices but to focus on the flashbacks of childhood abuse that were now making my life so difficult. We sat for several more moments in silence.

'Now, what is it you wanted to have a chat about?' she said, breaking the ice.

'I'm not exactly sure how to start,' I replied. 'It's not something I've talked about before.'

Her brow rippled and she leaned forward. I took a deep breath.

'I was abused as a child. Sexually abused,' I continued, 'by my father.'

'This happened once, Alice?'

'No,' I said. 'It happened lots of times. Hundreds of times.'

'Would you like to tell me about it?'

'Not really,' I said, 'but yes.'

She gave a faint smile and turned her head to one side.

I spoke for fifty minutes, my slot. I told her how my father had come to my room when I was a baby and had kept coming to my room as I was growing up. I told her that even as an infant I had been penetrated vaginally and anally, and now realized this probably caused my anal fissures and bouts of cystitis. I told her of my father's obsession with oral sex and how he liked to ejaculate in my mouth and over my face. I told her that he had taken me on numerous occasions to a large basement in a building that I had thought of as a castle but which was probably a warehouse or a factory on an industrial estate. I told her that there were men and women in there, a ring of paedophiles abusing young children, me included. I told her that as a child I had thought the abuse normal because I had never known anything different. And I allowed the abuse to persist because once the pattern was established it seemed unimaginable to break it.

I wasn't reliving these experiences, as in the bad dreams and flashbacks, but describing them as a third party. Psychology's rules are driven by the laws of cause and effect, the same as Buddhism, as Elaine had told me once at uni – it had stuck in my mind. In psychological terms, after being abused as a child and a teenager, the effect on me as an adult was ongoing bouts of depression, anorexia, drug and alcohol dependency, the combination creating low self-esteem, memory affliction and insomnia.

Roberta wasn't looking at me. She was looking down at my trainers. The sun was hot through the tall windows and I felt a trickle of sweat run down my back. My throat was dry and the fifty minutes was up. Roberta looked sympathetic, then looked at her watch.

'I think we should have another session early next week, Alice,' she said. 'Would that be suitable?'

'Sure.'

That was it. No pain. No gain. Not much of anything really.

I asked a bicycle messenger downstairs the way to the station and was back in my office in Huddersfield just after eleven. Gerald was giving a class, and Brian swivelled on his chair, said hi, and swivelled back to face his computer screen. Brian knew where I had been, and why, but didn't feel inclined to ask any questions. He had trimmed his beard, I remember, and was wearing a T-shirt featuring a muscled worker cutting off the head of a serpent with the word *fascismo* along its coiling body and CNT Comite Nacional AIT across the top.

'Fancy a cuppa?' I asked.

'Nice one.'

I'd read in the paper we were entering a mini-recession. 'How's your brother in the City, by the way?' I said.

'Don't ask.'

'He's not sick?'

Brian tapped his temple. 'Yeah, up here,' he replied.

I put the kettle on, produced a tube of Smarties I didn't recall buying, and went through my proposal deleting all the adjectives. I sipped tea from the chipped Newcastle United mug and could hardly believe my ears when I heard the bell in the old church strike two.

'Bye, Brian.'

'Adios, er . . .'

'Alice.'

'Nice one.'

I raced across town to the bus stop and watched a young mother with a boy of about five who reminded me of Billy. He was eager and inquisitive, full of male swagger and questions. Why is the bus green? Are all the buses in London red? Why's the bus always late?

'Oh for God's sake be quiet, you're making my head ache,' his mother said and drew on her cigarette.

I forced my nails into my palms to stop myself going up and giving her a good talking to.

This is the speech I rehearsed in my head.

'Do you know that your child's life will be shaped by all the things you say and do? You have the power to shape the future. From the moment your baby pops out screaming to the moment baby goes to playschool, you have to be there, watching, playing, talking. Keep baby in your own bed, or next to the bed. Be there when monsters real or imagined wake baby in the night.'

I pause. She's looking at me intently, hanging on my every word. Never has someone been so pleased to hear advice from a perfect stranger. If only I could be so erudite when I had to speak at a conference.

I smile and continue softly. 'If your little girl or boy of three of four or five is withdrawn and quiet, sit the little one on your lap and ask why. If she or he won't tell you, ask if it's a secret. If it is a secret, you already know what the secret is. Don't press the little person. Someone else is already pressing at their unformed minds and bodies or both or worse. If they want to talk, then listen. And believe.

'As many as ten per cent of our children are abused, usually in the home, usually by male relatives, stepfathers, half-brothers, new boyfriends. That means if you go into any classroom in the land, two or three or four of those children are suffering. Listen to the children.'

The bus came.

'Let's go upstairs. Let's go upstairs.'

Mother stamped out her fag and followed her little boy as he clambered up the stairs.

Perhaps she was a good mum having a bad day. How would I know?

The bus wound its way out of Huddersfield into open country. I hopped off at the end of the lane and trotted the short distance to Rebecca's cottage. I had by this time moved some of my junk with the itinerant teddies into the spare room; I was like a squirrel leaving bits and pieces all over the place. I put on my walking boots, some old jeans and pushed my anorak into my backpack.

It was one of those afternoons on the Yorkshire moors poets write about, warm but brisk, the wind carrying the hum of insects and the smell of things bursting into life. From the cottage, there was a six-mile walk that took me up a hill between collapsing dry-stone walls. I like stone. You can talk to it. You can trust it. It doesn't rot. It keeps its shape. All that lasts through time are the stone fortresses and cathedrals, the pyramids at Giza, the Great Wall of China – the only structure built by man that can be seen from space. So they say.

I thought back over my appointment with Roberta Stoppa. Nothing much had come out of it. But putting things into words and putting the words out in the open had a soothing effect; it was like being a cat and stroking yourself. I took a deep breath of that fresh Yorkshire air.

It felt good putting one foot in front of the other, the crunching sound beneath the soles of my boots like stone echoes, the sun losing its heat. I enjoyed the feeling in my legs, walking rather than running, using different muscles, the landscape spread out like a painting. The wind spiralled round me and, as I reached the top of the hill, I felt as if my whole body was dematerializing and becoming a current of air. I had stopped thinking, stopped watching myself, and it was in this vacuum that Billy must have come out.

I knew it was Billy because I was suddenly lying flat on my face with his plastic gun in my hand and a pain in my knees. I rolled over. I was dazed and stared at the clouds lowering from the sky. I didn't know where I was or how I had got there. I closed my eyes and traced back as one traces their fingers over the walls trying to find their way in a strange house at night.

I remembered being in the office editing my proposal. I remembered thinking. That's better. That'll impress Gerald. I could remember the words I had struck out. I could see them highlighted then vanishing as I hit the delete key. I could remember the illustration on Brian's Spanish Civil War T-shirt. But I didn't remember straying from my normal path or taking out Billy's gun from the backpack, something he did to feel secure. He must have taken a wrong turn, panicked, run off and fallen over. I gazed about me. I recognized nothing.

While Billy had been occupying my time, where had I been? I thought of it as away. But away where exactly? As I stood up, I had the sensation of growing back into my body, filling the space just as hot air pushes out the skin of a balloon, literally expanding. Billy at five was small and, when he took control, I had the sensation of shrinking and physically inhabiting the body of a little boy.

Kato was bigger than me. Like the Incredible Hulk, when Kato visited I expanded, my clothes grew tight. I felt stretched, tense, violent. I had sexual yearnings that could never be fulfilled because Kato didn't have a penis and I, as a consequence, suffered penis envy as well as fear of penetration. It was so frustrating. Kato took out his frustration by drinking, urged on in her cocky way by Shirley, slashing my arms with blades and broken bottles, punishing the whole ensemble of 'others' and further provoking the Professor and his lot.

My body, as well as my mind, had been 'invaded' by these kids. I was 'possessed', not by something external – demons, the devil, by spirits good or bad – but by alternative personalities that had surfaced without my prompting or moulding and which were growing more self-aware and confident.

The switches, I realized, had been happening for as far back as I could recall. At the age of two when my father shoved his willy in my mouth, I had sucked on it like a baby sucking a dummy. But I had also watched myself from outside myself, splitting myself firstly in two, and eventually into many parts. I could recall floating on a magic carpet watching a girl of four sitting on a blue sheet in the garden shed with spiders crawling over her plump naked body. I remembered thinking: I'm glad I'm up here and that's not me down there with those nasty spiders. At fourteen, I stood in the corner of the bedroom clutching a teddy watching a girl I now knew to be Shirley lying, with her eyes closed and her teeth gritted while the man rode up and down like a seesaw between her legs. Shirley knew this was wrong. That's why she drank. That's why she starved herself. That's why she hated herself.

I had always known there was something wrong with me. Always. I had not been aware that I housed a bunch of chattering kids, all these substitute selves, but it didn't completely surprise me when they started to come out in more open and obvious ways, not as observers but as players. I was surrounded by alternative personalities as if each reflected aspects of myself but concealed the real me, the whole me, from myself and the world.

My knees hurt. In pain we are in the present moment. I was very much me. The wind was blowing, but apart from that there was a marvellous stillness in the world and in my head. I had the same sort of feeling I had when I was in the Middle East, mind alert, shoulders straight, eyes on the horizon.

I put the gun in my pack. I tried to remember where the sun had been when I'd set out, but it had gone behind clouds and, anyway, I didn't have navigation skills. Billy had clearly turned off the path and climbed the hill into the next valley. As far as I could see there was nothing but jagged outcrops of limestone awash in seas of heather. It looked like a different country, the landscape treeless and primeval, with hills turning blue in the distance, no signs of life, cottages, church steeples, not even a path.

I went back the way I guessed Billy must have come, tracing his footsteps up to the ridge behind me. I stood in the wind. I had that feeling, like when you think you're going to sneeze then don't, but this was a feeling that I was going to have a panic attack and I let the feeling emerge and vaporize on the wind. There was no need to be afraid; nothing to be afraid of. It was spring. It wasn't cold. There were no wild animals except some grouse and grass snakes. I thought about getting the gun out again and then heard the sound of laughter. It was me.

In the far distance I could see what looked like the top of a truck moving across the landscape. Then another going the other way. That told me there was a road and I set out to walk in a straight line down from the ridge, into the valley and up again through the blue hills.

The shadows lengthened. The climb up the far hill was steep and at times I had to go down on my hands and wounded knees to scramble up to the peak. I ripped my fingers to shreds and sealed the cuts with a good lick. I rested at the top and made my way down the far side over a series of ledges carved, I imagined, during the Ice Age, a gigantic Jurassic sculpture against the inky-blue sky.

I was feeling oddly confident and was almost disappointed when I came across a narrow track, which I followed. I reached a crossroads and realized I was back on the route of the six-mile walk. I had tried to go in a straight line but had in fact gone in a circle, I thought that was typical, wherever we go and however far we go we tend to gravitate back to the source, as I would one day gravitate back to St Mildred's Church where I had been christened.

With the dry-stone walls to guide me, it still took another hour to reach the cottage. I had been walking for more than six hours and Rebecca was shocked when I turned up on the doorstep.

That night, over hot soup and oven-baked bread, I told Rebecca about the kids.

Now that I had begun to talk about the abuse, it was easier to breathe. My tics and twitches, a visual clue to my thoughts, were less pronounced. I had always felt ashamed, as if I had brought the abuse on myself. Battered women feel the same. That feeling didn't vanish but it did diminish and I woke one morning with a sudden compunction to call Dr Purvis, which I did from my office.

It took a while to trace her number. When I rang, she wasn't there. I left my number and sat at my desk trying to work and thinking back over my numerous sessions at the Naydon Clinic, Jane Purvis's wardrobe of bright costumes, *Quadrophenia* on the headphones . . . Whatever happened to that tape?

Brian had just entered the office and Gerald answered the phone when it rang.

'It's for you,' he said, and Dr Purvis's voice came on the line.

'Hello,' I said.

'Is that you, Alice?'

I thought for half a second. 'Yes,' I replied.

'What a nice surprise. How are you? What are you doing?'

She had the same girlish voice I remembered and the memory of her features and smile and soft lips swam back into my mind.

'I'm doing a PhD in Huddersfield.'

'Are you? That's really very good. I always knew you'd do well.'

There was a pause.

'There was something I wanted to tell you,' I then said. 'You asked me seven years ago if I had been abused as a child.'

'Yes, I remember.'

'I wanted you to know you were on the right track. I was being abused. Repeatedly. Even when you asked me.'

'Oh, Alice . . .'

'It's all right, it's all coming out now. I'm dealing with it.'

'I'm so glad.'

She asked me to look her up next time I was at home. We said our goodbyes and I returned the receiver to its cradle.

I glanced at Gerald. He had been listening, you could hardly avoid it in the small office; he pressed his lips shut and gave me a little shrug of sympathy.

'Cuppa, anyone?' said Brian.

We nodded our heads. Tea. It was the answer to all life's problems.

Once I had found the courage to tell Rebecca about the children in my head, it wasn't so hard in the coming months to tell Roberta.

On the train from Huddersfield one day in May I made a roll call of the usual suspects: Baby Alice; Alice 2, who was two years old and liked to suck sticky lollipops; Billy; Samuel;

Shirley; Kato; and the enigmatic Eliza. There was boy I would grow particularly fond of named Jimbo, who was ten, but like Eliza he was still forming. There were others without names or specific behaviour traits. I didn't want to confuse the issue with this crowd of 'others' and just counted off the major players with their names, ages and personalities, which Roberta scribbled down on a pad.

Then she looked slightly embarrassed. 'You know, I've met Billy on a few occasions, and Samuel once too,' she said.

'You're joking.' I felt betrayed. 'Why didn't you tell me?'

'I wanted it to come from you, Alice, when you were ready.'

For some reason I pulled up my sleeves and showed her my arms. 'That's Kato,' I said, 'or Shirley.'

She looked a bit pale as she studied the scars. I had a feeling she didn't know what to say. The problem with counsellors is that they are trained to listen, not to give advice or diagnosis. We sat there with my arms extended over the void between us like evidence in court, then I pushed down my sleeves again.

'I'm so sorry, Alice,' she said finally and I shrugged.

'It's not your fault, is it?'

Now *she* shrugged, and we were quiet once more.

Of course, I should have known the kids would pop out in the atmosphere of Roberta's office. That's what they do when Alice is under stress. They see a gap in the space–time continuum and slip through like beams of light through a prism changing form and direction.

We had got into the habit in recent weeks of starting our sessions with that marble and stick game called Ker-Plunk, which Billy liked. There were times when I caught myself entering the office with a teddy that Samuel had taken from the toy cupboard outside. Roberta told me that on a couple of occasions I had shot her with the plastic gun and once, as Samuel, I had climbed down from the high-tech chairs, rolled into a ball in the corner and just cried.

'This is embarrassing,' I admitted.

'It doesn't have to be.'

'It doesn't have to be, but it is,' I said.

The thing is, I *never* knew when the 'others' were going to come out. I only discovered that one had been out when I lost time or found myself in the midst of some wacky occupation – finger-painting like a five-year-old, cutting my arms, wandering from shops with unwanted, unpaid-for clutter.

In her reserved way, Roberta described the kids as an elaborate defence mechanism. As a child, I had blocked out my memories in order not to dwell on anything painful or uncertain. Even as a teenager, I had allowed the bizarre and terrifying to seem normal because the alternative would have upset the fiction of my loving little nuclear family.

I made a mental note to look up defence mechanisms, something we had touched on in psychology. I left the session pleased that Roberta wasn't freaked out about the kids *inside* my head, but irritated with myself that I still had a reluctance to tell her about the voices *outside* my head. They were with me even then in that room. They accompanied me down the stairs into the street and they persuaded me to lift my downcast eyes to gaze once more at the marble monstrosity of Leeds town hall.

You must die … Go on. Go to the top floor of that building and jump.

'Oh, bugger off,' I said.

Kill yourself, Alice. It's the only way you'll ever find peace. We are watching you. We are always watching.

On the train I carried on reading *The Magus* but the words lifted like a swarm of flies and settled as new words that spoke to me from the page.

Today I'm Alice

It was the Professor.

Don't think by talking to the woman you are going to get rid of me. She doesn't like you. I am the only friend you've got. I know what's best for you. Silly little Alice. You'll never get away from me.

I closed the book and stared out of the window. Every time things seemed to be getting better, the voices came back to torment me. It just wasn't fair.

CHAPTER 13
Human Touch

I adored my Toshiba laptop I had invested in, with the blue LCD screen and little mouse called Mouse.

'Hello, Mouse. How are you?'

'I'm very well, thank you.'

It was a polite mouse with a white tail and a mauve tip, really quite nifty the way with just a click it could sniff out menus and manipulate scroll bars. Every time I had Mouse in my palm I thought of Grandma, who had sent me a cheque for my birthday. I had invested the money in the laptop before Shirley and Kato got their paws on it. I wrote Grandma a long letter saying how much I missed her and how I was studying to be a doctor. It was a white lie but it would enhance her status at the nursing home.

I was ashamed to say I hadn't seen Grandma for ages. She had suffered a fall that had left her with a broken hip and, for reasons that were never completely satisfactory to me, my mother had moved her into a nursing home in Cliftonville. It's unacceptable, I know, but taking a six-hour bus ride across Sinai was easy whereas getting the coach to east Kent, which I kept planning to do, seemed complicated and I kept putting it off.

Clive was now a junior in a firm of solicitors in the City of London where several of the senior partners had gone to his old school. Stephen was the stepdad from heaven; I was always pleased when I called and he picked up the phone rather than Mother. She was usually out buying new shoes or about to go and have her hair done. Father was in my mind like a stain on a white cotton blouse. One day I bolted from the newspaper shop screaming when I found myself standing next to a man wearing Brylcreem, a fashion that may have been fading elsewhere but not among those obdurate Yorkshiremen.

The Toshiba stood on a table in the corner of my room in Kathy's house. I had been carrying floppy disks between the office and home and had all but finished my proposal ready for submission to the university board.

Of course the teddies, Snoopy dog and the red dragon didn't like the Toshiba. They were jealous of anything that took my time away from them, which was really juvenile seeing how the laptop was an inanimate object.

The Toshiba had been a friend. Then one day it turned nasty.

It was Wednesday.

There's something weird about Wednesdays. Wednesday's child is full of woe. Wednesday is sad and anxious about who he is, where he stands in the week. The word is weird. It should be Weirdesday. Wednesday would secretly like to be Latin but took his name from Woden, the Norse God. The Old English had to say Wednesdaeg, which is a bit of a mouthful. Funny things happened on Wednesday.

As I journeyed back from seeing Roberta in Leeds, there was a running commentary in my head.

See she's walking down the stairs. She's going to turn left outside and she'll glance up at the town hall as she passes. She's not sure if she likes the town hall or if she thinks it's silly having a Greek building in the middle of industrial England. She's going to reach the station, check she has her return ticket, stand three-

quarters of the way along platform two and she's going to look up at the sky and say, 'Oh, for God's sake, do shut up.'

'Oh, for God's sake, do shut up.'

You're useless. You're nothing. Why don't you do it today? When the train comes, just jump. You know you want to. It'll be good for you, Alice. It'll be good for the world. Move to the edge of the platform. Look down at those shiny silver rails. Can you see your reflection? Now, wouldn't it be nice to see yourself squashed like a tomato on the tracks?

Then the refrain: *Squashed like a tomato on the tracks. Squashed like a tomato on the tracks.*

Usual garbage. Just more of it. I tried to ignore the voices, tried to read the paper and tried to remember if I had ever seen Roberta Stoppa looking so – *happy.* She had been wearing a particularly feminine pale-pink suit with blue shoes.

Something was going on. I'd thrashed her three straight games at Ker-Plunk. It was almost as if she was letting me win.

'I really can't concentrate,' she said.

I looked at her pink lipstick and thought: You've been up all night fucking.

Then I blushed.

I didn't think about those things. Ever. Maybe Shirley did. Maybe I was projecting. Perhaps I wanted a boyfriend, a beau, a bit of the other. I did have tingles sometimes. Kato was messed up, a pimply teenager full of lust and testosterone. Was I projecting Kato's desires on to Roberta? Were Kato's desires my own? Projecting is a defence mechanism. I'd looked it up. Thieves imagine everyone is trying to rob them. When you don't think very highly of yourself you imagine other people don't like you. Paedophiles believe children are gagging for it.

'Who's Daddy's girl?'

Today I'm Alice

'I am.'

Defence mechanisms protect us from ourselves, from anxiety, trauma and social ineptitude. They make reality tolerable and provide a safe harbour from difficult situations and people. Everyone uses DMs. I certainly do.

I rationalize taking Kathy and Jim's booze by believing that they don't need it and won't miss it. I identify with the eggheads at Huddersfield to show I'm worthy of a PhD, just as my dad identifies with the successful men at his posh golf club. Identifying with others is the last refuge of bullies, cowards and those with low self-esteem. Regression is what my mum does when she plays the little girl to get her own way with Stephen. Repression is burying painful thoughts, feelings and memories in the subconscious where they grow vocal chords and chatter and natter non-stop.

Does it sound confusing? It was to me. My head was an incessant barrage of different thoughts, most of them belonging to the others, and a ceaseless barrage of alien voices that had been with me since I was doing my O levels at Dane Hill. My head was a radio station gone rogue, endless tapes spewing out interminable bullshit.

Wednesday: 11 a.m. Sun and cloud with a 40 per cent chance of precipitation.

Get off the train, think about going into the office, don't catch a bus up the hill. They're still at it, winding up like an old gramophone, the handle cranking, the needle scratching out the brittle sound of venom.

You, you, we're going to get you. You, you, it's time for you to die. You, you, there's nothing you can do.

'Oh, fuck off.'

The moment I got back to the house I switched on the laptop. The screen lit up but instead of the tropical fish normally decorating the desktop, I was staring into the face of a severe man with crinkly ripples of grey hair, fierce maniacal eyes and a look of holy zeal.

It was the Professor.

You think Gerald and Colin are going to like your paper. Don't make me laugh. You're useless. You can't do anything.

I sat there dumbfounded.

Yes, Alice. You. You're useless. You've always been useless. You're nothing. Go and steal Kathy's booze. Go on. Go and get a bottle of gin. Cut yourself. You know you want to. There's a big butcher's knife in the kitchen. Do us all a favour. Slit your wrists. Slit your throat. KILL YOURSELF.

I leapt up from my chair trembling and hid under the duvet cover in the corner of the room.

I could still feel the Professor's eyes like burning hypnotic rays and I could hear his voice droning away.

KILL YOURSELF. KILL YOURSELF. KILL YOURSELF.

I gripped the sides of my head and rocked backwards and forwards. My temples were exploding.

'Leave me alone. Leave me alone. Leave me alone.'

I should have pulled the electric plug from the socket, but I couldn't think rationally. I went instead to the kitchen, opened the cutlery drawer, gazed at the butcher's knife, saw my eyes staring back from the blade and slammed the drawer shut again.

I found a roll of aluminium foil, ran back upstairs and tore off strips. I spread them out over the duvet cover and pulled the cover over me but I could still feel the death rays beaming from the Professor's eyes.

We're going to get you, Alice.

I'm not Alice.

We're going to get you.

I want my gun.

*

When I opened my eyes it was dark. I was sweating. I was in the corner of my room under the duvet and there was crinkly tinfoil all over the place. What was that doing in my room?

I was shaken, afraid, paranoid.

I turned on the light and grabbed the *Oxford Dictionary of Current English* from the shelf. Derived from ancient Greek, paranoia describes 'a mind distracted'. The distraction, it adds, is caused by 'mental disorder with delusions of grandeur, persecution, etc.; abnormal tendency to suspect and mistrust others'.

Rubbish.

If you are afflicted with paranoia you *know* you are *not* having delusions. People *are* persecuting you. The Professor was alive. He was real. He had a face, he had a voice and he was joined by a choral hubbub screaming that I was useless. I should do the world a favour and top myself. All the same old spiteful stuff they'd been saying for years.

The kids in my head had kept them quiet for a while. But now they were back. Like a defeated army, they had gathered fresh forces and were on the march. The Professor and his lieutenants were working on an intricate conspiracy. I was the target. As well as my laptop, they inhabited the telephone and the newspapers, they spilled out of the television and they shouted from the pages of the novel I was trying to read.

I could hear the voices plotting against me.

Let's get her. We're going to get her. We'll trick her. She won't know what's hit her. She's alone. No one likes her. No one will miss her. Good riddance to bad rubbish. Get her. Get her.

My skin tingled with pins and needles. My brain was on fire. The voices were shouting through the flames. My body was wet with sweat and when I stripped off my clothes I could see burn marks where the light rays had zapped me.

*

For two days I remained locked in my room, staring at the blank computer screen, waiting to see if it came back to life. I didn't drink anything. I didn't eat. I didn't pee. I remained in the corner listening to the voices, the crinkling of the tinfoil, the light outside rising and falling with the passing of lost time.

On the third day I waited until I was sure Kathy and Jim had left for work. I pulled the hood of my anorak over my head and got the bus to the cottage to tell Rebecca what had happened. She didn't persuade me to tell Roberta. It didn't work like that. I had decided to tell Roberta but felt the need to share the decision first with Rebecca.

We went for a long walk. Summer was coming. I had been in Huddersfield six months and, against the odds, Colin Ince, my supervisor, was pleased with my progress. I was in the middle of my first major psychotic break with reality and couldn't help wondering how many other loonies there were creating new strategies to improve the health service.

At my next appointment with Roberta, I told her about the voices, but the attack had passed and I implied they were like chatterboxes in the back of my brain, talking to each other about me. She fluttered her fingers, a rare gesture (perhaps she was wearing an engagement ring?), and I admitted that the voices were with me almost constantly, narrating and commenting on my every move. I told her that sometimes I'd turn thinking somebody was behind me, but no one ever was. It was something that had occurred when I was a teenager and it was demoralizing now it was happening again.

Roberta sat silent, her usual modus operandi. I was about to add, 'You think I'm crazy, don't you?'

But she wound herself up, uncrossed her nylon-sheathed legs and leaned forward.

'Alice, I don't know that I have the expertise to help you

deal with these problems. Have you ever consulted your doctor about the voices?'

'Not really.'

'I'll support you as much as I can and we can continue with our sessions as normal, but I really think you ought to speak to your doctor.'

It was the first time she had ever given me advice. I was sitting on the floor and had put my head in my hands while she was speaking. I looked up at her, at her nice legs and good shoes, her patient face framed in wispy golden hair.

The light was behind her. A shadow must have crossed the sun. My throat was dry. My body was shrinking. My face was changing shape. I could feel the scaffolding below my cheekbones disintegrating and reforming. The sun came out again. Colours grew brighter and there was a nice lady sitting on a grey chair and I thought I knew her but wasn't sure.

'Who are you?'

'I'm Roberta.'

'Are you?'

'Yes.' She nodded.

'Where am I?'

'You're in my office.'

'What office?'

'It's my office, where we play Ker-Plunk, Alice.'

'I'm not Alice.'

'Of course you are.'

'I'm not, I'm not, I'm not. I'm Jimbo. You know who I am. I remember, you're that lady—'

'You're Jimbo?'

'Course, silly. I'm Jimbo. I'm Jimbo, but I prefer to be called JJ. I like ice cream.'

'Do you?'

'I don't like cake. I hate cake. I like ice cream. And I don't like spiders.'

'Why don't you like spiders?'

'They're horrible. They want to eat you. I saw a spider eating itself once. A man cut it in half with a big knife and the front half turned round and ate the other half.'

'What do you think that means?'

'It doesn't mean anything. It was just an itsy-bitsy spider.'

I didn't remember this conversation. Roberta told me what had taken place at a later date.

It was the first time that Jimbo had come out. I did not remember the details, but I did recall being aware of the slip at the time, that sensation of leaving and re-entering my skin. Nothing provoked JJ's appearance – it wasn't during a game of Ker-Plunk or in the midst of a regression session in therapy. It just happened and what was worrying is that I had never heard of this happening to anyone, ever, and I didn't know why it was happening to me.

I told Roberta this and she admitted she didn't know either.

'You need help, Alice.'

'You mean I need more help than you can give me?'

'I will help you as much as I can, but I really think you should talk to your doctor. Will you do that?'

'If you think it'll help.' I wanted her to make the decision. That was her job. 'But I'm scared of what he may think,' I added

'I'm sure your doctor won't judge you,' she replied. 'Our job is to be there and listen to people.'

I thought: She's putting herself in the same category as a doctor, but she's not. Counsellors only have a diploma. It was on the wall, three of them actually, with shields and gold seals.

I looked back at her again.

'If you want, I'll sit here while you ring to make an appointment,' she said.

Roberta found the number in the phonebook, dialled and gave me the receiver. The secretary said she had a free slot with Dr Michaels the following day at eleven.

'That's very good, Alice, you've done the right thing,' Roberta said when I hung up.

'Thank you, Roberta,' I said, and I didn't sound like me at all.

I was regressing again. We had been talking about JJ and I could feel JJ bubbling up inside me. He was an older, sharper, more inquisitive version of Billy, but then Billy was only five and JJ was ten, a self-confident boy who, if lost on the moors wouldn't panic and would find his way home.

This was my second visit in so many weeks to Dr Michaels. The last time had been for an ear infection, an odd coincidence since now I was going to talk about the voices whispering in my ear. Had they caused the infection with their halitosis breath?

I lay awake all night staring at the ceiling wondering what happened to the spiral mobile that had shadowed my childhood room. I remembered the way the coils moved in a mesmerizing way, how the spirals span faster when the door opened.

'Who's Daddy's girl?'

'I am.'

I got up at six, put on my abandoned jogging gear and was exhausted the moment I stepped out of the back door. I walked down the hill to the park, where I sat on a swing and swung as high as I could.

Go higher. Go higher. And jump. That'll cause some injury you can see the doctor about.

I was paranoid that the doctor would tell me I was wasting his time as I had no evident health problem. But then, the voices were a problem, even if you couldn't see them. As well as going to and fro on the swing I was going round in circles until I reached the decision to cancel the appointment. I'd go home and put some adjectives back in my proposal, something useful.

Kathy and Jim were having breakfast. I sat down with a cup of tea and some cereal. Jim was smoking a roll-up. Kathy was spreading marmalade on toast, the crumbs spreading across the table like insects.

I was still paranoid that Kathy and Jim were out to get me and at night lay in my bed wondering if there were a secret door between their room and mine. They thought I was a typical student boozing my way through uni with zillions of mates. They had no idea I was having a breakdown. I was living in my bubble. They were living in their own bubble, paying the bills, watching *EastEnders*, saving up for their holiday in Lloret de Mar, barely conscious of all we can be and do as humans and, like them, I wasn't doing or becoming those things either.

When they went to work, I blasted the house with Bruce Springsteen. The Boss's deep gravelly voice put the fear of working man New Jersey into the Professor and his band. I turned the volume to eleven and danced around the room singing along to 'Human Touch' from the new album.

The Boss's words faded from my head like the sound of a vehicle moving into the distance. I'd changed my mind again and was sitting staring at the clock in the waiting room at the Morningside Surgery, a big old country mansion with a warren of small rooms, each with an old fireplace that sucked cold air down the chimney.

Today I'm Alice

Tick tock, tick tock, Alice's going to die at eleven o'clock.

The little hand like a fat spider leg was moving closer to eleven. The palms of my hands were clammy, but eleven o'clock came and I was still alive. I'd made it. A few more minutes crept by and a Yorkshire voice sang out, 'Alice Jamieson, consulting room number two.'

Now, is this a trick? Is that the nurse calling? Or the woman from *EastEnders*? I took a chance. My heart was palpitating as I walked down the corridor that seemed as I set out to stretch like in a dream. I knocked on the door.

'Come in.'

I entered the room as if through a secret door, like the hidden door in the wall between my room and Kathy and Jim's room.

'Do sit down. Now what can I do for you, young lady?' said Dr Michaels

'I don't really know.'

The voices were sniggering in the background. They adored it when I was confused. The doctor had eyes like rays that were boring into me and I couldn't look at him.

'You'll have to tell me if I'm going to be able to help you,' he said. 'It's not that ear trouble again, is it?'

'No, no, I've been really stressed at university. People are plotting against me. They keep telling me to do things.'

'Who are these people, Alice?'

'You know, people . . .'

'And what are they telling you to do?'

I couldn't sit still. Ants in my pants, Mum would have said. I walked round the room listening to the voices whispering down the chimney and afraid to mention them. This was pure torture.

'Lots of people,' I said. 'And they're really bugging mc.'

Dr Michaels leaned on his desk and rested his chin on his

hand. He was a heavy man with a fat knot in a striped tie and a tweed jacket he must have bought in a shop that specialized in costumery for the medical profession.

'Do you have suicidal ideation?' he asked me.

There was a pause.

'What?' I said.

He repeated the question.

'Are you asking me if I want to top myself?'

'I am. I am trying to establish just who you think these people are, where they're coming from and what they're telling you to do. And I need to know if you're feeling suicidal.'

Hiding the truth about the voices took up a lot of time and energy. The pressure was building.

Dr Michaels leaned forward again and tried to make eye contact.

'Do you hear voices?' he asked, which took me back a bit. 'What are the voices telling you to do? Are you hearing voices now?'

I was, but I couldn't bring myself to tell him, to admit it. Was it some kind of trap?

'Not exactly,' I said.

'You know the voices aren't real. They're just in your mind,' he added, and I suddenly blew a fuse.

'They are real, I can hear them. I'm not *imagining* I can hear voices. I *am* hearing voices. I can hear them coming at me and they're as loud as the telephone ringing in reception, in fact, louder.'

'You can hear voices?'

'Yes. Can't you hear them?'

'Alice, if you can hear voices, they are only in your mind.'

'What do you mean *if*? I *can* hear voices. And they are not in my mind. They are not in my brain. They belong to people, real people, and they are not in my head.'

I felt angry at Roberta for suggesting I see Dr Michaels, and I was angry at Dr Michaels because I knew he had a preset idea of who I was and what my problem might be.

'People are persecuting me,' I said. 'They won't leave me alone.'

We batted about a bit more. People talking without saying anything. Like the voices. Finally my time was up, and Dr Michaels came to a decision. He said I was exhibiting classic signs of schizophrenia and did that thing doctors do best: he wrote a prescription for the drug Stelazine. He said it would help in the short term while he referred me to a psychiatrist. Counsellor, doctor, shrink. It was like climbing one of those step pyramids in Mexico.

I was drained, devoid of emotion. So I had schizophrenia? What did that mean? Maybe Roberta could enlighten me. My counselling was pretty intensive and I had an appointment with her later in the day I went to the university library before setting out for Leeds. I found a book entitled *Schizophrenia: The Facts*. The first chapter was 'What is Schizophrenia?'

I made notes.

According to the World Health Organization's International Classification of Diseases, schizophrenia and schizophrenic disorders are characterized in general by fundamental and characteristic distortions of thinking and perception, and emotions that are inappropriate or blunted. Clear consciousness and intellectual capacity are usually maintained, although certain cognitive deficits may evolve in the course of time.

The most important psychopathological phenomena include: thought echo; thought insertion or withdrawal; thought broadcasting; delusional perception and delusions of control; influence or passivity; hallucinatory voices commentating or discussing the patient in the third person; thought disorders and negative symptoms, which are feelings and abilities that most people have that schizophrenic patients lose due to their illness. These are:

- motivation
- the ability to interact socially
- enthusiasm
- appropriate emotional response

The facts:

- Schizophrenia affects 1 in 100 people.
- Some patients with schizophrenia only ever suffer from one psychotic episode and some have many over the years.
- The most common type of hallucination experienced by schizophrenia sufferers is auditory, but patients can also have visual, tactile, gustatory and olfactory hallucinations.
- Only one third of patients suffer paranoid-type symptoms.
- Approximately 10 per cent of schizophrenia sufferers will commit suicide.
- Signs and symptoms of schizophrenia usually first manifest in young adulthood and adolescence.
- Both sexes are at the same risk of developing the disorder.
- The majority of schizophrenic patients suffer throughout their lives whether it is ongoing or recurring.
- Only approximately 1 in 5 individuals recover completely.

I borrowed the book from the library and set off for the station with it under my arm. I could relate to much of what I'd read, but was fearful of the facts. My mind was spewing up questions. What causes schizophrenia? Is it really a disease? If I did have schizophrenia, with all my delusional perceptions and hallucinatory voices, would I ever recover or be cured?

In the calm of Roberta's office I reconstructed my meeting

with Dr Michaels. I was big on detail. I thrust my notes in front of her.

'What do you think?' I asked. 'Look at this. This is what some of the literature says. Do you think I have schizophrenia?'

Roberta wouldn't commit herself, but encouraged me to take the medication and see the psychiatrist. She praised me for going to see Dr Michaels; that's one of the tricks, reinforcing what the patient has already decided to do. She said we could talk more about his diagnosis at my next session, and I left in no doubt that Roberta Stoppa and Dr Michaels were in league with the Professor and part of the conspiracy.

I went home to collect some clean clothes. I'd decided to seek refuge at Rebecca's cottage where it was quiet and I would be able to study the book on schizophrenia and consider Dr Michaels' conclusions. Cold logic suggested that without a definitive understanding of the cause of the illness, there was no hope to cure it.

As I read, I began to understand that there is evidence that the causes of schizophrenia are at least, in part, genetic. Since genes regulate biological processes, including brain function, this evidence indicates that the biological processes are disrupted in the brains of schizophrenic people. On the other hand, the book suggested that psychological and social factors did not appear to play a prominent causal role, although they could be important 'modifiers' of the illness.

It seemed that I fitted the book's analysis like a hand in a glove, not that this was of any comfort to me. If anything, it made me more scared and paranoid as it implied that while people could get better from schizophrenia, there was no guarantee that they might not suffer a relapse. Was this something I had for life?

While I was reading I was subconsciously sipping gin from a litre bottle I didn't recall buying. I couldn't remember if I had already taken one of the blue tablets Dr Michaels had prescribed and was rattling the plastic bottle in time to the steady beat of the voices rattling around my head.

We'll get you. He's coming. You'd better prepare. He's coming now. Just wait.

'He' must be the Professor. He was the loudest and most scathing of my voices, a sort of Hitler or Mussolini. I waited and, sure enough, the Professor appeared.

See, people think you're crazy now. You'd better take all those tablets and drink some more. Then you'll go to hell. Where you belong.

'What on earth's the matter, Alice?' I heard a familiar voice say.

I turned, expecting to see no one, and found Rebecca behind me. I hadn't heard her come in. I didn't reply. I looked up. She looked so beautiful, so capable.

'What's in that bottle? Have you taken any tablets with the gin?' she asked. 'Come on, Alice, what's going on? You look like you've seen a ghost.'

I was hearing Rebecca's voice but it seemed distant as though she was calling across the moors.

Cathy? Cathy? Where are you, Cathy? Heathcliff. Heathcliff. Don't leave me.

I took a swig of gin and she took my hand to steady me as I got up from the floor.

'Things are falling apart,' I said.

She put her hands on my arms and they burned through my clothes.

'The doctor thinks I'm schizophrenic and I have to see a psychiatrist,' I told her and wriggled free. 'No one else can hear my voices. Only me.'

'I'm here for you, Alice, you know that,' Rebecca said. 'Why didn't you tell me about these voices before?'

'I didn't want you to think I was crazy,' I replied.

She shook her head and smiled. It was totally weird having a friend who really cared. We stayed up late again talking. Like Roberta, Rebecca didn't have a medical background but thought my seeing a psychiatrist was the best option.

Was she part of the conspiracy as well? I didn't want to believe it.

I took one of the blue Stelazine tablets before going to bed. I counted how many were left in the bottle and wrote the number down in pencil inside the back cover of the schizophrenia book. The voices were distant, but still they kept menacing me, muttering, nattering, chattering. I felt an emptiness inside, a void, a hollow space where another version of me floated in the nothingness of non-being. I didn't want much, not fame or fortune, power or success. I just wanted to be like everyone else.

CHAPTER 14
Shirley

My memory has many of the qualities of Raymond Babbitt, the character played by Dustin Hoffman in the film *Rain Man*.

This is what I recall.

The film came out in 1989, the year I was in training for the Birmingham Centenary Marathon. Written by Ronald Bass and directed by Barry Levinson, it stars Hoffman as autistic-savant Raymond, and Tom Cruise as his younger brother Charlie, a self-centred hustler. Their father dies leaving his entire three-million-dollar fortune to Raymond. Charlie plans to cheat his brother out of his inheritance and abducts him from the institution where he lives. During the subsequent road trip across America, Charlie is at first infuriated by Raymond's obsessions and repetitions, but gradually comes to admire his maths genius and feats of memory. In true fairytale fashion, the brothers form a deep affection for each other and live happily ever after with all that money.

Raymond had a photographic memory shot through with holes. Imagine a detective novel with pages torn out – the story has jumps, scenes are missing. Raymond was autistic. I'm not. Dr Michaels thinks I'm schizophrenic, but I can relate to Raymond's damaged memory, the graphic detail and blank spaces, closed closets containing chunks of the past I am unable to reach, while Billy, JJ, Shirley and Kato access those memories to live out their fantasy lives. It is in childhood where the adult is formed, and bits of my childhood seemed to be in the care of the kids.

As we know, the spanked child becomes a bully, the boy deprived of love may seek love in places where he shouldn't. I feel a deep and abiding grief over what happened to me as a child, without being ashamed of who I am. I couldn't be anyone else. I long for the missing pieces of my childhood as one longs for anything precious absently misplaced. I cherish those lost pages when they mysteriously turn up again.

Even the photographs from my childhood have all but vanished and I have taken to visiting car-boot sales and flea markets seeking out second-hand albums that may by some act of magic contain snaps of me as a little girl. Through the years and the moves, my mother has misplaced all but a few family pictures, me at three in the garden, at five with Clive in his school cap and striped tie. I stare at those photographs trying to see who I was then, as if in my expression I may find clues of who I was to become. Who I am. I would like to draw a dot in the past and another in the future and connect the dots with a straight line – not that anything in nature is ever straight, even time curves and our DNA is a spiralling set of helixes.

Why doesn't my mother have more pictures of me?

We were always taking photos in the garden, on holiday in Spain. Where are the pictures I took in Petra? In Israel? Where's that shot of me floating in the Dead Sea reading the *Jerusalem Post*? Photographs authenticate us, they remind us we existed in that place, at that time, and without photos from the past the present lacks roots, foundations, we are less real.

*

My appointment arrived.

I had a future.

I was to see Dr Eric Barne in Ward 10 at St Thomas's Psychiatric Hospital.

I went to bed feeling fretful, swallowed my Stelazine and Valium with a swig of water. The pills were bright blue and sunny yellow like the sky and sun in Billy's paintings. I dreamed of faded Polaroids of the castle and remembered dimly that one day someone had appeared with a camera to take pictures of the naked children. I woke with tingling fingers wondering whatever happened to those photographs. Would I find them one day in an album at a car-boot sale?

I showered, washed my hair, thought about becoming a brunette to confuse the teddies, and found myself sorting through the saucepan cupboard as Jim entered the kitchen.

'Not cooking now, are you?' Jim said as he lit a fag.

'Pancakes,' I replied.

'It's not Shrove Tuesday, is it?'

'No, Ash Wednesday.'

'It's not?'

'Doh,' I said.

He grinned as ash fell over his jersey and put the kettle on.

I cracked two eggs into a bowl, searched through the cupboard above the counter for some flour and borrowed Jim's lighter to light the gas under the frying pan.

What was I doing cooking pancakes?

I had no idea. I don't always know what I did yesterday and can rarely plan what I'm going to do today. Tomorrow is another country. That's why it's hard making friends, and it's even harder keeping the friends you've got when you are daily, hourly, knotted up in your own constantly changing emotions. I had confided in Rebecca, but had begun to avoid new relationships because I never knew when one of the kids was going to come out, or if I was going to lose time, or drink my way to unconsciousness.

When I did socialize it was spontaneous: a drink with Brian, who resided myopically behind his beard and class hatred. Gerald was a snail coiled in his own shell, and I was fortunate that Colin Ince had only ever seen me in my Alice costume, and had recommended me for a MPhil, the halfway stage to a doctorate.

Would I get through the next year? It was hard to predict. At times I lost control of who I was, slept in doorways, woke up in the park soaked to the skin, woke in Rebecca's cottage unsure how I got there. There had been a few more cutting incidents when, to avoid being admitted to A&E, I had struggled home to clean and dress my wounds. Along with my pills, I had a stash of antiseptic and bandages.

After an incident, my survival instinct would kick in, my left-brain would gear up and I'd work like a demon to catch up with my work. It wasn't a life, but a half-life with half a memory. Students I had never seen before would whisper something ambiguous and give me a wink across the polished wood tables in the library. I was a 'good little drinker', one guy said, and mentioned 'the boat race'. That was a drinking game Shirley must have taken part in but I didn't remember it at all.

I had become a skilled actress, coolly switching roles, retreating into the eccentric, the oddball, an intellectual with a book under my arm and my head in the clouds. Time, that blank canvas, didn't belong to me. My time was shared, and I realized that morning as Kathy entered the kitchen I was sharing it that day with Shirley.

She flipped a pancake and caught it perfectly.

'I wondered why you bought all these lemons,' Kathy remarked.

'You can never have too many lemons,' I replied, and thought: *I* bought all those lemons?

I had no memory of buying them, but I had no memory of not buying them either. Shirley and I were a bit like sisters; we cooperated sometimes, but not all the time. We had not become joined, or integrated, but we had found a way to work together subconsciously. We were both aware that we were sharing time, even though Shirley's presence was too subtle for Kathy and Jim to notice.

Jim squeezed juice through his big fist, covered the pancake in sugar and tucked in. They ate. I didn't. I'd lost my appetite. Shirley didn't have one.

It was useful having Shirley around and I decided I liked her after all. She was the imaginary friend I never had, and I felt her assured step in my calves and thighs as I marched along the street.

'Shall I walk down the hill to town?'

Nah, get the bus.

It was Shirley who bore the responsibility of my anger and psychosexual dysfunction. She carried the Oedipal hatred of her father aggravated by their incestuous intimacy and continued all those years later to suffer the pain and humiliation of those hideous memories. Like Raymond Babbitt in *Rain Man*, Shirley's phobias and fixations never varied. She was inflexible, unchanging. She was fourteen and would always be fourteen. A skinny, flat-chested girl who lifted her arms for Daddy to pull the nightdress over her head and opened her mouth for his penis to find its familiar slot. He held the back of her head, screwing her hair into his hand, and she looked up at the foil condom packets like a hand of cards in his fingers. He was smiling.

'What colour do you want, red or yellow?'

Shirley had the temperament to submit to Father as she would submit to alcohol and starvation.

I was beginning to understand that Shirley, the same as Kato, Billy and the others, had come into being to shield me from the fears and feelings I was unable to face. She wasn't my enemy. She was me. She held the keys to the locked closet of emotions and memories too painful for me to store.

I was slowly working things out for myself. Given time, I might, through the university library, have been able to diagnose my own disorder. Sadly, the medical profession wasn't going to allow that.

St Thomas's rose into sight through the bus window and I felt drawn to it by some uncontrollable inevitability.

The hospital's domed entrance was like the portal to the spaceship in *Close Encounters of the Third Kind*. I admired the controls, all those flashing lights and ringing phones, all those chirpy medics in their colour-coded uniforms. I dawdled along the corridor passing zombies with blank expressions and found Dr Barne waiting in Ward 10. He closed a file (mine, I assumed) and jumped straight in.

'My name is Dr Barne. You're Alice, I assume?' he said and I thought: You can assume whatever you want. How would I know?

'Yes,' I said. My throat was dry and I felt that tic in my neck twitching.

'Do sit down. I would like to ask you some questions, if that's OK?'

'I guess that's why I'm here.'

A nurse popped in. 'Coffee?' she asked.

I smiled and she gave a neat little twist and was off again on her white shoes. I didn't feel like me, but knew I had to behave normally if I was going to stay out of reach of the shrinks and finish my doctorate.

'How are you today?'

The psychiatrist had a deep voice that reminded me of the

Professor. Be careful, Alice, I thought. I tried another small smile.

'All right, I guess,' I said.

'Now I just want to take down some personal history. When were you born?'

'Tenth of January 1969.'

'So, you're . . .'

'Twenty-three,' I said. He clearly wasn't good at maths.

'Tell me a bit about your parents.'

'Mmm, I guess they're the sort of people I never wanted to be,' I replied and shrugged. 'Mum's OK, I suppose and, well, I hate my father.'

'You hate your father?'

'That's what I just said. He abused me as a child.'

'How does that affect you now? Does it upset you?'

I looked up at Dr Barne. What a stupid question. He had little piggy black eyes behind black-framed glasses, and his enormous beard hid his expression.

'Of course,' I answered.

'Do you remember many things from your past?'

'Where's this questioning leading?' I snapped.

'I'm sorry,' replied Dr Barne. He looked surprised and changed the subject. 'Maybe you could tell me about your diet?'

'My diet?' He nodded and I continued, 'I eat quite healthily.'

'Do you smoke?'

'Smoking is not for the likes of me, those whose brains must remain pure and responsible.' What am I talking about?

'Have you ever been hit on the head or knocked unconscious?'

'What are you trying to say?'

'Have you had any serious accidents?' he continued.

I thought for a moment, scrunching up my lips, holding my chin.

'In 1991, the Iraqis tried to assassinate me with a bomb. It only ruptured my eardrums. I was saved and that proved that I was on the right track. I felt established more firmly in my mission.'

'Do you drink?'

'I like my gin and tonic,' I answered, though I didn't tell him just how much I liked my gin and tonic.

'Do you take drugs?'

'No, I don't.'

'Do you feel as though you need anything now?'

'Right now?'

'Right now.'

'I'm feeling OK right now.'

'Do you have trouble sleeping?'

'Yes, sometimes.'

'Do you have any hobbies?'

'I like listening to music, writing poetry and reading. Actually, I'm reading a big book about schizophrenia at the moment.'

'Ah.'

'It's called *Schizophrenia: The Facts*. It's like *The Magus*, but without so many twists and turns.'

We were interrupted by the nurse, who brought in two cups of coffee and some packets of sugar in a bowl. Dr Barne shovelled three packets of sugar in his and stirred vigorously. I watched the coffee going round and round in spirals.

'What do you do for a living?' he then asked.

'I am on a bursary, studying for my PhD at the university.'

'Do you enjoy that?'

'Not really.'

'What do you want to do ultimately?'

'I am destined to become a diplomatic agent for the UN and bring about peace in the Middle East.'

'How much money do you earn while studying?'

'A pittance.' I paused. 'Like, really . . .'

'Do you know why you are here today?'

'Not really, no. Why?'

'I thought you were having some problems.'

'I guess I've been upset recently.'

'By what?'

'People making me nervous.'

'Who makes you nervous?'

'Certain persons.'

'Tell me more.'

'Do you know anything about the spies?'

'No, tell me.'

'Well, they've been watching me.'

'How do you know this?'

'They follow me, for one thing,' I told him.

'Why do they spy on you?'

'They want to get false evidence to frame me.'

'Can you give me an example?'

'No, they may be listening in on our conversation.'

'Not in here.'

'They have bugging devices. It's very sophisticated.'

'Do they know you're here in the hospital?'

'Of course they do.'

'Do you have any friends?'

'A strong person is mightiest alone,' I remarked.

'You didn't answer my question.'

'Yes, I have one good friend.'

'That's good.'

I took a moment to sip my coffee. The shrink did the

same. He slurped in a vulgar way and cleaned coffee from the corners of his hidden lips with two fingers.

'What do you think of this interview so far?' he asked. His beard opened to reveal a little pink tongue, and I thought: If I were casting a movie he'd make the perfect Neanderthal man.

'It could be better,' I said.

'I'm sorry.'

'That's all right. Ask me some more questions if you like.'

'Do you ever feel unreal?'

'Why do you say that?'

'Do you hear any voices?'

'No, I don't,' I said fiercely.

'Do you have hallucinations?'

'No, I don't. You must think I'm like the other patients here.'

'Are you a patient?'

'No, I don't belong here.'

'Do you need to have treatment?'

'No, I told you, I don't belong here. Anyway, Dr Michaels has given me some medication.'

'You appear sick to me, Alice.'

'Somebody should teach you a lesson in interviewing.'

'That's as maybe. I must say I don't think you're normal. Do you think you're normal?'

'Probably none of us are entirely normal.'

'How do you feel right now, Alice?'

'I'm a bit pissed off.'

'Why are you pissed off?'

'This has been a rotten interview.'

'What can I do to help?'

'Nothing,' I said and drank more coffee. I didn't actually like coffee, but Shirley did.

'Do you have any questions you would like to ask me before you go?'

'No.'

'Well, if it's OK with you, I'd like to see you again next week. I want you to continue taking the Stelazine that Dr Michaels prescribed and we can talk some more about how you feel next week.'

'OK,' I said, getting up from the chair.

He looked at his diary. 'Let's say three o'clock next Wednesday.'

Oh, no, not bloody Wednesday.

I walked the long corridor among the imbeciles and dead heads inhaling the scent of brimstone, the sulphur stench of death and decay. I could hear the clatter of metal trolleys, the cry of patients. The walls were that shade of cream that may once have been white. The floor was sticky beneath my running shoes. The zombies were hissing at me, mesmerizing me, drawing me into their clan.

They're going to get you, Alice. They're going to get you.

'Yeah, yeah, yeah. We've heard all your shit before.'

I saw a nurse with a syringe big enough to tranquillize an elephant. She gave me the evil eye as I passed. They were out to get me, all of them, the dead patients with brains sucked from their skulls, the malevolent nurses in league with Dr Barne, Dr Michaels, Roberta Stoppa, Gerald Brennan, Mao-Tse-Brian, Kathy Higgins, Jim Whatnot with secret potions in his Golden Virginia.

Through the door and out into God's fresh summer air.

No way. Absolutely no way.

That was them, the voices. For once we were in agreement. I and we and they all knew that if I ever went back to St Thomas's again it would be the end of everything, me in all

216

my varieties, my doctorate, my sanity, my hopes for the future.

I turned back like Lot's wife for one last look at Bedlam and we ran down the road as fast as we could, a song I didn't know playing in my head. 'Oh me lads, you should've seen us gannin'/Passing the folks along the road/And all of them were starin'/All the lads and lasses there/They all had smilin' faces/Gannin' along the Scotswood Road/To see the Blaydon races.'

Scotland. That's it. That's the answer. We should keep running across the moor, over the hills and dales, up through the limestone peaks and heathery seas until we reach Scotland and ask for asylum. Alice McJamieson PhD. I've come home.

I kept running and found myself back in the city centre and was shocked that all the buildings we'd blown up with Molotov cocktails had been rebuilt. How do they do that? So quickly. It was part of the conspiracy, obviously. They did it to confuse me.

If only I'd worn my anorak with a hood. I didn't want anyone to see me as I hurried into the library. I flashed my card like a secret agent and scurried into the medical section. I knew me well enough to know that my current state of paranoia would progress into full-blown delusions and hallucinations if I wasn't careful. Another big book with a black cover. I took the gun out of my backpack and hid it in my lap. I wasn't taking any chances.

Paranoids, I discover, display a lack of trust stemming from the absence of warm and trusting relationships with their parents.

Now that does surprise me!

The parents of paranoids are often controlling, rigid, distant, even sadistic.

'Yes,' I screamed.

'Shush,' someone hissed.

As children, paranoids develop a feeling that they would be betrayed, that their parents would not help them with disappointments and frustrations. They grow up feeling that the environment is hostile, and develop hypersensitivity to imagined slights.

Yep, that's not far off the mark.

I closed the book feeling pleased with myself. I thought about showing my face in the office and decided not to.

On the way home, I bought a bottle of gin and only when we started drinking did it occur to me that Shirley had taken part in the conversation with Dr Barne. Shirley had drunk the coffee. I had just sat there like a lemon (another one of Mum's sayings).

I, we, drank the drink and listened to the voices as we trudged exhausted and drained up the three-mile hill.

You must die, Alice. One way or another you must die.

I felt as though I was on fire, as though I was a pan of bubbling water boiling over. I was suffocating in the sweltering steam, in the stream of poison filling my head, my thoughts, my memories, the kids, Grandpa, the past, vicious, ugly, unkind, unrelenting voices growing louder and louder.

You must die. You must die.

'Oh, for crying out loud give it a break.'

I dropped down on the pavement and rested against a wall inscribed with graffiti – fuck you, wanker, bollocks, Man U are fucking bastards, fuck, fuck, fuck – a poetic stream of Tourette's obscenity and despair that made perfect sense. I found the bottle of blue pills in my rucksack and tipped a couple into my palm, then some more, and some more, until a blue-stepped pyramid stood in my hand.

Stelazine is a tranquillizer and an anti-psychotic. If two a day keep you in balance, what would the whole bottle do? I lifted my hand to my lips, pushed the pills in and swallowed them down with gin.

The voices moved off like a gang of football hooligans. I felt instantly energized, furious, full of spitting, venomous hatred. A great irrepressible anger was building inside me like a volcano.

I swallowed the rest of the Gordon's and brought the bottle down on the pavement, smashing it to smithereens. I pushed up my sleeve, selected a piece of glass and drew the sharp edge across my white skin.

It hurt at first, but then it felt good. It was like lancing a boil and all that poisonous frustration came flooding out with a stream of red blood that I watched as it wended its way down my arm. I made another cut, just for fun, and pushed myself up. I gazed up the hill, at the blue sky rising endlessly into forever, and my eye was drawn back to the wall – fuck you, wanker, bollocks, Man U are fucking bastards, fuck, fuck, fuck.

CHAPTER 15
Bedlam

Bright lights. The smell of drains. The capable clip of heels. I am horizontal in a bed that's tightly tucked.

'The girl in bay two needs an escort for St Thomas's.'

My ears pricked up.

Am I the girl in bay two?

I tried to sit up. My head spun and I slid back down again. I closed my eyes, took a deep breath and made a plan. I turned back the bedclothes, kept my eyes closed and jerked upwards into a sitting position. I swung my legs round and slipped from the bed. I was wearing a pale-blue nylon nightie and my arms were bandaged. The floor moved beneath my feet and two ghostly figures costumed as nurses lifted me up, tucked my legs under me, spread me flat like a fish and pulled the bedclothes back in place.

'The consultant's given the all clear,' one of them said. Then she added, 'They are going to take a look at you at St Thomas's.'

Well, you didn't succeed in your pathetic attempt that time. Now you'll be with the loonies.

I gave my head a good shake.

'What?' said the nurse.

'Nothing,' I replied.

She took my blood pressure, stuck a thermometer under

my tongue and the consultant appeared like God surrounded by acolytes in white coats. He drew the curtain round the bed, sat and took my hand. He had nice teeth. As he spoke, I looked away from his face and stared at his hand holding my hand.

I had been found unconscious in the gutter, my arms leaking blood, and some kind person had called an ambulance. My stomach had been pumped, my cuts sutured and bound. I'd had a narrow escape. I was out of danger and was, said God through his nice teeth, being transferred to St Thomas's for an assessment. The acolytes nodded wisely.

'But I'm all right, really,' I said. 'I wasn't trying to commit suicide. I was just a bit confused.'

'We don't want it to happen again, now do we?' he said, and continued before I could speak, 'Dr Barne will see you later today.'

The consultant rose to his feet and pulled back the curtain as if he were unveiling a painting. The flock of white coats shuffled out and I listened to the swish of their shoes moving across the ward. I could hear the ticking of a clock, a hacking cough, scissors clattering in a dish. Voices were murmuring round me and inside me. I was being watched, of that I was certain. I scanned the ward for cameras until my eyes grew heavy and closed. I was tired in the way Pheidippides was tired after running to Athens.

Time passed, peeling away like dead skin until the nurses came and made me get out of bed. I was stripped of the pale-blue nightie and dressed in the bloodied clothes I'd been wearing when I was rushed to the Royal Infirmary.

I was driven off in an ambulance with an escort, a woman who read notes in a manila dossier and who never exchanged a single word with me, a Ministry spy, obviously. I gazed out at the rebuilt streets of Huddersfield as if from the window of a hearse and this was my last journey. As we neared the hospital, I sighed with relief. I could see the spaceship rising before me and got the idea that I had been chosen. I was one of the lucky few. It had all been a test and I had made it. I was going to be taken away to a better place.

Whoopee, cried Billy.

I can't tell you how disappointed he was. We were back in St Thomas's with the mad people. Not the outpatients. The inpatients. I was assigned the bed next to the nursing station so I could be under constant observation. This is what's known as special obs, and if you're under special obs they take away your shoelaces and belt.

Blood loss and Gordon's had stolen my energy. I dozed until someone shook me from my dreams and marched me like I was in Stalag 13 down the corridor to the torture chamber they called the dining hall. I was squeezed between two real crazies and the nurse sat behind us watching as mounds of grey fetid foodstuff was served into metal dishes. I thought this was probably a test: they wanted to see if I was truly mad and so willingly I tucked in. Some of the loonies did actually eat this stuff but most just threw it over themselves.

The voices told me to make a run for it, which I did, but was soon caught by three nurses who pinned me to the floor in the corridor.

'I'll page the duty psychiatrist,' one of them said. She mumbled something else that I didn't hear because the fat one sat on me.

I didn't give up. That's not how you run marathons. I carried on kicking and punching, Kato's power and his surge of testosterone took over my skinny frame.

'You wankers, get off me. Fuck off, you fat bitch. You fucking tossers, I'll smash your fucking faces in.'

Kato was angry, violent, persecuted, but he had a gentle side too. He was and is protective of the kids, he makes sure

Billy always has his gun in my rucksack; he comforts Samuel when he cries. Kato cuts me and protects me. Is that contradictory? Yes, I suppose it is. That's the way it is.

A male orderly came to help, and Kato was dragged screaming and kicking to what they call the seclusion room, a small, square space that smelled like a toilet and contained a solitary white vinyl mattress on the bare floor. There was a single window covered with mesh. On the ceiling, too high to reach, was a mirror, tilted so that anyone observing from outside could look through the plate-glass window in the door and have a clear view inside the room.

A few more heavies joined the fray. The fight was over. Kato left me. Before I could catch my breath, I was held down, someone grabbed the zip on my jeans, my jeans and pants were pulled down, and I was given an intramuscular injection in my backside.

Did they not know that I had been sexually abused for sixteen years and being half stripped in this way might not be such a good idea, not for someone in my current mental state, not in my case?

It doesn't work like that. You're just another nutter.

The fat one was grinning. As the needle went in she said, 'That's a jab well done,' and I thought: You cow, and knew she must have said this many times before, that being fat she felt a need to be funny.

'Increase the meds by ten milligrams,' said the woman who had injected me.

'At every injection?' queried the orderly.

'Four times a day,' answered the woman. 'That's what the doctor signed for.'

The nurses took everything away from me, jewellery, shoes, the things in my pockets. As they locked the door and left me alone on the white mattress I felt a moment of triumph. It didn't matter how much or how loudly the voices encouraged me to kill myself, I wouldn't be able to, not in that room. I also felt proud that I had not succumbed to the poison in the dining hall and thought it hardly surprising the halfwits who ate the stuff were in an asylum.

One of the benefits of the anti-psychotic they had pumped into me was that I was scarcely aware of my surroundings. In that empty space I felt as if I had entered the inner mystery of the Rubik's Cube. I curled up in the foetal position on the thin mattress and slept while time did its thing and passed.

I was woken again. They led me down the corridor to another room where I assumed I was going to be tortured. I had information. They knew that. They were keeping me in solitary in case I organized a prison break. They softened me up with a biscuit and some tea that tasted like fish soup. I perched on a plastic chair scratching myself like a dog with fleas. The nurse explained that the itchiness was caused by photosensitivity, a side effect of Chlorpromazine, the drug I'd been given.

She told the doctor about the itching and my meds were changed to Haloperidol. This is a powerful anti-psychotic tranquillizer that blocks the receptors in the brain's dopamine channels, those mysterious vents that darken in schizophrenia and, to make life for psychotics more interesting, controls bodily functions and movement such as talking, walking, raising a cup to your lips.

I exposed my rear for the next jab without a struggle. The Haloperidol kicked in, my body went numb and I collapsed on the mattress. I slept the sleep of the marble knights in St Mildred's Church and was woken as if from a medieval curse for another shot. 'Every six hours,' I heard someone say, although it could have been every few days, few years. Time had stopped curving and turned circular like the spiral above the bed.

During waking moments I was aware that my throat was

dry and my lips were cracking. My eyes were glued shut. I slumbered on, Sleeping Beauty with sticky eyes, split lips, itchy skin. I might just as well have been in a straitjacket because even when I was awake I was unable to move.

Even motionless and asleep I was considered a danger to myself and didn't learn until those long-lost days were over that a member of staff had sat outside throughout, the shifts changing hourly, their sole responsibility to stare at the reflection of my prostrate form in the mirror above the mattress.

It came to an end. Prince Charming must have kissed my cracked lips and I was taken to a room and placed in a chair facing the hirsute Dr Eric Barne.

He was behind a long table with some faceless functionaries, six of them, I recall: women in pearls, men in ties. They talked among themselves and I would have said, 'Hope I'm not disturbing you or anything,' but my lips were glued shut. I was lost, drained and thin and was wondering if Colin Ince was in on the conspiracy. I understood now. I understood it all. These people had vested interests in keeping the health service running just the way it was. They didn't want me coming along with my PhD and changing everything.

They spoke for about ten minutes and it seemed like for ever. After being comatose for so long, the voices in my head rose full-throated from their siesta and were suddenly coming at me from all directions so that my mind was tossed like a mixed salad.

Dr Barne finally spoke.

'Do you remember who I am?' he asked.

I nodded my head.

'Do you know what day it is?'

I shook my head.

'Do you know what month it is?'

'Water,' I mumbled.

'I'm sorry?'

'Water.'

'She wants some water,' one of the jellyfish women said.

'Ah, yes, of course.'

They sorted out a glass of water, which I sipped.

'It's 1992,' I said.

'I'm sorry?'

'If that's the next question, it's 1992. I'm twenty-three. I'm studying for my PhD. My name is Alice McJamieson.'

'Ah, yes.'

'Alice Jamieson,' I corrected myself.

'Let me ask you another question,' Dr Barne continued. 'Do you hear voices?'

'Yes.'

'What are they saying to you?'

'I can't begin to tell you,' I answered.

'You must be very tired,' he said. 'I think it's time you left seclusion, but I'd like to keep you on special obs for a while.'

The rest of the bunch nodded and I remembered the student doctors who'd done that. Once I was in charge, I was going to stop all that nodding, get rid of all those pearls and tweeds, stop male orderlies pulling down your jeans.

In the main dormitory, I was put in the bed next to the nursing station. A nurse asked me if she could call a relative to bring me some clean clothes. After five days without changing I must have reeked. I gave her Rebecca's home number and closed my eyes.

My new bed was far comfier than the mattress in the seclusion room. I was pleased that life was getting better. I had already forgotten what life really is, we work hard and study hard, we run for the bus and we eat pizza, we have friends and read books, that it is a struggle. This is life.

Today I'm Alice

I had no appetite at teatime. I was given another injection and it was back again in no man's land. Later that evening, Rebecca arrived and I was overjoyed to see a friendly face, someone from real life. We chatted about who knows what and she promised to call at Kath's house to get me some clean clothes.

As she was leaving I heard her say to one of the nurses. 'That's not who Alice is. Look at her eyes. She's so drugged up she's in a trance.'

'She needs to be sedated right now,' the nurse told her. 'She's paranoid and exhibiting signs of psychosis.'

Rebecca stood there for a moment. She looked back and gave me a little wave. I waved, but I was thinking: Psychosis. *Psycho-sis*. The word conjured up images of Norman Bates in a frenzied knife attack in the shower scene in *Psycho*. That wasn't me. I wasn't a psycho. Kato's not a psycho.

The clock struck ten and it was meds time again. The fat nurse bustled through distributing tablets.

'Dr Barne has taken you off the injections for the time being,' she told me. 'You'll need to drink this in front of me so I can be sure you swallow it.'

It was green like fungus.

'What is it?' I pleaded.

'It's the same stuff you've been receiving, but in liquid form,' she replied, and added with a lift in her voice, 'I imagine it's preferable to all those shots.'

The green stuff looked like liquidized leftovers from the dining hall. I drank it down and climbed between the sheets thinking the sort of people who work in psychiatric hospitals are not the sort of people who ought to be working in psychiatric hospitals. I had to remember that. Write it down. Write an essay on my Toshiba. I missed Mouse.

Another nurse appeared, pulled up a chair and sat beside

the bed where she or someone would remain all night. I was still on special obs.

The thing with hospitals is they won't leave you alone. I was dreaming about rock sculptures or something when I was woken up by a nurse holding a tot with my medication. Morning must have come.

I drank it down and asked if I could have a shower.

She had to think about this. It was as if I'd asked if I could borrow five quid.

'I'll have to sit in the shower room with you . . . not under the shower though,' she said.

Hahaha.

And off we trooped. I washed the glue from my eyes and changed into the clean clothes Rebecca had dropped off on her way to work.

They still kept giving me drugs. I didn't want to take them, but knew if I didn't they'd pin me down and stick a needle in my backside. You can't win. I was followed by a nurse into the dining hall where I ate a few spoonfuls of cornflakes from a new packet that hadn't been tampered with. It was like being at a chimp's tea party. As I watched the lunatics trying to feed themselves it occurred to me that if you weren't careful, you'd end up like them: institutionalized.

From the dining hall we journeyed deeper into the joys of bedlam. This was my first visit to the day room. There were about twenty patients on the ward, men and women all mixed up in one apple turnover. I realized with sudden horror that *I* was a patient now.

There were a few people my age, most were older. One man spent the entire morning urgently pacing in circles; others sat rocking a leg back and forth in a motion I recognized as my own. In my psychotic world, I didn't realize until I worked it through my brain that, like me, the other patients were medicated. The constant pacing and inner restlessness is known as akathisia, a common side effect of anti-psychotic medicines.

The routine never varied. Breakfast was available between eight and nine. Lunch was at noon, tea at five. There were group activities between meals and visiting times, which were between four and eight. I kept away from the other patients and sometimes watched as two people with akathisia played table tennis.

Watch out for that one. He could kill you.

Even drugged with anti-psychotics, the voices persisted and would persist, perhaps for ever.

When I tried to read, my eyes wouldn't focus.

'It's a side effect of your medication,' said the nurse specialing me at the time. 'It often causes blurred vision. It's nothing serious.'

Nothing serious? If I couldn't read I'd surely go crazy in this nuthouse.

You'll go crazy, crazy, crazy.

Reading was my one respite and now that I couldn't read I stared out of the window and watched the light changing as the world turned. In your day-to-day existence you forget the sheer magnitude of time. It slips by, fast and slow, dragging and hurrying for deadlines, Mondays followed by Tuesdays, weekends, holidays, Christmas, another birthday, another year. In bedlam, time becomes an unvarying eternity, a vast pale-blue haze too heavy to hold; this is what people mean when they talk about the weight of time.

When you stop thinking about time you stop thinking, and non-thinking is a form of death. When you are young, you don't think about death unless, like Kato and Shirley, there is some intolerable pain that torments your mind to a degree that makes death the only solution. It was Kato and Shirley who had conspired to take those pills, drink that gin, break that bottle and break through the flesh on my forearms. I understood why and forgave them.

At teatime, a biscuit and the usual thick gruel that tasted of fish, I caught a glimpse of my reflection in a chromium tray – there were no mirrors, no glass to cut yourself with – and I didn't look like me at all. I was both older and younger, careworn like the children one sees in documentaries labouring in fields or huddled over hand-driven sewing machines. The sound of my own voice blocked out the voices inside me and I realized I was talking to myself.

Dinner, sunset, lights out. Between the death sleep of drugs the long hours are longer. At night you have silence and the screams of patients being pinned down and drugged. Their screams are piercing and brilliant like shooting stars; the silence falls like snow in a thick muted blanket, a black cocoon in which you dream bad dreams and awake afraid and helpless.

As I was now on the main ward rather than in seclusion, I was granted more privileges. I contacted Roberta Stoppa on the outside line and apologized for missing our last session. She said she had been worried about me and claimed she didn't know I was in hospital.

My privileges quota shot up even higher a few days later when I was taken off special obs. I was now allowed to shower and go to the loo without an escort, although someone still came to check on me every fifteen minutes.

They were still stuffing me with anti-psychotics. I slept a lot. My hair grew longer. My running shoes needed a clean. During conscious moments in the day room I listened to the internal chatter and watched my mind moving like a prison-camp spotlight over different scenes from my life: that little girl with spiders on her belly, with her dad's willy pushed inside her rectum, that girl with pink cheeks reflecting the pink rocks of Petra, that girl in a cap and gown receiving a first-class honours degree.

It was important to work out who I was so I didn't become someone else. The other patients were always sniffing and dribbling, coughing, spitting, jerking, twitching, walking in circles. One would set off another and the day room became a theatre of the absurd with all these mad people, as if in a lavish routine, staring, punching the floor, wetting themselves, laughing, screaming, hitting their own heads with table-tennis bats. If you are sane, or believe you are sane, you start to wonder. I didn't want to catch any bad habits from the other patients and kept away from them.

I constantly asked myself the same questions. Should I listen to every voice? Act out every impulse? Should I make my thoughts a reality? The drugs and the environment are no help when you're trying to hang on to your sanity. If someone that summer of 1992 had said, here's £400, go to Israel for a month, I'm sure I would have been perfectly well. It confirmed to me as I stared through the window that there was a plot to stop me meddling with the NHS.

Different psychiatrists saw me on different days on their ward rounds, each, as if it had been rehearsed, or they were testing for a role, unscrewing the tops from their fountain pens to jot down analytic notes to add to my file. A slender woman with long, sensuous legs and well-cut clothes said to me one day in a French accent, 'Freud says we are all someone else underneath, and the real person underneath has different feelings.'

She shook her gorgeous hair and smiled.

'What?' I said, but she was gone, her long legs on stilettos like scissors cutting a path through the ward.

During the next six weeks Kato, when he was 'out', rebelled against the system. He'd fight with the fat nurse and I felt like a pawn tossed about in someone else's battle. After these fights, we'd end up back in the padded cell because I was 'considered a danger to myself', and my medication would be changed once again.

Finally the shrinks made their diagnosis.

I sat at the long table facing Dr Barne, who was sitting in a line with his cronies.

There was a long pause, pregnant with possibility.

I was, he finally announced, 'psychotic with auditory hallucinations'.

I hunched my shoulders and scrunched up my toes. I hated the word psychotic, and hallucinations meant I was hearing voices that didn't exist. That was all very well, but if the voices didn't exist, how come they were nattering all the time? Even then, at that moment.

Dr Barne refined his diagnosis at our next session. He looked jolly pleased with himself as he told me that I was suffering from paranoid schizophrenia, or, put another way, 'schizophrenia with pronounced paranoid ideation'. I had, he concluded, non-existent voices with a warped way of forming ideas and images.

A smile appeared in his black beard. 'The thing is, Alice, the symptoms can be treated with medication.'

Well, that was a relief. Wrong, but a relief nonetheless.

I'd already tried three different anti-psychotic drugs, which hadn't been very effective. He now prescribed Clopixol.

The new drug did quieten the voices and relieve my paranoia. Dr Barne was 'thrilled' with my progress and I began to mix more with the other patients.

One day I got chatting to a girl named Sophie, who was the same age as me. Like me, she had been admitted to St Thomas's because she was considered a danger to herself and had twice tried to commit suicide. She had also been exiled on various occasions in the seclusion room. I thought she must have voices like me, but she confided that she had been abused as a child by her father and had two children by him.

Sophie could never forget what had happened to her. There were two children to remind her every day. The pain was so great that at those times when they bundled her into the seclusion room she would let out a piercing scream that came from the depths of her wounded soul and made you imagine all the nightmares and horrors of eternity.

I recalled a fragment from fourth-year Shakespeare:

> Give sorrow words. [For] the grief that does
> not speak whispers to the o'erfraught heart,
> and bids it break.

I lay in the black night, sleep gone, remembering that I, too, had been abused and inside me there was a gaping wound full of grief, sorrow and hurt. A time would come when, like Sophie, I would need to find the scream inside me and let it out.

CHAPTER 16
Regression

Now they *thought* they knew what was wrong with me, those eight weeks of humiliation at St Thomas's came to an end and I was sent back into the world with a bag full of drugs, a cold chill slicing through my anorak and a date with a community psychiatric nurse.

She was a pink-cheeked Yorkshire lass by the name of Lynne Tucker and, like Mum and her hairdresser, I would see her once a week for a chat. Lynne was a big-boned woman who talked solely about herself as if this would show her patients that disturbed they might be, but at least they didn't have to put up with her bad back, her daughter's tonsillitis, and so on.

'And how are you today, dear?'

'Freezing,' I replied.

'It's the weather.'

Hahaha.

The summer had gone. Vanished. I didn't see it passing. The view from the window at St Thomas's never contained the sun, just a pale watery haze the same shade as my faded jeans.

I was surprised to discover that my proposal for an MPhil with a view to extending my thesis for my doctorate had been accepted by the university board. I had made it through the first year at Huddersfield and was back on the spiral stairway to doctorate heaven. In that restrained English way, Gerald Brennan, Brian and Colin Ince never mentioned my absence at the end of the summer term. I realized that being a nutter and doing a PhD were not incompatible.

I resumed counselling with Roberta Stoppa. She had already introduced games like Ker-Plunk to draw Billy out and now, when he appeared, she encouraged him to talk about his dreams and secrets. As part of her NCH training, Roberta had learned a procedure developed by Penny Parks, the author of *Rescuing the Inner Child*.

Simply describing your nightmares is not enough, she explained. Only by reliving those nightmares was I going to get on the path to healing.

Through carefully constructed questions and promptings, yet never using hypnotism, Roberta was able to make me regress to childhood. The kids all held different memories, each compartmentalized to protect me, Alice, from those memories. Now that the memories were allowed to resurface, the kid remembering would suffer the agony and anguish of reliving those memories of abuse. As those memories filtered into my consciousness, I suffered the same torture. I went into counselling a perfectly normal young woman, sort of, became a five-year-old boy, or a two-year-old girl, and came out a quivering wreck.

When I left these sessions I was completely drained, and sobbed as I made my way back to the station. I would stand three-quarters of the way along platform two watching the train growing larger as it charged over the silver rails. I'd clench my fists and direct messages down to the soles of my feet: Stay still, wait for the train to stop; stay still, wait for the train to stop.

I tried to be normal. I tried not to drink, wound myself, overdose. But the temptation was beyond my control; it was inside me. When a tightrope walker inches across the abyss, he carries a pole that he holds parallel to the ground to keep him steady. Clopixol was my pole. But I was still balanced on a thread, poised over the abyss. Occasionally I fell. I lost time. Missed appointments. Drank. Fell over. Slept rough.

One morning, Rebecca dropped me off in Leeds for an appointment with Roberta. I waved as the car turned and had no idea where I was. I grabbed my gun.

Bang. Bang.

You're dead.

There's a marble temple, a red-brick building, three flights of stairs. It must be Wednesday.

I thought yesterday was Wednesday.

Where am I?

Jump, Alice, jump. You know you want to.

'Fuck off. Just fuck off.'

Time was spinning out of control.

I was back on platform two watching the train hammering down the line, experiencing Billy's fears giving way to Kato's rage, his anger distorting my features. I'm going to fucking punch somebody in a minute.

Jump, Alice, jump. You know you want to.

The Professor was like an old gramophone record stuck in a groove. He'd repeat *Kill yourself, kill yourself* in a humming voice like a drill boring holes in the protective shield of my anti-psychotics.

That night in Kathy's house, the hidden doorway artfully concealed, I lay in bed with Valium taking me into sleep. As I was dozing off, I realized rather than recalled that I had been at a therapy session with Roberta that day, but as the time had been consumed by Billy and Kato, I had no clear memory of what they had said and suffered. Their memories were raw open wounds. As those memories slipped into my sleeping mind I woke to a sickening flashback of the physical act of my father entering my bedroom, taking off my clothes, lubricating his penis in my mouth and violating me anally, turning me over and pushing his moistened erection into my little-girl bottom.

I lay there awake, me, Alice, trembling, sweating, nauseous, afraid. I had come to understand that sex, like Bach in his 'Goldberg Variations', has many themes, deviations, tangents and digressions. I couldn't imagine taking part in a three-some, but at least I now knew what it was. Billy's recollections were the foggy nightmares of a five-year-old, but they came back to me as the clear and vivid memories of a twenty-three-year-old woman.

I pushed back the bedclothes, ran down the hall and threw up in the toilet. The pain of these memories was excruciating. It was like having your teeth drilled without novocaine, an immersion in pain that was overwhelming, constant, unbearable. I felt disgust at the touch of my own skin, at my hands as I watched them moving over the Toshiba keyboard, in the blank look I saw in my eyes on those rare occasions when I caught my reflection in the mirror.

Two questions kept running through my head: How much longer can I put up with this torment? How long is it going to be before my mind is healed?

Lynne Tucker didn't know. Roberta didn't know. I called the Touchline emergency number at the National Children's Home. The counsellors didn't have any answers, but they were good listeners. I am a telephone person. You can talk more freely down the copper wires, your voice is detached from the prison of your body. You don't have to hunch and hide, wipe away your tears, clean the vomit from your T-shirt.

I called Stephen. I told him I was experiencing flashbacks of previously repressed memories of being abused as a child and was summoning up the courage to finally enlighten my mother. He promised to support me when I did. My stepdad, I'm sure, had always known there were taboos in our family psyche. He had always been sympathetic and that helped me more than he knew.

The desire to tell my mother what my father had done to me had been in my head for ten years. I wanted her to know every foul, unpalatable detail.

'Who's Daddy's girl?'

'I am.'

That long tongue licking my private parts, pushing into my bottom, his cock in my mouth, oiling the thing, relaxing the sphincter at the entrance to my anus, pushing that greedy cock into my vagina, pumping his warm semen over my face, kissing my lips. When I read in a book by Anaïs Nin that prostitutes never kiss the clients I understood why.

I wanted my mother to listen. I wanted her to believe me. And I wanted her to identify this 'covert' truth instinctively, with that instinct mothers have when they hear their babies cry in the night. I wanted to take the skeletons out of the closet and, what's more, I wanted Mother to understand that what I was revealing wasn't an attack on her. I wasn't blaming her.

During the next couple of weeks, I wrote in a notebook everything I could remember about the abuse. One bleak midwinter Thursday I took the train to Birmingham to spend a long weekend at home.

It was late by the time I arrived. We ate supper from trays on our laps in the lounge. My tummy was clenched like a fist and the spasm in my neck was throbbing. I took my tray through to the kitchen then sat down again. Mother had sensed something was in the air.

'Mum, there's something I want to tell you,' I said.

She gave herself a little shake. 'You don't have to stand on ceremony with me, Alice,' she replied.

'I know. But I want you to hear me out without interrupting.'

'Don't I always?'

'Let's listen,' said Stephen.

I opened my notebook. I could hear my heart thumping in my ears. The room was as still as a theatre as a play is about to begin. I had the feeling my mother had been anticipating this moment for a long time. I told her everything. Every wretched contaminated detail from the degrading mess that had been my childhood: the spiders, the castle, the man in the Rolls-Royce, the multicoloured condoms; those times when I was locked in the Bird Cage with a tin of spaghetti hoops; the anorexia, the beaker of alcohol I'd taken daily to school, my visits to Dr Purvis, the child psychiatrist; the eight degrading weeks I had spent at St Thomas's drugged up to the eyeballs.

She sat in silence, the blood racing from her cheeks. I closed the book and started to cry. I cried and cried. I wept bitter tears and those tears came from Baby Alice and Samuel, they came from Shirley and Kato, they came from Billy, from JJ and they came from me. I cried and my mother came to sit beside me on the settee. She put her arms round me. She patted me and through my sobs I heard her say she believed me, she believed me, she believed me.

In the prolonged denunciation of my father I avoided mentioning the rape when I was twenty-one. I don't know why. We give a bit, we hold a bit back. I sat on the settee and let the opportunity slip by. My mother had her arm round me. She believed me. I desperately needed to take short-term comfort in the fleeting moment. But I did say I wanted to confront my father and asked Stephen to go with me.

Why did I need to confront him again? I am obsessive. I

repeat myself. I can't help it. I live alone in my head. I have few friends and lose the friends I do have. People think I'm weird, and I am, I suppose. I wanted my father to see with his own eyes that the little girl who had lain on her face while he split the walls of her anus pushing his penis up inside her was still alive, still fighting, still struggling to be normal, to be happy. I had been incarcerated in the concentration camp of my pink-walled room but, like my friend Esther, I had survived.

We drove to his house on Friday evening. I stood in the porch and said my piece. What I said I have no idea; it came spewing out of me like poison. My father trembled. His shoulders were shaking. He looked old and mad standing there being confronted with the horror of who he was and by what he had done. Nothing, nothing will ever balance the injustice of what my father did to me, but at least my outpouring of poison gave me a moment of self-respect.

My father could see Stephen sitting in the car and remained in the open doorway meekly taking everything I could vomit out of my gut. He didn't go and get a knife from the kitchen. He didn't threaten me. The thing about bullies is that they are always cowards. Always. I turned away. I strode straight-backed down the path and closed the gate quietly. The kids, I'm sure, were proud of me.

While we were driving home, my father telephoned my mother to plead his innocence and my mother told him that she believed me, not him.

Now I had told my mother and confronted my father, I was able to regress more easily with Roberta. I often put my thoughts down on paper. Once I wrote:

Roberta, there are some questions I need some answers to:
  1. Why are the kids there? (Although I think I know the

answer to that anyway, perhaps because I feel I was
never a child?)

2. How do I make them go away or get them to grow
up or whatever?
3. How can I do it quickly?

Some more things I need reassuring about:
Please tell me you believe me.

Do other people feel like this, or is it just me being stupid/
going crazy/not facing up to some awful aspect of myself
(like maybe I'm a pathological liar or something)?

Finally, can Billy wear his cap next week and have some
birthday cake even though it's not his birthday yet? And
can he maybe scribble or colour? I know it sounds silly,
but Billy would really like that. I know you probably think
it's stupid, but it's because I'm sad. I was never a kid and
it's not my fault that things are like this now. Billy is a
good boy and it's not his fault he wants to play. Do you
mind if he plays when he comes to Leeds, or will you get
fed up with him and think that he's not trying? (Even
though he is trying really; he's trying really hard.)

On my actual birthday, I entered the counselling room to
find sandwiches, crisps and a birthday cake with candles and
presents including a set of farm animals and a Lego truck.

Billy was 'out' in a flash. He was fascinated by Lego. On
several occasions when I'd set about working on that slowly
evolving research project at the cottage, I'd stir, as if from a
dream, grow back into my clothes, and find myself cross-
legged on the floor assembling a car or a castle from my
growing collection of Lego – bought or stolen. Where it all
came from and how it kept growing I wasn't sure.

*

I was still spending a lot of time at the cottage, walking on the moors in climbing boots those cold winter days, having snowball fights with Rebecca and Zoë. Christmas had come and gone. It was 10 January and I was a year older; twenty-three had seemed young; twenty-four felt old, and the world seemed to be growing old with me.

Back at the birthday party for Billy, Roberta told me later that she and Billy had had something of a tiff. She insisted that if Billy had been five, he must now be six. But he wasn't. Billy was right. Billy will always be five, just as Kato will always be a pimply lad of sixteen, and JJ a swashbuckling little ten-year-old. I don't know how I knew this, I just did, in the same way I knew Billy was named Billy and Shirley, bizarrely, Shirley.

Of course, the day Billy was five again, Samuel was six still. After regressing at the birthday party, I remained in child-mode at the end of the session. As I closed the door behind me, I started panting for breath and was struck suddenly with paralysis. I was overcome by the most unbearable sorrow. I slipped to my knees, rolled into a ball and wept. I wept until Roberta found me clinging to the bars at the top of the stairs. Luckily, she had met Samuel before and knew how to comfort him with the scruffy pink teddy.

She cancelled the rest of her appointments and spent the afternoon with Samuel delving into the absolute worst aspects of abuse: those times when my father took me to the castle and shared his trusting little six-year-old with the coven of paedophiles playing at devil worship. The memories were like a jigsaw of 10,000 pieces slowly transforming from the fragments in Samuel's head to a solid picture growing in my subconscious.

By the end of the day, I had transmogrified back to Alice and Roberta took me to A&E where I saw a psychiatrist –

odd that there's a shrink for accidents and emergencies, but there you are. I have no recollection of what was said, how I escaped from the claws of the psychiatric establishment, or how I eventually got home.

What I did learn that day was that there was more contact between the kids than I had first thought. I knew that Shirley and Kato communicated. Now it seemed clear that they were all tuned in to a telepathic current and knew each other's thoughts. Sometimes I was included in the team, but at others the fuse blew, the current ruptured and I was alone with just myself for company.

I remember Grandpa telling me not to let things in life embitter me, but to let them enrich me.

I'd lost sight of this. In fact, I couldn't see how my troubles could possibly enrich me. I had a psychiatric label, I had spent months in an institution and was psychotic a lot of the time. I was glad Grandpa wasn't there to witness my suffering. This is what I wrote in my diary:

> I just want to sleep and block it all out. This isn't fair. Today's another of those days when I'm remembering the abuse. The truth feels too painful to bear. It torments me mentally and emotionally. Physically my body feels retraumatized. Help! Help! I feel such isolation. I need someone's touch (safe touch); to hear someone's voice; to know someone's there. Help! Help! Please don't let me be alone with this again. Oh God, I hurt so much. And now I remember this is how I felt so many years ago. It all comes back to me now ...
>
> HELP! HELP!
>
> I want to cry, but feel like stone, cold and hard. I cannot allow myself to experience the depth of my feelings, so I just turn my emotions off. But now a commentary from somewhere in my mind tells me this is real. It did happen. Oh shit, it

happened all right. Then the voice seems even more intense and repeats: 'Oh God, please help; someone help!' Again: 'Help! Someone help!' And again, with more urgency. Then everything falls silent. I've gone numb and feel like stone again. The only trace of emotion is the crying in my head. The crying of a child. Bitter, sad tears. Tears of despair. I want to reach out and touch the child, but I can't. I sit and listen to the crying and I want to shed tears too. But I can't. Yet it doesn't detract from the feeling of despair. I hurt. What the hell is happening to me? I feel like I'm going crazy!

That same month funding for counselling from NCH was cut for everyone on their lists. Samuel was shattered. He trusted Roberta. He couldn't understand why he would never see her again and spent hours curled in a ball, staring at the wall, big tears running down his face.

Alice appears. She stays in bed with a wet face dozing, drinking, scribbling poems, drawing, reading. She is, as Blake wrote, 'among those to misery born.'

I was building up to my second nervous breakdown. Or was it my third? I'll get the calculator. Check the diaries. Call Touchline. Send that letter to Patrick O'Hay. I wasn't living. I was barely existing. I was sinking down inside myself as if down a mine shaft leading to the mystical depths of my being. To my soul.

Roberta once said: 'Something's broken and it's got to be fixed,' and what I saw that day was a vision of shattered pots in sun-warmed museums.

Other times, I was suffering from what they call a fugue, a dreamlike state where normal life seeps away like sand through an hourglass, the light changing to darkness, the darkness to light, the teddies alternatively chirpy with bright smiles, wicked with evil grins, the hole in the wall between my room and Kathy's opening and closing like the eye of a giant fish. The flashbacks of the abuse were coming and going like wind-tossed kites. Sleep vanished.

People get on with their lives, go to work, pay the bills, save up, get tonsillitis, get married, have children, get divorced, feel depressed, go to work, save up, fall into the abyss. I began pacing like one of the imbeciles at St Thomas's. I've got to keep going, keep moving, keep forging ahead.

Kill yourself, Alice, kill yourself.

The voices. Always there. Always.

The house is quiet. The hole's sealed. Kathy and Jim are at work. Long shower. Collect my prescription. Stock up. It's Monday. I'm not sure why this is important, but if anyone asks, 'What day is it today?' I'll be able to answer, it's Monday.

I make my way to the office. At the bottom of the hill there's a baby in a pushchair outside a shop crying, a long, mournful sobbing cry . . .

I couldn't work out what I was doing standing on the platform at Manchester Piccadilly railway station.

Did I get a train?

My clothes felt tight.

Kato was popping Clopixol like Smarties. He got on the next train, slamming the door as hard as he could. Some old fart shakes his head and Kato just glares. He keeps popping pills as the train rocks and bumps over the sleepers. He punches the palm of his hand. He feels sweaty and angry. He wants to do something, but he's not sure what.

Birmingham New Street. Slam the carriage door. Push on down the street, breath fading, limbs growing heavy, throat dry, eyes fuzzy.

Just keep going.

I read somewhere the horizon is twenty-five miles away. You keep walking to reach the horizon and it just keeps moving back. Life's like that. You never reach your goal. It's always moving away from you. We are doomed to disappointment because in our pursuit of perfection we are constantly reminded that we will never reach it. The goal like the horizon is beyond our reach. If you run the marathon there's always another minute to knock off.

A bus drops Kato at the end of the street. He counts down the houses, stumbles up the path, rings the bell and collapses as the door opens.

Is he dead?

How Mum managed to get Kato in the car no one will ever know. She did. She got him to hospital and all those anti-psychotics he'd swallowed got pumped right back up again. They sent him home to Mummy.

And he did it again. Twice more in a week.

Kato can't take the pain. Kato borrowed my body when I was sixteen. As a girl who should have known better, but didn't know how to stop what was happening because it had always happened, he, as me, watched as Daddy unrolled the condom and lay back with spread legs and small breasts for Daddy to do that thing daddies do.

CHAPTER 17
Body Memories

They always smile when they jab the syringe in. It's as if the plunging action is directly connected to a muscle that brings a grin to their open lips.

I was back in the nuthouse. Not a nice space-age nuthouse like St Thomas's with blow dryers in the bathroom but a Victorian asylum where I stared unblinking at the water-stained ceiling and listened to the rats moving behind the walls. They'd stuck me in a dormitory with the lunatics around me screaming, sobbing, moaning, talking to them-selves. Even the building was groaning; the ancient bricks made from dead grandpas and dinosaur bones were turning back into dust. I was on special obs again and a motionless nurse, who may have been a waxwork sat at the bedside. My mind was racing.

Shirley had found a piece of glass behind a pipe in the bathroom and hidden it under the mattress. The waxwork nodded off to sleep. Shirley slipped from the bed, extracted the shard of glass and went running down the corridors slashing my arms and splashing the walls with blood.

The waxwork came to life, rounded up a posse and gave chase, yelling, waking the drug stupefied loonies, who screamed and joined the chase. The red stuff poured out of me in spurts, turning the corridor floor into an ice rink of fresh wet blood. I was caught, pinned down, tranquillized and slept like a dead bird.

It was not an auspicious start. Bandaged and sedated, the shrinks at the asylum told me if I did it again I'd be sectioned, a word that strikes fear in the hearts of all loonies. Under the Mental Health Act that meant they could keep me banged up while I received compulsory treatment for as long as they believed was necessary. Nurse Ratched. Jack Nicholson. *One Flew Over the Cuckoo's Nest.* All knowledge can be found in the movies.

Shirley shrank back into the shadows – typical – and I promised to play by the rules.

The duty psychiatrist took it upon herself to ignore Dr Barne's diagnosis. She found in me no signs of psychosis and cut the anti-psychotics from my diet. I was permitted Prozac, Diazepam and Temazepam – sleeping pills.

Dr Adele Armstrong, the consultant psychiatrist, turned up two days later. She was stern, poker-faced, unbending; a Victorian schoolmistress for a Victorian asylum. If you have mental-health problems it's a serious matter, nothing to joke about.

She told me she intended keeping me in hospital for a week for observation, and then I was to attend a day hospital in Naydon Clinic – every day.

'But I can't do that, I have to get back to Huddersfield.'

'You don't have to do anything of the sort.'

'But I'm halfway through my PhD,' I explained.

'Not any more you're not.'

They can be so cruel.

I returned to the womb, a child with my mummy and Uncle Stephen to look after me. We collected my things in Huddersfield.

'Where'd you get all this Lego from?'

'Dunno.'

We left Kathy and Jim standing on the kerb, the car boot full of boxes. I glanced back without nostalgia at the house on the hill with its smell of Golden Virginia and Bruce Springsteen buried in its DNA.

Samuel welled up in tears when we said goodbye to Roberta Stoppa. We were able to spare five minutes for Lynne Tucker, Gerald Brennan and Brian. Keep in touch, they said. We'll see you again soon. But I had come to realize that when people say they'll see you again soon you know you'll never see them again. Friendship is like fire, you have to keep stoking it or the fire goes out. We drove across the moors to the cottage. When Rebecca Wallington put her arms round me I felt a cut across my chest as my heart split in two.

It was Sunday. No time for tea. Just as Stephen had driven me up the motorway to start my doctorate he drove me back, completing the cycle in order for me to get up early on Monday and complete another cycle.

The day hospital was in the same building as the clinic I had attended weekly as a teenager to see Dr Purvis. Eight years had gone by and my brain was still playing up.

Mother dropped me at the entrance.

'Have fun,' she called. 'Work hard.'

It was as though she was dropping me at school and I was Billy. She came to call the hospital the Fun Palace and it did provide what the shrinks must have considered fun stuff for people off their trolley. There were about fifteen patients in various states of mental decay and to help heal our minds there were arts and crafts, puzzles and Scrabble. When I saw the table tennis table it confirmed there were hidden cameras filming these akathisian games for entertainment at psychiatric conferences.

Three times a week, on Mondays, Wednesdays and Fridays, I had a two-hour session with a therapist named Jo

Lewin, whose style of counselling was different from that with which I was familiar under the NCH system used by Roberta Stoppa in Leeds. Jo was a vibrant, slender woman with a rounded face, vivid blue eyes and a penchant for black, which made her look elegant but sombre. She had her way and her way was what she called the 'chair'.

The chair is introduced when the therapist believes the patient is ready to confront their unwanted and undefended feelings. You begin with breathing exercises and when you're relaxed the therapist asks you if you want to sit on the chair. Once you do so, through the therapist's careful questions, you are encouraged to get in touch with your deepest feelings, your most painful and repressed memories. You must relive what happened in the past in order to get those feelings out into the present. If, or when, this is achieved, when you stand up, you leave your bad feelings and memories behind you on the chair, and they will never seem quite so painful again.

That's the technique. But the thing is, I didn't like sitting on the chair and wanted to sit on the floor, as would a child. I continually asked Jo why the rubber-backed carpet couldn't act like the chair and allow me to relive my memories. To a child, a chair and a carpet would do exactly the same job.

I didn't want to tell Jo about the kids. I kept them hidden for as long as I could, but switching was an automatic response to things beyond my control. The crying baby outside the shop in Huddersfield had set Kato off on his trip home by train, the overdoses taking us to the asylum, the day hospital and the sudden termination of my doctorate, which broke my heart. What set Samuel off I'm not sure. It could have been the smell of the therapy room, the pictures on the wall, the concentrated look in Jo's blue eyes. Samuel was besieged by a sudden memory that transformed into an excruciating pain. He banged his head on the table and wept for two hours.

Jo was aware this wasn't normal regression or acting out behaviour. She got off her own chair to sit on the floor with Samuel, and he allowed her to comfort him in her arms.

Roberta Stoppa had begun the process of coaxing the kids at NCH out. Jo Lewin first met Samuel, then Billy and some of the others. She knew there was something going on that didn't fit the normal pattern. She saw me for several more sessions, she did her research and finally she called Dr Armstrong.

After that call, everything changed.

Like misplaced family photographs, the fault in a troubled mind can be hard to find.

Thanks to Jo Lewin's call, and thanks to her knowledge, she was able to guide Dr Armstrong to diagnose my complaint as Multiple Personality Disorder (MPD), usually referred to as Dissociative Identity Disorder (DID) by the psychiatric community. Finally I was told that I wasn't crazy after all. The voices of the kids inside my head were echoes of dissociated memories of sexual and emotional exploitation.

Throughout my childhood and adolescence, I had seen various GPs, paediatricians, a psychologist and a consultant child psychiatrist. Each of them had a different piece of the puzzle. Put together, the pieces added up to corroborative evidence of long-term abuse, but no one had enough pieces to work this out.

The consultant child psychiatrist had asked me if I had been abused, but because of my 'dissociation' (a new word for me) as a fifteen-year-old, I didn't *know* in the normal sense I had been abused. As we were living in the nice house in the perfect nuclear family, I wouldn't have admitted it anyway.

After being diagnosed with MPD/DID, I went off in my usual way and did my own research.

Alice Jamieson

The American Psychiatric Association's *Diagnostic and Statistical Manual of Mental Disorders (DSM-IV-TR)* defines MPD/DID as a mental illness in which a single person displays multiple identities or personalities, sometimes called alters, each with its own pattern of perceiving and interacting with the environment. When I – Alice – switch into one of the other personalities, he or she takes complete control of my behaviour, and I experience memory loss for the time that the alter is 'out'. I had been aware of this for as long as I could recall, but had never been able to pin a label on it or understand why. I did my research and everything began to make sense.

In the textbook *Multiple Personality Disorder*, published in 1989 by the Canadian psychiatrist Colin A. Ross, I came across this paragraph on page 2 of the introduction:

MPD is based not on defect but on talent and ability. The patients have used their ability to dissociate to cope with overwhelming childhood trauma, which usually involved both physical and sexual abuse. MPD is a creative and highly effective strategy for preserving the integrity of the organism in the face of chronic catastrophic trauma.

On pages 55 and 56 Dr Ross poses a startling question:

What is MPD? MPD is a little girl imagining that the abuse is happening to someone else. This is the core of the disorder, to which all other features are secondary. The imagining is so intense, subjectively compelling, and adaptive, that the abused child experiences dissociated aspects of herself as other people. It is this core characteristic of MPD that makes it a treatable disorder, because the imagining can be unlearned, and the past confronted and mastered.

What jumped off the page were the words MPD is 'a little girl imagining that the abuse is happening to someone else'. I knew all about that. I had always known. Always known and always dismissed my own knowledge, my feelings, my intuition. You hear voices and recall horrid, unbelievable things and you can't help thinking you're crazy, that it can't be real, that there's something wrong with you. And there was. And now I knew what: I was a multiple.

I wasn't surprised to discover that the majority of MPD/DID sufferers are women. It is little girls who are most frequently abused, usually at home, usually by male members of their own family. Male multiples are often reluctant to seek treatment and routinely end up in prison or mental institutions.

Dr Ross adds in his text that, in his experience, complex multiples with numerous alter personalities and complicated amnesia barriers are associated with a 100 per cent frequency of childhood physical, sexual and emotional abuse. 'I have never met or heard about a complex multiple who had not experienced all three.'

I sighed. I felt that thing people call joy. Thank you, Dr Ross. You saved my life. I am not a freak after all. There are others like me, girls who suffered unremitting 'physical, sexual and emotional abuse'. I had suffered all three. My father had not hit me with his fist, but I had been anally penetrated aged two and, to me, that constitutes physical as well as sexual abuse, and all abuse is in itself emotional abuse.

I survived. I'm still here. With treatment, counselling and drugs, I would get better.

I turned up for my next session at the day hospital and began to feel like a mouse on a wheel being tested and analysed as Dr Armstrong and Jo Lewin set about making me better.

Jo had no experience of dealing with a multiple, but she

was a smart woman and learned how to cope with my 'switching'. Having first met Samuel, she began to build a rapport with him. I'd go into counselling, sit on the chair and regress almost immediately.

I'm not sure of the exact date the diagnosis was made but it was shortly before my grandpa's birthday. Grandpa had been the only male influence in my young life that I'd trusted and I had never properly grieved his passing.

Samuel stored my memories and experiences with Grandpa. He told Jo that he was sad because he had never been able to say goodbye. Jo made an age-appropriate analogy and explained to Samuel that Grandpa was like an old car and his body had just stopped working. That wasn't enough for Samuel and I could hear his heart-rending sobs in my mind. I was deeply affected by this. I had blocked out all my emotions associated with Grandpa's death, and now I had to learn how to deal with it.

Samuel, in deep regression, wanted to write a letter to Grandpa. Jo helped him to spell the words:

Dear Grandpa
I miss you lots and lots. I didn't want your body to stop working because you are my best friend and you teach me lots of things. You teach me about the plants and the leaves and you show me the tomatoes in your greenhouse. You told me the bestest ones are money-maker ones. I miss you and I want you to come back, but I know your body stopped working and so I just remember you waving goodbye and smiling at me and I try not to cry and be sad.
    Lots of love
    from Samuel xx

Samuel picked out a card showing bluebells growing in the woods and copied out the words in his best handwriting.

Today I'm Alice

Samuel knew Grandpa would like the card because Grandpa had taken pride in his garden and had always been at peace with nature.

I still have the card and find it weird that Samuel's hand-writing is nothing like my own. I have notes written by Kato (mostly apologies for lacerating my arms), his lettering heavy and underscored. Shirley's writing is ponderous, her thoughts illustrated with sickening imagery as they spill out on the page in prose poems that I would later read with a lump in my throat.

I was grateful to Samuel for remembering Grandpa so vividly, but also for making me remember that Grandpa had always deeply cared for me.

In my diary, I wrote:

I'll always love you, Grandpa. Today I will be thinking about you; it's been 8 years since you died and I still miss you. I will always remember you with affection.

Something must have happened in the next twenty-four hours. This is the following entry:

Oh God, what do I have to do? Billy is firing his gun all over the place and Samuel is thinking about two TV programmes I used to watch when I was a child – Rent-a-Ghost *and* The Phoenix and the Magic Carpet. *Samuel holds his nose like the man in* Rent-a-Ghost *who just disappears or floats in the air on a magic carpet so he no longer feels anything, but can watch what is happening to his body. Abuse. This is Samuel's way of coping.*

Samuel was popping out more often and it encouraged Alice 2 to do the same. Alice 2 cried non-stop. It made me sad as well as agitated. I was twenty-four years old and I had these stupid kids inside me. If I wasn't walking around firing my gun and blowing things up, I was shoplifting or drinking, or playing with Lego, or putting the baby to bed with a bottle.

As with a fever, I was going to have to burn in the fires of hell before the fever broke and I began to get better. In the meantime, the Professor and his lot were still raging on about death. Every night, every single night, I had to fight my inclination to sleep the sleep of the dead and overdose on Temazepam.

Sometimes I went with my inclinations, slipped from the tightrope and fell into the abyss.

Mum was extremely distressed and did everything to help me get through this period. She slept with her door open and popped in frequently to make sure I was all right. If I wasn't, and it happened several times, she would dial 999 in the middle of the night. An ambulance would rush me to A&E and I'd wake to the sight of the strip lights on the ceiling, my throat sore from having my stomach pumped, or my arms would be bandaged, or both.

Dr Armstrong would switch to the uncompromising head-mistress and limit the amount of medication I was prescribed at any one time so I couldn't overdose again. Jo Lewin would sit me on the chair and like the mouse on the treadmill I'd run in circles trying to work out what trigger had provoked the latest relapse.

Dr Ross makes it clear that MPD treatment is painful, gruelling and prone to setbacks. The ultimate aim of treatment is the integration of the alters. But that, Dr Armstrong told me, was going to take years of analysis and counselling. In the meantime, she put me back on anti-psychotics. I had first been prescribed this type of drug when I was diagnosed as being schizophrenic. MPD/DID is a completely different kettle of fish, but still, these drugs were aimed at combating auditory hallucinations, in other words the external voices of the Professor and Co.

Did the drugs help? Not much. Pandora's box was open. The jack-in-the-box was freshly oiled, and the kids were as excited as if it was school holidays; they just couldn't wait to jump out.

One morning, Billy came jogging with me. There were sadistic things in his mind that day. He wanted to shoot and torture the men we passed. It was an odd sensation, Billy's thoughts running parallel with my own, the two independent strands of thought overlapping and intermingling. I could hear Billy's voice and his memories were filtering into my own consciousness. And I understood. I understood Billy very well. Billy hated men – he hates men – and that morning we had to stop running so he could just stomp up and down.

Bang. Bang.

He wanted to blow up the whole world. Hold people as hostages like we saw on the news. As we were walking across a zebra crossing, he pictured himself pressing his gun in the back of the man in front and marching him to the torture chamber. Bang. Bang. Bang. And on to the next person. Bang. Bang. The streets are on fire. The buildings are blazing. I am in control.

I was terrified and energized by the power of Billy's imagination. In his fantasy, he carried a machine gun and drove an army truck patrolling the flaming streets. He wanted to wipe out all the men in cars. He hated Rovers and white cars most of all. He wanted to drag the men out of their cars and tie them up so they wouldn't know what was happening to them. Maybe he'd blindfold them and then tie them up.

But that frightens Billy. He remembers when he was tied up with a rope. It was coming back to him, to me, and it was so painful we pulled out the gun and just shot all the people driving by in their cars.

Bang. Bang. Bang. Bang. Bang.

We arrived home and Billy threw my books round the room. Then he sat in the corner and cried like Samuel. I wanted to cry too. Or else be sick. Or just suck my thumb and sleep. No more bang, bang. I'm only little and I don't know about all that. I'm tired. I want to have my bottle and play with my teddies. I want to sit on Daddy's knee and watch telly.

24 May:

I think Alice 2, Billy and Samuel represent three things that I've lost: the innocent, fragile baby; the spontaneous, playful and mischievous child; and the shy, timid side to my nature. Today, I feel sad and am grieving for the fact that I was never allowed to be a kid. I can't explain. When there is sex, sex, sex in your childhood, then you don't have a childhood. I just feel sad and empty. And also alone – cut off from the world, in the sense that I'm merely existing while there is life around me.

Why can't all this pain be over quickly? Please give me a date when things will be OK. Oh God, I'm trying so hard, but it hurts like hell. Nobody will give me any answers. I don't know and I don't really want to think about it. Please just let me sleep – or let me face the horror of it all straight on, so it can be over and done with, even if it is horrible.

Now that Jo and the shrink were meddling in my subconscious, the memories came flooding out in scenes that were so lucid I could feel the draught as the door opened, the mobile above the bed winding in spirals, the smell of Old Spice. I could feel my father's hands on me, stroking my body, running his finger over my lips until my lips opened and he inserts his finger in my mouth.

'Look who's here.'

I didn't need to be told what to do. I was a Sindy doll. I went up on my knees, opened my mouth and his cock slipped between my lips. I sucked as hard as I could because it was better when that creamy stuff emptied into my mouth, or he sprayed it all sticky and warm over my face. Then he didn't need to put it in my front botty or my back botty, which really hurt.

They were the memories of a five-year-old. At five I wasn't a baby any more. There was confusion in me, and anger, too, a sense that I didn't like doing this any more, but that's what my daddy did and I didn't have the power to stop him. There was between us a pact, a secret, an inevitability. This is what happened in my bedroom at night in the dark. It had always happened. It was normal. I loved my Daddy and I watched from the magic carpet or from the corner of the room as that girl swallowed the white stuff and Daddy kissed her good night. It wasn't me. I'm Billy. I'm Billy and I remember all this happening as if it happened to me, but it didn't happen to me, it happened to her. Alice.

I would come out of regression drained and exhausted, a shadow of myself.

One afternoon after my session, Mum picked me up, took me home and then went out again to the shops. I heard the door click shut. The sound of the metal clasp slotting into place triggered the memory of her rowing with Father, then him locking me in the Bird Cage.

It was *my* fault they'd argued. I'm a bad girl. I deserve to be punished. Tears poured down my face. The psychological and emotional sensations that had gripped me as a child held me in their iron grasp twenty years later in what I came to think of as body memories. I felt sick and weak. The unbearable pain I had suffered in my little-girl body as I was penetrated by my father I felt again. It throbbed through me like an echo.

As therapy progressed, the memories came flooding out like black pus. I watched Jo's pencil scratch furiously across the page. Sometimes I vomited over the carpet. It was confusing, surreal, a horror movie, a fugue: climbing from the car outside the castle, holding Daddy's hand as we descend the steps, the flickering glow of candles . . .

My name is Lucy. I am four. And I am very brave. I like Nurse Nancy from my comic and I am going to be a nurse when I grow up. Nurse Nancy injects me at the children's hospital and I don't cry when I go in this big machine where they look inside me at my kidneys and my blood. I've got cystitis. And when I was little I couldn't do a poo for two weeks and eight nurses had to hold me down so they could look in my back botty. I don't like people looking at my botty. My back botty hurts because I've got a tear in it. I don't like it in the dungeon.

Lucy! Lucy? Who the hell's Lucy? She popped out at one the counselling sessions and Jo's pencil almost caught fire as Lucy gave way to Billy, and Billy to Eliza.

Confusing?

It is to me too, and it would take several months of counselling for Jo Lewin and me, Alice, to get straight.

Lucy at four, Billy at five, and Samuel at six all remember snatches of going out with Daddy in the car to the castle. They take Daddy's hand and go down the steep stairs to the dungeon.

Eliza was initially in my mind as the Devil's Child, a name

that had been given to her by 'the people in black'. She remembers the ritual abuse in scenes of devil worship and made it clear, screaming at the top of her voice, that she is not the Devil's Child. Her name is Eliza. Eliza is seven, but occupies a body – my body – that was ten years old at the time of her most vivid and flamboyant memories.

What to Lucy, Billy and Samuel was a castle, to Eliza is a closed-down factory on an industrial estate a short drive from home. She was taken there many times. There were other children too. Naughty children, like her, who needed to have the naughtiness driven out of them in secret ceremonies that no one must ever know about.

The basement is decorated like a gaudy church with tapestries, an altar and a large inverted pentagram on the back wall. Candles make long scary shadows. The children have wide eyes. They are frightened but obedient. The adults wear dark hooded robes because they know how to deal with the demons in naughty children.

A bell rings. The people start chanting. Eliza can't understand what they are saying. One of the people, someone important, takes the Holy Bible, pulls out the pages and burns the book in a metal dish on the table behind the altar. Someone gives her a set of bound printed sheets, like a hymn book, but with symbols and words she can't understand.

Eliza remembers that once one of the men in robes told her to take the silver cross she was wearing off its chain. He threw it on the floor and stamped on it. She was made to take off her clothes. She lay stretched like a starfish on what they called the torture table, really the altar, and just like the other children she was licked and sucked and penetrated. Men shot their semen over her; women poked things inside her – the handle from a hairbrush, a fork – that really hurt.

She remembers thinking this is what it must be like when Mummy does Tampax, and she remembers thinking that she never wanted to grow up.

The adults played with the children and sometimes the children were made to play with each other. Eliza recalls Lucy at four playing sex with her Sindy doll and Clive's Action Man. That's when she went to the dungeon the first time. When she was four.

Eliza in deep trance recalls Shirley at fourteen in that candlelit basement wearing a mask to frighten the little ones. She recalls the time when a coffin stood on the altar and a naked woman appeared as if rising from the dead. Her face was covered with what looked like earth or dust, but her white body gleamed like porcelain and her breasts were full with hard pink tips. The people were chanting through their hoods and masks and you had to make sure you didn't cry or squirm away because if you did, they'd put you in the coffin and close the lid. It had happened to Eliza once and she thought they were going to bury her alive.

Satanic abuse? Ritual abuse? Calling up the devil?

No. No. No.

It is clear from my retrieved memories and Jo's notes that as a child, and as a teenager, my father allowed me to be abused by a paedophile ring, by adults who got their kicks out of hurting and frightening children. The devil stuff was a cover, a trick that seemed real to the children. But then children are easily tricked. Through my skills of dissociation, I tricked myself and in the alter personalities of Billy, Lucy, Samuel, Eliza, Shirley and Kato, I was able to switch off 'Alice' and the kids took the pain and abuse for me. That is the essence of Multiple Personality Disorder; the alters are protectors who begin life as devices and slowly grow personalities, preferences and dreams of their own.

It was Shirley who scribbled in the diary after a session at the day hospital her memory of the time when her father took her to the factory. The basement was in total darkness. She was led to a smaller room where she had never been before. It was lit by a single candle and, as she turned, she looked into the face of the man who drove the white Rolls-Royce. It was terrifying.

He shuffled her into the centre of the room where there was a mock altar. On the altar there was a sheep. The man gave her a long knife and, with his hand guiding her hand, she slit open the sheep's stomach. They kept cutting into the animal, the blood spurting over her face. They reached the beast's heart and cut it out. The man removed the other organs. They were placed on a silver plate and everyone present ate of the sacrificial lamb.

Shirley wrote in the diary:

I was not surprised that this was happening and I cut the sheep open as if it was no big deal.

Kato at a later date wrote:

It's hell in there. You always have your head down waiting for the next atrocity. After a while you have nothing left, not even the fear and sickness you first felt. You become like a dead person. You don't even expend the nervous energy worrying about what'll happen next.

The counselling became more detailed, more intense, and at the end of each session Jo Lewin was as pale and exhausted as me. The abuse had started when I was six months old. Everything that can be done to a child, to a woman, had been done to me.

Are my memories real? Can they be trusted?

This is what the kids recall and these recollections are true to the part of me, that fragment, that alter, that splinter of my personality that holds the memory. I have no reason to doubt that these atrocities took place. If the language is childlike or dreamlike or complex, it is because the memories come from children, from me as a dissociated child.

The repressed memories were brought to the surface through relentless sessions of therapy, as Dr Armstrong had warned. They did not arise under hypnotism, nor were thoughts planted by therapists. They came from me.

I could go on and on for pages and pages, an endless pornographic litany that makes me sick to remember and sick to see these words going down on paper. I will leave these memories behind with a haunting poem called 'I'll Never Forget and I'll Never Forgive.'.

I did not write this poem. Shirley did. When I found it in a notebook, I was shocked, terrified, bewildered, and sad.

PART 1

At only 14 years old,
Some man
got me pregnant.
Weeks later,
He aborted the embryo,
Made me eat it . . .
Made me a murderer.
Words fail me . . .
How can I make poetry out of this?
I don't even know whether I should share it . . .

Today I'm Alice

PART 2

I felt doomed to death,
But in a flash,
Before I could reduce my thoughts
To an emotion,
I felt a mass leave my body:
Departing.
Then my mind becomes anonymous
As is each night.
Just unfinished thoughts,
and a deep sickness inside,
As I was forced to swallow it,
Something I've tried to bury deep inside my
psyche to this day.

PART 3

At this very moment
The voice that is my guide
Is silent.
There's just an avenue of mirrors
Reflecting an infinity of fear
Things multiplying in my mind
Wherever I look
Even when my eyes are tightly closed
Loom memories
Of that baby
That I ate.
The life I was forced to take
The voice is still silent
Just a heaving feeling
And now I have been sick

Alice Jamieson

Sick because of this enduring memory
And finally, the voice inside says,
'I will never forget and I'll never forgive,
For will I ever be free?'

CHAPTER 18
Complex Multiples

The word is dissociate. There is no 'a' before the 'ss.' People invariably say dis-a-ssociate, which, if you're suffering Dissociative Identity Disorder/Multiple Personality Disorder, can be irritating. People then want to know how many personalities I have and the answer is: I don't know.

The first book about Multiple Personality Disorder to make an impact was Flora Rheta Schreiber's *Sybil*, published in 1973, which carries the subtitle: *The True and Extraordinary Story of a Woman Possessed by Sixteen Separate Personalities*. Corbett H. Thigpen and Hervey M. Cleckley published the controversial *The Three Faces of Eve* much earlier in 1957, and Pete Townshend from The Who wrote the song 'Four Faces'. People seem to feel safe with numbers.

The truth is more complicated. The kids emerged over time. Billy, the boisterous five-year-old, was at first the most dominant. But he slowly stood aside for JJ, the self-confident ten-year-old who appears when Alice is under stress and handles complicated situations like travelling on the Underground and meeting new people. The first *entity* to visit was the external voice of the Professor. But he had a choir of accomplices without names.

So, how many actual alter personalities are there? I would guess more than fifteen and less than thirty, a combination of protectors, persecutors and friends – my own family tree.

Some alters are what Dr Ross describes in *Multiple Personality Disorder* as 'fragments', which are 'relatively limited psychic states that express only one feeling, hold one memory, or carry out a limited task in the person's life. A fragment might be a frightened child who holds the memory of one particular abuse incident.'

In complex multiples, Dr Ross continues, the 'personalities are relatively full-bodied, complete states capable of a range of emotions and behaviours.' The alters will have 'executive control some substantial amount of time over the person's life'. He stresses, and I repeat his emphasis, 'Complex MPD with over 15 alter personalities and complicated amnesia barriers are associated with 100 percent frequency of childhood physical, sexual and emotional abuse.'

Did I imagine the castle, the dungeon, the ritual orgies and violations? Did Lucy, Billy, Samuel, Eliza, Shirley and Kato make it all up?

I went back to the industrial estate and found the castle. It was an old factory that had burned to the ground, but the charred ruins of the basement remained. I closed my eyes and could see the black candles, the dancing shadows, the inverted pentagram, the people chanting through hooded robes. I could see myself among other children being abused in ways that defy imagination. I have no doubt now that the cult of devil worshippers was nothing more than a ring of paedophiles, the satanic paraphernalia a cover for their true lusts: the innocent bodies of young children.

It is hard to bring paedophile rings to justice. Thankfully it does happen. Perhaps the most horrific recent case came before the High Court in Edinburgh in June 2007. It involved a mother who stood by and watched as her daughter of nine was gang-raped by members of a paedophile ring in her home in Granton, in the north of Edinburgh. The mother, Caroline Dunsmore, had allowed her two daughters to be used in this way from the age of five.

Sentencing Dunsmore to twelve years in prison judge, Lord Malcolm, said he would take into account public revulsion at the grievous crimes against the two girls. He told the forty-three-year-old woman: 'It is hard to imagine a more grievous breach of trust on the part of a mother towards her child.'

Morris Petch and John O'Flaherty were also jailed for taking part in raping the children.

Child abuse nearly always takes place at home and members of the family are usually involved.

Dr Armstrong continued to be my consultant. Having identified the disorder, her principal treatment was prescribing drugs. I tried them all in diverse combinations, a feast of anti-psychotics and anti-depressants that sometimes made me feel marvellous and at other times paranoid and suicidal. Under severe stress, Shirley grabbed a bottle, or Kato pushed into my clothes, and I'd relapse into sprees of binge drinking and self-harm. In all, I have overdosed about 100 times and had 600 or more stitches to my arms; battle scars, we call them. How I have survived those battles a believer would describe as a miracle.

Why do I take a blade and slash my arms? Why do I drink myself into a stupor? Why do I swallow bottles of pills and end up in A&E having my stomach pumped? Am I seeking attention? Showing off? The pain of the cuts releases the mental pain of the memories, but the pain of healing lasts weeks. After every self-harming or overdosing incident I run the risk of being sectioned and returned to a psychiatric institution, a harrowing prospect I would not recommend to anyone.

Alice Jamieson

So, why do I do it?

I don't.

If I had power over the alters, I'd stop them. I don't have that power. When they are out, they're out. I experience blank spells and lose time, consciousness, dignity. If I, Alice Jamieson, wanted attention, I would have completed my PhD and started to climb the academic career ladder. Flaunting the label 'doctor' is more attention-grabbing that lying drained of hope in hospital with steri-strips up your arms and the vile taste of liquid charcoal absorbing the chemicals in your stomach.

In most things we do, we anticipate some reward or payment. We study for status and to get better jobs; we work for money; our children are little mirrors of our social standing; the charity donation and trip to Oxfam make us feel good. Every kindness carries the potential gift of a responding kindness: you reap what you sow. There is no advantage in my harming myself; no reason for me to invent delusional memories of incest and ritual abuse. There is nothing to be gained in an A&E department.

It is necessary to make this point in answer to the 'iatrogenic' theory that the unveiling of repressed memories in MPD sufferers, paranoids and schizophrenics can be created in analysis; a fabrication of the doctor–patient relationship. According to Dr Ross, this theory, a sort of psychiatric ping-pong 'has never been stated in print in a complete and clearly argued way'.

My case endorses Dr Ross's assertions. My memories were coming back to me in fragments and flashbacks long before I began therapy. Indications of that abuse, ritual or otherwise, can be found in my medical records and in notebooks and poems dating back before Adele Armstrong and Jo Lewin entered my life.

There have been a number of cases in recent years where

the police have charged groups of people with subjecting children to so-called satanic or ritual abuse in paedophile rings. Few cases result in a conviction. But that is not proof that the abuse didn't take place, and the police must have been very certain of the evidence to have brought the cases to court in the first place. The abuse happens. I know it happens. Girls in psychiatric units don't always talk to the shrinks, but they need to talk and they talk to each other.

As a child I had been taken to see Dr Bradshaw on countless occasions; it was in his surgery that Billy had first discovered Lego. As I was growing up, I also saw Dr Robinson, the marathon runner. Now that I was living back at home, he was again my GP. When Mother bravely told him I was undergoing treatment for MPD/DID as a result of childhood sexual abuse, he buried his head in hands and wept.

Child abuse will always re-emerge, no matter how many years go by. We read of cases of people who have come forward after thirty or forty years to say they were abused as children in care homes by wardens, schoolteachers, neighbours, fathers, priests. The Catholic Church in the United States in the last decade has paid out hundreds of millions of dollars in compensation for 'acts of sodomy and depravity towards children', to quote one information-exchange website. Why do these ageing people make the abuse public so late in their lives? To seek attention? No, it's because deep down there is a wound they need to bring out into the clean air before it can heal.

Many clinicians miss signs of abuse in children because they, as decent people, do not want to find evidence of what Dr Ross suggests is 'a sick society that has grown sicker, and the abuse of children more bizarre'. He continues: 'A popular superstition in North America is that children are the most valued resource and that the intact nuclear family is a good

271

place to grow up. For many children this is a lie. The intact family, for many North American children, has been a war zone of physical and sexual abuse, a private Vietnam.'

We have new wars for our analogies now. Dr Ross's book was first published more than twenty years ago. If our sick society, in Europe and the United States, was growing sicker then, what about now in this new millennium, in the age of the World Wide Web?

In my passage through those grim psychiatric hospitals I have met many young women who, like me, have been sexually, emotionally and physically abused, nice words for raped, silenced, kicked and throttled, their bodies used as punching bags, their flesh as ashtrays. I remember the confused, battered women at the refuge in Liverpool, and I will never forget the primal scream that erupted through the corridors of St Thomas's when they pinned Sophie down to tranquillize her. Her crime? She had given birth to two children by her father.

Who is looking after Sophie's children while she is in a psychy ward? Their father/grandfather? Her distracted mother? The wardens at a council care home? Are Sophie's children living in a war zone? Is Dr Ross correct in saying that our sick society has grown sicker?

It has certainly grown sexier, as we can see in every movie, TV soap and ad campaign. In women's magazines the perfect woman is one breath from childhood with inexplicably full breasts, a narrow waist and vaguely bruised, unfocused eyes. Her clothes resemble bondage costumes designed more to reveal than conceal. If you want to find a man, keep your man, please your man, there's Botox, cosmetic surgery and creams that deliver the promise of eternal youth. Young is sexy.

At the time of writing, a leading UK company is selling padded bras for seven-year-olds. Little girls have been turned into consumers. They don't play, they shop. We have allowed the commercial pressures of a sick society to rob little girls of their childhood and to create in their minds the sense that they are sexual objects. If girls of seven are encouraged to 'look sexy', it shouldn't surprise us when sex is the outcome.

Why do men take advantage of little girls? How does it start?

Little girls, little boys too, are soft, pink, beautiful, innocent. Daddy tickles baby and she giggles. She likes it. Daddy rubs his nose against her nose and she giggles even more. She *really* likes it. She likes being fondled, touched, teased. He kisses her little round belly and can't resist touching the tip of his tongue to the crease of her vagina. Baby is still giggling and that man, her daddy, the babysitter, the warden, has an erection. He can't help it. And some men can't help going further. She likes it, she wants it, the little slag.

The majority of men have self-control, morals, decency. But there are an awful lot who don't. Once a man with power over a girl gets a taste of using her as a sex object, he becomes addicted to this power and will continue to abuse her in ever more subtle and terrible ways. Sex with a child crosses the taboo barrier and, once crossed, the temptation is to push the barrier back further, to cloak the abuse in the mantle of ritual. Virgins were sacrificed in pagan religions to appease the gods. Men, it seems, are fixated on virginity, with young, unsullied flesh, and those men, incapable of forming normal relationships with adult women, will rob a child of its purity to satisfy this sick obsession.

The Internet has allowed the authorities to track paedophiles who groom children. The downside is they find each other, these kiddy fiddlers, flashers, pederasts, those rock spiders skilled at finding their way into hairline cracks. They move with sly ease across the Web exchanging pornographic photos of damaged children, and find a perverse legitimacy knowing that their lusts are shared. Hey, what the hell, everyone's doing it.

Dr Ross is surely correct in his analysis. Our sick society *is* growing sicker.

I didn't want to be the receptacle for all this unpleasant knowledge. I just wanted to be a normal girl with friends and a nice family. I was coming up to twenty-five, in therapy, addicted to prescription drugs. I was twitchy, nervous, jumpy, sexually ignorant, sexually perturbed – a victim of our sex-obsessed culture. I was living at home, unable to work. I was stumbling blindly around the edge of the abyss and daily resisting my fixation on long drops, steep stairs, plastic bags, broken glass and the thin blades in the craft room at the day hospital.

What chemical imbalance ignites a relapse? Is it just dark clouds blotting out the blue sky? A moment's edginess from Jo Lewin? The look in a stranger's eyes? The teddy's eyes? That's right, twenty-five and still sleeping with stuffed toys.

As irony would have it, I was going through a good period. I had become reacquainted with Jacob Williams, a bright, shy boy who had been in my class at school and was now attending the day hospital suffering from bipolar disorder/ manic depression. We had always liked each other and had always been too shy to find anything to say. Now, united by mental-health issues, we had been hanging out, having the occasional coffee or drink, and talking about our treatment. Jacob knew that I had suffered abuse as a child, but had avoided telling me what lay at the bottom of his depressions.

Jacob was on my mind as I was walking along the hospital corridor and the next thing I was in the toilet, blood pumping from my arms. I was dazed, my lips were tingling from a panic attack. In moments I was in my own blood bath. My left forearm was cut in several places and my right was scribbled with fine deep cuts made by a craft-room blade. I could see it glinting up at me like a triangular silver eye in the spreading pool of blood on the white-tiled floor.

Luckily, JJ welled through me and, in his voice, a terrified scream, like Sophie's scream that time in St Thomas's, brought the entire hospital to silence. Three nurses arrived in seconds. I had lost at least two pints of blood by this time. While the nurses were stemming the flow with thick cotton-wool dressings, Dr Spencer, the registrar to Dr Armstrong appeared, her nice legs on show in a black pencil skirt. She raised my right arm above my head and applied pressure as blood escaped from the swabs and splattered her white blouse.

I was rushed by an ambulance with wailing sirens to A&E again where the brachial artery in my right arm was clamped, sutured and stitched. I had to have several saline drips to avoid the need for a transfusion and was returned, under the supervision of a member of staff to the day hospital, in a taxi with my arms bandaged like an Egyptian mummy. Dr Armstrong was waiting for me in her office wearing a pinched smile. She sat on the edge of her desk.

'You don't need to bother to come in until Monday, Alice,' she said.

'You mean you don't want to see me tomorrow?' I asked.

'No, no, no, best not,' she replied. 'Let's leave it till Monday. You need to have a good rest. I'll give you some more sleeping tablets.'

'Really?'

'Yes, Alice.'

We stared at each other in silence. We were always arguing about my tablets, their numbers and strength. I hurried to the pharmacy before it closed and went home on the bus. The voices were chattering away; I wasn't listening. The rain beat against the window. I thought about Dr Armstrong.

Even though she had diagnosed DID, my consultant psychiatrist couldn't entirely grasp that it wasn't me slashing my flesh, it was an alter personality in pain – something I understood and forgave. It was Kato who had harmed me and JJ who had saved me. I was one of the team.

As for the sleeping pills, because there was always a danger I might overdose, I had been issued scripts, as junkies call them, on a twenty-four-hour basis. I would occasionally save them up and sleep away the entire weekend rather than face Mum and Stephen. They were doing their utmost to be patient with me and engaged with the alters when they made an appearance, perhaps at dinner.

'I don't like this.'

'Then don't eat it, Alice.'

'I'm not Alice. I'm not Alice. I'm not Alice.'

'Who are you?'

'Billy. Billy. Billy.'

'This is like living in a madhouse.'

Bang. Bang.

Poor Mum. On days when my thoughts were clear and I was just Alice, I could see by the look in her eyes that she was hurting for me, that all she wanted for me was what any good mother would want for her daughter. She never fully understood the disorder and didn't take the counselling offered to families of victims and survivors of childhood abuse after trying a couple of sessions. She thought I just needed to be 'bucked up'.

'Where's that girl who was going to become a doctor, that's what I want to know?'

'Pardon?'

'What happened to my Alice who used to run marathons?'

'She can hardly walk these days.'

'I'll tell you what, I'm going to get someone I know a new pair of trainers.'

She was doing her best. She picked me up after work next day and we bought a pair of Nike's with pink trim and laces. Even trainers were getting sexy.

Now that I was back roaming the streets, I met old friends from school, most of whom once they knew I had mental-health issues drew back as if the disorder were contagious. It's useful to know who your friends are, and I was pleased to have Jacob in my life.

Jacob and I went to movies, nervously hugged, knitted our fingers together under wine bar tables. There was a frisson, but just as I had been unable to act on my log-jammed instincts with Patrick, I never allowed Jacob to get closer than touching cheek to cheek, stroking each other's hair, the sad involvement of damaged people.

Jo Lewin became my friend as well as my therapist and spent as much time with me as she could. In Shirley mode, I would make a lasagne at home and take it to Jo's house to spend the evening with her and her son. We went on walking trips in the Lake District. In the sessions at the day hospital she peeled back layer after layer of buried memories that often left me distressed and in physical discomfort. The 'body memory' of feeling as if a rod of iron has been inserted in your rectum creates a very real pain you cannot fabricate or explain.

It was a relief that among the clinicians I was considered a victim and survivor 'of the most awful abuse one can suffer', as Jo Lewin once said. But that acknowledgement didn't diminish the torment of sitting on the rubber-backed carpet at the day hospital witnessing scenes inside my head of that big man lying on top of a small girl and forcing her to have sex.

Those same pictures that developed in therapy come back into my head now, today, at odd times, at any time. Imagine seeing your child being run over by a car, your mother being stabbed to death, a missile exploding on your house as you hurry home through the streets of Baghdad or Jerusalem. Those pictures are always there. You try and pick up the shattered scraps of your life but the scars remain.

Sometimes when I am lying in my bed at home, I hear the neighbours ascend the stairs next door and I cannot stop myself recalling the sound of my father climbing the stairs when I was a child. The door opens, the mobile moves. He throws the teddies on the floor and lowers the zip on his trousers with a grating rasp that puts my teeth on edge. I can see myself coming up on my knees, my mouth dropping open, his willy jerking back and forth for what seems like an eternity. He holds the back of my head to make me swallow his sperm, or he lets it seep from my lips so he can rub the 'cream' over my naked belly. Sometimes he would bugger me and then ejaculate in my mouth. Daddy liked that. I remember the foul taste, the tangles in my knotted stomach, the feeling of being lost, isolated, a little bubble floating alone in a big black universe. I remember now. I remember it all. There was no perversion my father didn't inflict on me, his little daughter.

Different personalities emerged by dissociation at different periods of my life, each holding unique memories of abuse, a virtual library of obscenity and evil. Kato and Shirley were more reluctant to describe my father's cruelty than the younger alters, who had less understanding of its implications. I was protected by a deeper amnesia by unnamed alters with memories buried too deeply to be expressed verbally. These materialized in 'automatic' paintings I created in the art room at the day hospital. They were crude scenes of black-robed figures highlighted with brilliant patches of scarlet. The paintings repelled and fascinated me.

Like Kato and Shirley, I developed an obsession with

blood. I was shocked to recall that at fourteen (Shirley's age) I had been making preparatory nicks and cuts on my arms just to see the blood, a recovered memory confirmed by my old schoolfriend Lisa Wainwright.

The memories ebbed and flowed; a tide of human depravity nice people couldn't begin to imagine. Mum would pick me up from the day hospital or I'd make my way home on the bus reciting my PhD proposal to myself. The streets appeared as a cityscape from a dream, so hyper-real as to appear unreal. Mum had taken control of my medication. She dealt with the incidents of overdosing and self-harm. My mother knew the abuse had taken place, that the memories were real. She knew the extent of the abuse, and she did her best during the two years I lived at home to help me survive the trauma of therapy.

Two years had drifted by. Gone. Just like that. Burned like refuse in Grandpa's garden. I know it was two years because I was suddenly eligible for a council flat and moved the teddy gang into a little one-bedroomed box with a sigh of relief echoed, I'm sure, beneath the roof of my mother's house.

It was around this time that my father mysteriously sent me a cheque for a very substantial amount of money, about the amount it costs to buy a brand-new car. When it arrived, I pinned the cheque to the corkboard in the kitchen and stared at it as if it were a scrap from the Dead Sea Scrolls.

That *huge* sum of money. From my father. Out of the blue.

It was hush money, obviously. Having set out to silence me, it had the opposite effect. I photocopied the cheque and began to compile a dossier of his attempts to make contact with me in neat plastic display envelopes in a binder that would grow to be two inches thick. I don't do anything by halves.

My first instinct was to send the cheque back. I went with

a more sensible decision and put the money in the bank for a rainy day. Although I spent about £50 buying wine, food, new music and two red candles with glass holders. I baked fish with green vegetables and Jacob came to my flat for a romantic twosome. We ate almost nothing, drank the wine, drank some more wine, sat on the sofa Mum had given me, and thought about sex. Nothing happened. Neither of us knew how to start, where to start. We were afraid of our feelings, afraid that we might feel nothing, afraid of hurting each other. We were a mess.

Jacob now told me that he, too, had suffered from abuse when he was a young boy at school. I was horrified to learn that the perpetrator was a teacher I remembered. I burst into tears. We hugged, we sort of kissed, but there was no sex that night, or any night, actually.

My attendance at the day hospital had been reduced to three times a week on my therapy days. To fill my time and keep the therapy going, I started to go to the drop-in centre for mental-health-service users. I became particularly friendly with a lively, formidable blue-eyed woman named Megan Sorensen who was a member of staff. She had great skill in drawing out the alters, especially JJ, and engaging with them. One time, Kato emerged and, when in conversation she hit a raw nerve, in his hostile way Kato slapped Megan's arm.

I have no idea if this slap was hard or not. Kato is his own person and does stupid things that I don't approve of and have no control over. In fact, I didn't know anything about the notorious slap until the director called me into her office and informed me that Megan would not be able to see me again.

I welled up in tears. I adored Megan. 'But why?' I asked.

'Because you slapped her arm, Alice, and she didn't like it.'

'But I didn't.'

'Megan said you did.'

'Yes, of course I did. But it wasn't me.'

'Look, I'm not going to sit here arguing with you.'

I sat and sobbed. It's another downside of MPD/DID: as well as disagreeing on treatment, psychiatrists, counsellors and mental-health professionals sometimes 'forget' you're a multiple. You can't 'see' the disorder like a dodgy heart or a patch of malign cells on an X-ray. You look normal. I was trying to be normal, and obviously succeeding in as much as the director treated the slapping episode as you would under normal circumstances.

But the appearance of a troubled sixteen-year-old boy in Alice's mind and Alice's female body is not normal. It's abnormal. The disorder is not as rare as once thought, but complex multiples can only be 'cured' if the alters can be integrated through a process requiring years of therapy, constant adjustments to medication and superhuman patience and understanding.

That day at the drop-in centre I felt like a leper in the Middle Ages, an outcast with a ringing bell to announce my pariah status. I went home, swallowed a handful of pills and slept and cried without getting out of bed for four days.

Kill yourself, Alice. Nobody likes you. Take an overdose. Cut your arms.

Just because I was in therapy and taking anti-psychotics didn't mean the voices were stilled. Confused sometimes, silent never. I would still take the occasional three-hour shower and scrub my skin raw, press my jeans, wash my trainers, start reading a book in bed at night and find myself still reading as the sun came up the following morning, the hours gone, the words forgotten, the months slipping from the calendar.

Four days after taking to my bed, I finally dragged myself out to attend an appointment with a new psychiatrist standing in for Dr Armstrong while she was away on maternity leave. The shrink was willowy and assertive with a cut-glass accent that quavered when she discovered I was taking 60mg of Temazepam rather than the recommended dose of 10mg. She made some phone calls, whispered authoritatively in her nice voice, and I was found a bed in the Josiah Jennins psychiatric unit for a supervised detox.

I am not sure how I came to be taking so much Temazepam. I had to spend eight days in the unit to wean myself off the stuff. The chemical compound in Temazepam creates a trance-like effect, so you can easily fall and hurt yourself. I spent the first twenty-four hours in bed, and then each day spent a few more hours up in the day room or prowling the corridors wondering if I was ever going to get well. I was discharged with a new prescription for Welldorm (chloral betaine), not a benzodiazepine and not so addictive.

Jacob visited me in hospital, as I would visit him in the future when he had his manic calamities. He brought me his Walkman, a copy of John Steinbeck's *The Grapes of Wrath* and a bunch of grapes because, he said, he was 'feeling bacchanalian'. I was thrilled to receive his themed gifts and was still wondering what he meant by 'bacchanalian' when he came to take me home the following day. A single word can get into your mind like an insect in an apple and you chew away on it for days.

Now that I didn't have my Temazepam, I started drinking, wine at first, then spirits, the usual cycle that led to a new dependency which was irritating because I didn't like dipping into the money in the bank, my safety net. I hated waking after broken nights with a terrible headache. I had met a guy in the psychiatric unit doing an alcohol detox and decided to go to Alcoholics Anonymous with him. It was amusing listening to the people as they sat in a circle admitting to themselves and the world that they were alcoholics. But it wasn't for me. I was just a binge drinker missing the chemicals.

Drugs, alcohol, sleep, lack of sleep, overdoses, self-harming. In therapy, the alters were encouraged to spew out their memories. Narcotics in all their variations were the only relief from the agonies of remembering. My mind brimmed with recollections of the abuse and my body was wracked with the body-memories of physical and mental torture.

Would Billy ever get over the experience of being buggered by strangers in the dungeon of his mind? I had created the dissociation device, as Dr Ross describes it, to remove myself from the pain of those violations, but they had still happened. They still had to be confronted if I was ever going to integrate and get well. This insight kept buzzing round my head like a bothersome fly.

One day, I was passing the police station. I stopped outside and looked at the open doors, the noticeboards, the posters. The weather was warm, the sky bright with a few puffy clouds like you see in children's paintings at school. Back straight, eyes focused, voices distant, I ambled up the steps.

'Good morning,' I said to the desk sergeant, a portly pleasant-looking man. 'My name is Alice Jamieson. I would like to report my father for abusing me sexually when I was a child.'

The plump sergeant lowered his head and looked at me over the top of his glasses. He came to his feet.

'Come this way,' he said, and opened the counter to let me into the heart of the building.

I was taken to a small, bright room where I explained to a young woman detective that I had suffered persistent child abuse at the hands of my father and others. She was patient and sensitive. She made notes, she made some phone calls.

We arranged for me to make a statement on neutral turf at the Callaghan Centre, a resource for people with mental-health problems, with my then mental-health social worker as an appropriate adult. The interview went on all that day and continued the following morning until mid-afternoon. I didn't want to miss anything out.

The police investigated my allegations by accessing my medical and psychiatric records.

As well as copies of reports from my GP, Dr Robinson, and my consultant psychiatrist, Dr Armstrong, the police went through my social-work records and investigating my allegations, which included my father raping me when I confronted him. The police obtained statements from the people who had been involved in my life at that time such as Louise Lloyd-Jones, Dr Graham Sutton and the psychiatrist Dr Simpson as well as from Rebecca Wallington and the professionals who had been involved with me while I had been in Huddersfield. They even went as far back as delving into the notes of Dr Purvis, the child psychiatrist.

My father was arrested and had to wait six long weeks before the Crown Prosecution Service (CPS) decided not to proceed with the charge.

The CPS had come to this decision after weighing up a number of factors:

- The amount of time that had lapsed between the 'alleged' abuse taking place and my reporting it to the police ('alleged' was a legal prefix that would now cling to 'abuse' like a shadow).
- The fact that I had been under the care of various mental-health professionals before making the report.
- I would probably not be able to endure the defence lawyer's cross-examination in my fragile state of mental health.

The decision was distressing, relieved only by the consolation I felt when the detective constable in charge of my case scribbled on a piece of notepaper that she was confident that I had given a true account of the abuse that my father had inflicted upon me. The fact that I had suffered frequent bouts of cystitis since the age of four took on a new significance. Cystitis is the inflammation of the lining of the bladder as a result of infection, irritaiton or damage. It can afflict men, but is more common in women, particularly during pregnancy, menopause and when women are sexually active. Women are more likely to suffer cystitis than men because the urethra, the tube that evacuates urine from the bladder, happens to be shorter and its opening is located close to the anus, which means that infection can occur more easily.

Cystitis is not the sort of thing that normally effects little girls. But I spent so much time in the waiting room at the doctor's surgery with this ailment, before my fifth birthday, I had taught myself to make a car with moving parts from Lego while Mum became an expert on hair products and makeup reading women's magazines. Persistent cystitis can cause kidney damage. It only took about six years, the wheels of the NHS grind slowly, but finally I was referred to the Children's Hospital in Birmingham for tests. Mum took me once a month for more than a year and a stream of consultants and students in white coats gazed at me as if a child with cystitis was one of the mysteries of the universe. No one to my knowledge ever suggested that the condition could have been the result of irritation caused by ruptures or infection in the area adjacent to the exit to my urethra. Eventually the tests came back. There was no kidney malfunction. I was a freak of nature. There was another intriguing piece of evidence. At the age of two, I was so severly constipated, I had to go into hospital to be treated. When I was examined, it was discovered that I had an anal fissure. That note was a reminder of what I had suffered and survived. It went in the file and would be instrumental when the possibility of reopening the case against my father was suggested some years later.

I just had to go through hell first.

After the slapping fiasco with Megan, I didn't return to the drop-in centre for a long time. When I finally went back, the director put me in touch with Mike Haydock, a senior psychotherapist. Mike set firm boundaries for therapy: I had to sit and remain sitting in a chair, and there was to be no social contact outside therapy, the opposite to my relationship with Jo Lewin. I found it hard at first to conform to this regime, but over time I began to be aware of some real positive changes.

I saw Mike once a week. His approach to therapy was more psychoanalytical. With his remote air and persuasive voice, he was able, even if I resisted, to draw me smoothly into regression. He set out to uncover the unconscious elements at work in my mind and investigate their interaction with those that were conscious. For example, although he did not especially focus on self-harming, he encouraged me to think about what purpose this served and the unconscious forces that drove me to do it.

He was different to the other therapists, too, in as much as he did not refer to the alters by name. He placed less emphasis on the separateness of the kids, and more on the functionality and reason for their separateness. In this way, the focus on integration, or becoming whole, as a goal of therapy could be viewed as an on-going, gradual, discreet process of developing personal insight and growth.

Through Mike's subtle methods, I learned over the weeks

and months to make more of an effort to get to know the alters, to appreciate the traumas they had suffered and carried with them into my adult life. By getting closer to Shirley and Kato, I would be in a better position to persuade them not to relieve their mental anguish in the physical act of slashing my arms.

The process is complex and protracted, easing thoughts like shifting balls in a bagatelle to different parts of the brain, from left to right, from the sub-cortex, where the emotions are stored, to the neo-cortex, the rational side where, according to Mike, there is little capacity for depression. He taught me a simple technique: if you feel down, just think of something that will make you smile – Mr Happy standing on his head, or the kind eyes of my old friend Esther in the kitchen at Kibbutz Neve Eitan. The procedure switches mental activity and the blues blow away. That's the idea. Think happy thoughts, be positive, be grateful. I tried.

MPD/DID therapy aims finally at integration. Mike Haydock believed the *journey* to integration was just as important, that I would feel a sense of recovery simply by moving on, by accepting that the abuse had happened, by grieving for what I had lost, and feeling the various emotions associated with the abuse so the pain became less acute. In this way, the therapy resulted in some of the alters integrating, but the most important consequence was that I was able to function better and was comfortable with myself as an adult, integrated or not.

I spent more time with Jacob, and was able to focus on him, and his needs, rather than use our time together to focus solely on myself. He had always been patient when one of the alters popped out. Now the psychoanalysis was making me stronger, I tried to be there for him when, during his spells of illness, an impenetrable wall went up round him.

Jacob was keen to change both the public and professional view of mental health and had become involved in new mental-health legislation. This inspired my own interest. At that time the local Primary Care Trust was creating a fresh mental-health strategy. I joined the committee as a mental-health service user and was able to make a contribution drawing upon my own experiences. Had I completed my PhD, of course, I may well have served on such a committee on the other side of the table.

Jacob and I continued to act like a couple but, due to the medication we were both taking, any attempt at having sexual relations were unsuccessful and left us numb with anguish.

On Valentine's Day that year I received my first and only card, a cherished possession like Grandpa's *The Waving Palms of Tropic Isles*.

Dearest Alice,

I have never been in a relationship that has given me such great hope for a lasting unity.

I love you so much that it has conquered any doubts I had in the past about allowing myself to be vulnerable.

Know that I want us to be together for ever and that I truly want to be there for you.

All my love, Jacob xxx

Even though Jacob and I had made a commitment and Jacob had written about how he had conquered his doubts about being vulnerable he was, of course, still vulnerable. So was I. I trusted Jacob more than I had ever trusted any man, but I was terrified and incapable of letting myself go completely and settling into a normal relationship. It's the fear of damaged people. You hold back. You hide yourself. Protect yourself. It's as though you have been submerged in a barrel of tar. No amount of cleaning or therapy seems to wash it all off. You remain fragile and you damage others whether you realize it or not.

When I secured a placement working voluntarily a few hours each day with the newly formed local mental-health outreach team, I became so engrossed I didn't notice Jacob was becoming quieter, more withdrawn. We saw each other less and less without my realizing it. Every morning I had a team meeting with community psychiatric nurses, social workers and other mental-health professionals so we could decide on appropriate interventions for mental-health service users who had been referred to them specifically. It was the most useful work I had done since leaving my job in Swansea.

By this time I had my first mobile phone, a big clumsy machine with an aerial on the side. One morning, when it rang during a meeting, the tone was so insistent it urged me to rush out to the corridor to answer it. It was Oliver, who had once shared a flat with Jacob.

'I'm so sorry, Alice. It's about Jacob,' he began to say.

I don't know how I knew, but I knew. I stood in that corridor and sobbed my heart out. Jacob had committed suicide.

CHAPTER 19
Charlie

Cocaine, my love –
it took only one line
to get me hooked.
Since then
I've never looked back to see,
cocaine,
how you've got a hold over me.

You can zip through your savings in a few months when you have a £400-a-week habit. I loved the white stuff. I wrote poems for the white stuff. When you're in love, you'll do anything for the white stuff.

Anything.

Jacob had filled my life and left me empty again. We had been two people on a rockface joined by a rope and we needed each other to climb up into the clouds. Jacob had taken a dive. I understood this. I understood better than most people, but you can't help blaming yourself. If I hadn't been afraid of commitment, of sex, maybe we could have lived the dream and got better. Life's like that: you dream, you wake – then there's nothing.

I was thinking about Jacob as I left my flat and was shocked to find, as I opened the front door, a guy with no legs sitting on the doorstep of my first-floor flat. Maybe he had legs but they didn't work. He was paralysed, paraplegic. He was OK. But what was he doing there?

I went upstairs to tell my neighbour, a kindly, elderly man who I called Uncle Joe and who played the violin. We stood talking for ages. I've no idea what about. He went inside, I stood for a while gazing out of the window at the clouds, wondering if Jacob was up there, and then became aware of two paramedics running up the stairs towards me. They were cheerful guys in bright jumpsuits, puffing as they approached.

'OK. OK. You're going to be just fine.'

'What? It's not me. What are you talking about? It's him.'

I could see my front door and the guy with no legs was still curled up on the doormat.

'Look, he's in agony,' I called.

One of the paramedics slid his arm gently around my waist. He was good-looking. I looked into his eyes and he smiled.

'Listen, the man needs help,' I told him.

'There's no one there.'

'Yes, there is, look he can't move, he's paraplegic.'

'Let's just make sure you're OK.'

'It's not me, it's him,' I said again.

We argued like this for a while. I remained adamant that there was a guy with no legs downstairs. I took some convincing, but after checking inside my flat, in the cupboards, in the broken fridge for him, we finally locked my front door. The good-looking man held my arm as we descended the stairs to the car park and I stepped into an ambulance.

'You have to go and find the guy, he really needs help,' I said.

'We'll make sure he's all right, don't worry.'

I trusted him. It's easier trusting good-looking people, for some reason. I sat down in the back of the ambulance and heard the door lock shut. Where did the legless guy come from? Where did he go?

Next thing I knew, I was lying in bed staring at the cobwebs drifting over the ceiling in the Josiah Jennins psychiatric ward. They'd stuck a needle in my bum. They always do that.

I'd suffered a 'brief psychotic episode', and was stuck back in the bin for five weeks. My neighbour upstairs must have seen I was in a state and called an ambulance. They'd arrived at the speed of light.

In hospital, I was prescribed a new anti-psychotic called Olanzapine (Zyprexa) – two white 10mg tablets daily – with my usual Prozac and Valium. I don't recall eating the institutionalized grey stodge and starch they slap on your plate at mealtimes, but I suppose I must have done. I put on about three stone in weight and went up from a dress size 8/10 to 12/14. I felt like Kato squeezing into my clothes. I looked like a whale, an elephant, a dirigible. I'd never looked like me. Now I didn't look like anyone.

There was a hippy chick on the ward named Sam who didn't eat. She was covered in piercings and had vacant eyes like Buddha. We got talking one day in the TV room about supermodels staying thin and she said they all snorted coke.

'I could do with some of that,' I said.

'No problem,' she replied.

I hadn't done any street drugs since smoking hash in Sinai and popping a few E's to be sociable. That night Sam's boyfriend, Andy, appeared. He gave me his mobile number and I called him when I was discharged, fat as a pig, ten days later.

Today I'm Alice

We met at the Wylde Green pub on the Birmingham Road. Sam was there. She'd got out a week before me. I didn't think there was anything much wrong with her. She was just a skinny hippy who did a lot of drugs. We had a few drinks and watched football on television. When we left the pub it was bucketing down and Andy drove me home. Outside my flat, with the rain hitting the car windows like arrows, Andy took a CD case from the glove compartment, a credit card from his wallet and produced a small plastic bag like the ones in which extra buttons are stored when you buy a new jacket. He tapped out a little pile of white powder on the CD case and chopped it fine as fairy dust with the edge of the credit card. The ritual was mesmerizing.

'Fancy one?' he asked.

I'd seen cocaine being snorted on TV shows like *Miami Vice*, so I knew what it was all about. Andy divided the white powder into three thin lines about 3 centimetres long, then rolled a ten-pound note into a tube. Bending over the CD case, he pressed his finger against his left nostril and snorted the line up the right one through the tube. He inhaled deeply to get the full strength of the hit.

He handed the CD case to Sam. She did the same. One line remained. It was the key to belonging, to new friends, a new life, a sense of purpose. I felt cool.

As I snorted the coke my nostril tingled at first, as though it had been touched with chilli powder. Then I felt an incredible buzz, a clarity. I felt as if I were fully awake for the first time in my life. The voices vanished. My troubles vanished. It was the most exhilarating experience I had ever had and I loved it. I wanted it. Multiple Personality Disorder. Incest. Dead boyfriends. Nothing matters when you've got Charlie.

Andy gave me the remainder of the coke as a sample

and next day I was on the phone ordering a gram bag costing £50. I had more than £10,000 in the bank. I was rich. Olanzapine made me feel bloated and depressed. Cocaine made me feel alive, not just existing like a rat trapped in the revolving door of the mental-health system.

I stuck stars on the ceiling that glowed at night, and by day I cruised with Andy, Sam and Matt, a friend of Jacob's who I'd known at school. Andy was sharp, designer dressed, cocaine confident, a Manchester United fan who'd done time in jail for dealing. We spent hours in pubs analysing soccer games; hours in flats doing lines, listening to music with Sam half naked and the tattooed snakes on her arms coming to life and wriggling over her white flesh. I gazed at the dancing snakes and remembered there was once another girl named Alice who had watched a snake charmer in Petra, women in veils, donkey carts with long-suffering donkeys, the peppery taste of the street food that never made that girl ill. Matt played guitar. He was sweet and lost, a loner, beautiful with olive skin, brown eyes and shoulder-length wavy brown hair. I really fancied him, but he didn't know that.

My scripts from Dr Robinson filled a carrier bag. But then you can never have too many drugs. I was on 60mg of Prozac – the highest dose; Valium – 15mg in three 5mg daily hits; Zopiclone, for sleeping; Olanzapine, a 20mg antipsychotic; Gaviscon for heartburn.

I liked to mix and match these with the illegals. Ecstasy makes you dance, even when you're alone. Speed makes you alert and paranoid. It's a pleasant dichotomy, like taking part in a threesome, I imagine, at least that's what went through my mind when I saw that girl from school at the pub. She was wearing six-inch stilettos, a dress about the size of a handkerchief. I thought: what a state. Still, I could talk.

Today I'm Alice

The thing with amphetamines is you can stay awake for days, you lose time, inhibitions, talk to strangers. The come-down from speed leaves you with nothing to live for, so you drink a few pints, smoke a joint. You deal with it. I tried heroin. I mean, you have to. You put a pinch of brown crystal on a piece of aluminium foil. You heat it with a cigarette lighter and, as the crystal turns to a misty vapour, you chase the tail of the dragon up your nose. Try it and fly. Try it and die. H kills pain. H silenced the voices. H confused the kids. H terrified Alice. H is like returning to the womb. It's warm and safe. I never look like me, I never feel like me, but with heroin I didn't feel like anyone else either. You just kind of float as though you're on a magic carpet.

That's what drugs are all about. You want to get out of yourself. Out of your body. You want to get away from being who you are, and if there are twenty little people and a choir of aggressive aliens in your head, the further away the better. It doesn't matter what drug you're offered, if it's going to change your perception of reality, you want to stick it in your mouth or up your nose, get it into your bloodstream, live the trip and talk about it. Drugs make you talk a lot. It's weird, but you can oil your throat with as much alcohol as you want without getting drunk. Alcohol keeps the buzz simmering like a low gas under a pan of water. Best of all, you have friends.

One night Matt appeared with some ketamine, which he chopped up in fine sparkling white lines. K is a horse tranquillizer that eats the membranes in your nostrils. Most druggies are sniffers. After ketamine, no matter how dehydrated you are, there's always a bead of dribble waiting to drip from your nose. You hoover up your line and close your eyes. A spear cracks the reality barrier between your ears and you're sucked into what they call the K Hole. It's a deathlike experience where you feel your essence leave your body to float above it, a spiritual trip for some people, for me an insight into dissociation.

I tried to walk across the room after that fat line of K, but the floor had become sponge sucking at my limbs. I thought Matt was going to play his guitar, but his hands had frozen, his fingers grown longer. I felt weightless and slipped down on to the floor. Matt was staring at me. As I stared back, my mouth tingled in panic. It wasn't Matt sitting there; it was the Professor. I recalled his face from my computer screen in Huddersfield, old, distorted, full of anger and hatred. A scream left my throat. I tried to get up, to flee, but my weightless body wouldn't move. I was bathed in sweat. I couldn't focus, but my eyes seemed to have been fitted with the adjusting lenses of binoculars. As they came back into focus, I realized I had made a ridiculous mistake. It wasn't the Professor at all. I was being paranoid.

It was Grandpa.

He smiled. There's was so much love in his face I suddenly understood. I understood everything. I wasn't alone. He was always there. Somewhere. I could let go now. I watched myself hovering above. I looked happy. I was glad I was up on the ceiling not down there in the grips of reality.

Matt was beautiful, gentle, like Grandpa. With Matt I could have broken my paranoia about sex, but on drugs sex slips from your mind and all you think about is drugs. We hung out. We were together, glued by our desire for constant self-medication, our permanent paranoid need to get out of it.

We went one night to see Kevin, a gay friend of Matt's who worked as an air steward out of Birmingham Airport, and who needed cheering up because his boyfriend had chucked him. Kevin had a garage at the bottom of his garden where our dealer, Andy, kept his stash in the boot of an old car without any wheels. We did a couple of lines and then went to the garage to sample some of Andy's goodies: coke, weed, Ecstasy, GHB. That car boot was an addict's pharmacy and when no one was looking, a 5-gram bag of Charlie worth £200 slipped into my pocket.

The adrenalin rush of stealing was such a hit that a week later, when Kevin was at work and Andy was in London getting fresh supplies, I suggested to Matt that we go back to that garage with some tools and break in. You don't think of the consequences when you're stoned, and the crime turned out to be surprisingly easy. Andy didn't know we knew he kept his stash in the garage. Kevin wasn't going to tell him and, anyway, people were always breaking into garages in that area. We escaped with £1,000-worth of drugs and partied for a fortnight. It was to be my last big drug binge.

My therapy was going down the drain. I rarely managed to get it together to go and see Mike Haydock. I rarely made contact with Mum and Stephen. I didn't need them. I didn't need anyone. I had a lover.

> Cocaine –
> a rich person's game.
> Just one line
> gives you an unbelievable high.
> Now it's an addiction of mine.

Kato didn't like drugs. He didn't mind Shirley drinking. But he didn't like Alice getting high. He didn't like the sense that things were getting out of control and fought back the only way he knew how with razors and knives, cutting into arteries and muscle tissue. I'd come round in A&E with a drip bottle above my head and those sticky magnetic pads on my body linking wires to an electrocardiogram. Bleep. Bleep. Bleep.

Andy and Sam would come and pick me up. They'd have a bag waiting for me and I'd go to the bank. It's great being rich. You don't worry about petty, bourgeois things like money.

Then it runs out.

Worse, I owed Andy: not wise when your dealer's done time. Friends will let you have a line once, twice, but their first love is coke. It's not you. You're someone to take coke with, borrow coke from, borrow money from. No coke. No money. You're a non-person.

Sam would turn tricks if she had to. A girl with nothing has always got that; there's always some bloke who'll give you a line of coke for a poke. I put on some red lipstick and studied myself in the mirror. What a joke. I hadn't even managed to make it with Matt. I remembered that first line of coke in the car with the rain beating on the windows, the feeling of euphoria. It was always good after that first time, but it was never quite as good. That's Charlie's trap. He gets you, he keeps you in his embrace and he squeezes tighter and tighter.

I had all these alters revving up inside me, head spinning, body aching, walls pressing in on me, the Professor peering through the kitchen window, that legless guy back on the doorstep, the Olanzapine was making me feel sick. Let's try another.

And another.

And another.

There was a tall, slim Asian man with twinkly dark eyes looking down at me. Ah, yes, it's Dr Thandma. I'd seen him doing the rounds on the Josiah Jennins psychiatric ward. What went through my mind was: How come you're wearing a pinstriped suit, not the disposable apron more appropriate in a place awash in human blood?

He was waiting for me to speak. I kept silent.

'So you believe the devil slashed your arms, do you?'

I had no idea what he was talking about. 'No,' I replied. 'It was most likely one of the *others* who did it.'

'Who are you now?'

'What?'

'And who are these *others*?'

'I'm Alice Jamieson. I have DID. The *others* are different personalities or what you medics refer to as *alters*,' I replied.

'One of the nurses told me you are often here after lacerating your arms. So what made you cut yourself this time?'

He was probing the topic of deliberate self-harm, which, in my experience, is generally misunderstood by doctors and is often an issue used to stigmatize and label you. It was also clear that he knew little or nothing about DID.

I sighed. The effects of the lignocaine injected into my cuts to anaesthetize the wounds while they were stitched was wearing off. My arms were sore, my head hurt and I really didn't want to have to spell out my diagnosis to a psychiatrist.

Dr Thandma moved on to risk assessment; I'd been waiting for it.

'Are you feeling suicidal?' he asked.

'Not at all.'

'Then why did you cut your arms again?'

'I suggest you read my notes,' I replied.

'I have already read a brief history. I think in view of the fact that Dr Armstrong is on leave, you should come into hospital for a while so we can keep an eye on you.'

Back in the bin. No way. I took a breath, calmed myself. On the previous day they had removed the stitches and bandages covering the cuts that had been inflicted by Kato less than a fortnight previously. I tried a smile.

'I don't think that will be necessary, Doctor, really.'

He stood very still, holding his fingers to his chin while he thought. 'As long as you can give me your word you are not intending to cut yourself again, you are free to leave,' he finally said.

'Thank you, Doctor.'

I called Matt and he came with Andy to pick me up. I stayed alone in my flat for a couple of days and it was as though someone had wound back the clock, not hours, not days, but years. I had been diagnosed with Multiple Personality Disorder in 1993. More than ten years had gone by. Burned. Wasted. Drugged.

Most of that money sent mysteriously by my father I had saved through the years by scrimping, by shopping at Oxfam, by taking my holidays in my head. When Jacob died I transferred all the love in my heart to the white stuff, the marching powder, cocaine. Now the money had gone. All of it. Every penny. I had to go cold turkey. I could do it. I'm strong as well as weak. I had to get the cocaine out of my body, but I soon became aware that even if you do, it never leaves your mind. There's always the memory of feeling free, of creeping into McDonalds to pinch a few snorting straws, of rashly breaking into a garage to steal a drug dealer's stash, of living on the edge with the outlaws. I remember the music sounding better. I remember dancing like a breath of wind. I remember sitting in the back of Andy's car with the window open and the night air on my face.

What's it like going cold turkey?

It's like being a cold turkey, straight out of the fridge and straight in the oven. You're featherless, headless, flightless. You sweat and you freeze. You shake and you cry. The voices come back.

Today I'm Alice

You're nothing. You'll never be anything. You're a failure. You should kill yourself, Alice. Do the world a favour. Do it today.

There was no chance of that, not with my debts. I was behind with everything: rent, council tax, utility bills, credit card bills and interest, my dealer. The television had given up the ghost. My bike had vanished. I had £95 a week Incapacity Benefit and £315 a month Disability Living Allowance – enough to dabble and keep the anti-psychotics in balance.

It may sound like a contradiction, but even after you've gone cold turkey, even when you give up drugs you don't completely give them up. It's not like that.

I was back at the day hospital, this time with a psychologist who I'd learned not to get too close to. I went home occasionally to see mum and Stephen so I could talk about myself, though never about my use of illicit drugs or my debts.

Years of drug addiction, self-mutilation, odd weeks and months in the nuthouse. In my life I have studied the inner architecture of several different psychiatric hospitals, high-tech post-modern, decaying Victoriana – I could write a book and call it *Let's Go Loony*.

You look at me, you look at my medical records, and you say to yourself: what's wrong with that girl? What's wrong is that from a baby to a teenager I was constantly raped, buggered and abused. You don't get over it. You just don't. It wasn't something I had done. It was something my father had done to me.

CHAPTER 20
The Other Side

Drugs are like a warm bath, a good night's sleep, a sunny day, a smile. Drugs are fun. That's why people take them. They don't take drugs because they're addicts; addiction is a side effect. People take drugs because they want to get out of their heads. Drugs change reality. And if your reality's crap, it doesn't matter how many times you decide to quit drugs, the temptation is always there, calling you like the Sirens luring mariners to steer their ships to disaster.

After going cold turkey and giving up the white stuff, to my shame I followed the Siren's call and started again. I ran up more debts and to stretch my meagre resources switched from cocaine to bombing 'base', which is wrapping a pinch of amphetamine paste in a Rizla and swallowing it with a slug of water. This gives you a sore throat, a nose leak and a feeling that you could run a marathon in three hours. In truth, it would be hard to run 300 yards without falling over.

It didn't take long before my consultant psychiatrist had me back in Josiah Jennins for a drug detox, which lasted a fortnight. While I was there, the shrinks decided to change my anti-psychotics again. The new drug was pale blue and green like the plumage of a lovebird. I lay hollow as a hole in special obs, Jacob hovering above me like a phantom. I blamed myself that he was up there, not down here with me between the sheets.

Could it have been different?

Each one of us is the master of our own ship and Jacob Williams set sail in his own good time. On the last occasion I saw him, he had been very quiet, quieter than usual. He seemed to have an inner stillness, a peace, an emptiness, perhaps. He had already made his plan. When I left his flat that night, he gave me a big hug and that hug meant goodbye.

Matt came to pick me up from Josiah Jennins and we sat upstairs on the bus snorting speed and talking nonsense. At least the new anti-psychotics didn't make me fat. I was back in my old clothes. I was me, the me who hung out and didn't read, the me who missed counselling appointments and lay on the floor listening to Pink Floyd's *The Dark Side of the Moon* over and over again.

I was the loony who had lost the path. Time was running away from me; not months but years. I wasn't a girl any more. I was suddenly thirty-six years old. My birthday raced by on a gram of coke – well, it *was* my birthday – followed by a sleepless night. I walked the streets in the morning watching the kids making their way to school, the girls in blue blazers with a badge showing St Mildred in a circle of light. It felt odd that I was big, not small and dressed in the same school uniform.

Time turns to dust and the dust vanishes on the wind. One blow, and it's gone. At thirty you are connected to twenty-nine with all those years of hope and optimism going back to childhood. At thirty-six your fate is fixed. You are what you are. I wasn't sure who I was when I found myself sitting in a torrent of tics and quivers in St Mildred's Church with the light through the narrow windows putting a silvery sheen on the old granite floor.

I looked about me. Everything was curiously strange yet

familiar like a shimmer of déjà vu. The last time I had been in a church was in Florence during my Italian tour. I had no idea what I was doing in St Mildred's or how I had got there. I was holding a tube of Smarties and the handle of Billy's gun was sticking out of my bag. I glanced at my watch then remembered I didn't have a watch any more.

Jesus stared from the cross with a forlorn look and I gazed at the blood trickling from below his crown of thorns. I had been christened in this crumbling old church, the dates slowly eroding from its tombstones as if to remind us time is eternal. The sweet smell of incense recalled the Christingle services of my childhood, the times when I thought I was that lucky girl from the big house with the nice mum and dad. The Christingle is an orange tied with a ribbon and pierced with cocktail sticks holding cloves, raisins and sultanas to represent the earth and its fruits. There is also a small candle that, when lit, symbolizes Christ as the light of the world.

After my coke birthday party with Matt, I was feeling perceptive and paranoid, senses comfortably numb, memories appearing like pictures in a flick book. The voices whispered over the arched ceiling.

You're shit. You're nothing. You'll never be anything. People hate you.

An old woman was looming over me below a mass of furious white curls, her quizzical face screwed up like a lemon.

'Are you all right, my dear?' she asked.

'Are you talking to me? There's nothing wrong with me,' I snapped, and rattled the Smarties at her.

She left me with a sour look. I watched her green cardigan and long kilt sway away on sensible shoes down the aisle to a small door behind the organ. She returned with a man wearing a navy-blue crew-necked jumper over a white shirt and grey trousers with sharp crease that instantly reminded me of Grandpa.

'Can I help you?' he asked.

'Sure,' I replied. 'You could get me a glass of water.'

He smiled at me, then smiled at the woman to show all was in hand.

'I'll be back in two seconds,' he said and disappeared through the same door behind the organ. When he returned with the water I drank it down in one.

'You're dehydrated,' he observed.

'I don't know why,' I said, but of course I did. It was the drugs.

He sat on the pew in front of me and turned to face me as he spoke. He talked about the history of St Mildred's, stuff I vaguely recalled from school. It added to my sense that the dust of time was blowing backwards. I was high on a dab of base I'd bombed to help me through the coke withdrawals. I wandered about the old building in a daze when he offered to give me a tour. I followed him down some narrow steps into the chapel, then into the sacristy full of silver and paintings showing scenes of despair and pain.

'Why don't they paint something more ... uplifting?' I said, and the man shrugged and turned to me with a smile.

'You know something, I've always wondered that myself,' he replied.

We looked at the last of the paintings, looked for a moment at each other. There was nothing more to say. The light through the stained-glass windows was growing dimmer by the time we made our way back up the aisle to the main doors.

'Come and see me again,' he said in parting. 'I'm always here on Mondays and Thursdays.'

*

I didn't plan to go and see him again, but the following week, time slipped out of joint, I lost my bearings and found myself running out of a rainstorm through the open door of St Mildred's. He was standing in the aisle as if he had been expecting me, back straight with blue eyes like flakes of sky and pale blonde hair parted on one side. He puffed up as if he were pleased to see me. In his tweed suit with a green waistcoat, he made me think of a budgerigar.

I had assumed he was one of those clergymen who didn't bother to wear clerical garb, but he turned out to be a church warden by the name of Alec Menzies. He had a faint Scottish accent. Edinburgh, he said. He was a good talker and a good listener, although I can't imagine what we had in common or what we talked about that week, the following week, or the week after. Sometimes Alec wore gold-rimmed glasses like Gerald Brennan, my director of studies in Huddersfield. He had nice hands. I always notice hands, and often when we sat together talking I rested my hands in his palms as though I was a little bird and his hands were a nest.

About a month later I asked Alec to lend me £30, and shared a wrap of speed with Matt. I asked for £20, which Shirley spent on a litre of gin. I borrowed £200 to pay off a debt to Andy, the dealer. I asked Alec for small sums, I don't know how many times.

'Could you lend me twenty pounds, Alec?'

'What for this time?'

'I'll pay you back,' I said, but I never did. Addicts never do.

It must have been two or three months later when the come-down from a speed trip sent Kato off in a rage of paranoia and violence. He was gripped by the memories of a sixteen-year-old entwined with his father, my father, pumping away between his legs, my legs, the Brylcreem smell a soporific, my father's body stiffening in climax. My dissociated self watched that girl's features turn into Kato's face as it twisted in despair and self-hatred.

Kato had visions of taking a knife to bed, hiding it under the mattress, and stabbing that man, my father, as he expelled his foul seed into a condom. Kato imagined lifting the knife and bringing it down again and again, the blood spurting in showers, coating his pallid flesh, the bed, the walls. Kato hated himself because he had never found the courage to take the knife from the magnetic rack and give life to his visualization. He lay there like a girl and Father fucked him.

Kato wanted God to understand his pain. He stormed into St Mildred's one Thursday morning, jumped up on the altar, grabbed the three-foot silver crucifix and threatened everyone who came close. A little crowd gathered just out of reach: Father Roger came running up on his small feet; some ladies in pearls, come for the service; church guides; tourists.

'Get away from me, you bastards. I'll kill you all.'

Alec Menzies appeared and stood close enough for Kato to pulverize him.

'Come down, Alice,' he said.

'I'm not Alice. I'm me. Me. I'm going to kill you.'

'No you're not. Come down and talk to me.'

'You bastard, I hate you. I'm going to kill you.'

Kato swung the crucifix at Alec and Alec caught it without flinching and held it steady. People gasped, and I burst into tears.

Kato had gone. I felt weak, tired, limp, drained and relieved in my left-brain Alice persona that I hadn't harmed myself or anyone else. Alec helped me climb down from the altar and took me into the back room where I sat and sobbed. He calmed me, as he had done before, and would do again. Many times. Without planning or knowing what I was doing, I was testing Alec Menzies as heroes were tested in a Greek myth or the Bible.

He was being tested by the church too. The clergy had become aware of the friendship between the thirty-six-year-old crazy girl – woman, whatever I was – and the church warden, a married man with three grown-up children. There were people in the congregation who thought, far from needing help, I was the devil's spawn in need of exorcising, banning from church, burning at the stake. I was the traveller on the road from Jerusalem to Jericho set upon by robbers and Alec Menzies was the Good Samaritan who didn't pass on by.

Alec wasn't an analyst but he had the patience and insight to ask the right questions. That day after Kato took to the altar I began to tell him about the abuse, the loss of my PhD, my DID/MPD, my addiction to street drugs and prescription drugs.

'Why do you take so many drugs?' he asked.

'To forget.'

'The abuse?'

And the debts, I thought, but didn't say so. I had an overdraft, a broken refrigerator, a £100-a-week speed habit to fend off a potential £400-a-week coke habit.

'Lots of things,' I replied. 'The pain. The past. The memories. There are always things to forget.'

'You need some new memories to replace the old ones,' he said, and closed his palms to squeeze my hands between them.

People are rarely interested in the minutiae of other people's lives, their airport nightmares, hospital dramas, the uncaring bank. Alec showed interest in me, me Alice, and me JJ, Kato and Shirley, whatever me popped up to test him with a new quirk, a new demand. He drove me home and in the car park outside my flat, where Andy had given me that first line of coke, I leaned back through Alec's open window and kissed him on the cheek.

One night not long after that I plucked up courage and called Alec at home. His wife was in the south of France, where they had a stone cottage. We met at a pizzeria in town. We shared a bottle of wine and for the first time I listened as Alec talked about his life, how he had joined the army at eighteen and had risen through the ranks, taken a commission and retired aged fifty-three, a major.

I saluted and he grinned.

He was thinking of setting up in business as a security consultant and had volunteered as a church warden. His wife was fluent in French and, with the children grown up, she went off to the cottage in Provence he had built with his own hands whenever she could. He seemed to be hinting there was some strain in the relationship and then changed the subject.

'It seems daft,' he said, 'but when you appeared in the church that first time it was as if I'd known you all my life.'

He paused. I didn't want to hear this. I was messed up. I didn't want to get more messed up.

He smiled. 'You looked like a lost lamb,' he added, 'and I suddenly felt like a shepherd.'

Unlike Alec, I am not blessed with faith. I have had my head in too many psychology books for that. But I realized that night as we drank red wine in the candlelight that I had a feeling inside me I had never had before. It was small, fragile, a baby bird. It seemed as if Alec actually loved me. And there was something else, something terrifying and bewildering: this feeling was reciprocated. It frightened me. I was suddenly tired. I was afraid of hope. I saw no chance for lasting happiness: no way to renegotiate my fate.

That night I lay in bed gazing up at the moons and stars

on the ceiling telling myself I was stupid. Alec didn't love me; he couldn't. Not in that sense. He was doing what Christians are commanded to do: loving your neighbour as yourself. Alec Menzies would let me down. Men always do. Grandpa died. Jacob killed himself. Matt was a junkie. My father raped me.

I had promised to call Alec next day so he would know I was all right. I didn't make that call and didn't return his calls or texts. I stayed away from the church. I avoided Matt. I was determined once and for all to get clean of drugs, clear of dependency. On anyone. Or anything. I had squandered my potential. I had given up therapy with Mike Haydock and wasted the opportunity of further integrating the alters and finding peace within myself. MPD is a house of mirrors and everywhere you look you see your own distorted reflection. Only by working on myself was I ever going to be able to have normal friendships without making unrealistic demands of the sort I had made on Jo Lewin and was now making on Alec Menzies.

I had to change my mindset. Reading was my drug of choice. I liked buying books, making annotations, giving books as presents. There was no money for that so I sat in the library lost in the novels of Ian McEwan, Martin Amis, Bret Easton Ellis. I read *American Psycho* in one sitting, aware from the first page that the writer had studied dissociation before creating his anti-hero Patrick Bateman. The book made me appreciate that there were people a lot crazier than me. When you can hold on to that thought, you aren't exactly on the road to recovery, but you can see the road.

To avoid drugs, I had to fill every second of my time. I dug out all my old CDs and, when I wasn't reading, I lay on the sofa listening to music, the same albums, the same tracks, with my enduring OCD, which never goes away. I must have listened to Eric Clapton singing about 'dirty cocaine' a million times. You're right, Eric, it is dirty. I wanted to get clean.

I took my Prozac and anti-psychotics. I *almost, almost* stopped taking non-prescription drugs. I poured the gin down the sink when I found it where Shirley had hidden it in the cupboard or behind Mr Happy in the corner of the bedroom. The teddies were on the shelf and the voices were muttering. I blew the dust from my laptop. During my research into DID, I had come across the psychiatrist Dr Joan Coleman, who runs RAINS – Ritual Abuse Information Network and Support – a counter-organization to the British False Memory Society, which was formed in 1993. This organization, to quote its literature, 'Serves people and professionals in contested allegations of abuse.' It disputes the reliability of recovered and repressed memories and makes a case against what they describe as false memories.

Dr Coleman called me after I'd left a message on her answerphone. She assured me that paedophiles commonly create satanic scenarios as a cover for their true intentions. Children are both confused and convinced by the ritual, by the sense that they have been chosen to take part in these adult ceremonies. I wasn't crazy. I hadn't made it all up: my medical history showed that. All these years after my father raped me and ejaculated over my face, I still thought: Why me? It's not fair. How can such a thing have happened? *It can't have happened.* You can't put an end to these thoughts. You can't stop the record replaying in your head.

We ended the conversation talking about Alec Menzies. Dr Coleman didn't advise me to go and see him again. That's not her role. But she did say that I was unwise cutting myself off from anyone who, as she put it, 'extended the hand of friendship'.

*

After my conversation with Joan, I continued to stay away from Matt. I stayed away from drugs, and I started a course to learn how to be a fitness instructor for people with mental-health problems. The mad leading the mad, I know, but I was trying.

Most of all, I stayed away from St Mildred's. I stayed away for nearly a year and then, one day, feeling bubbly and wearing a garish yellow tracksuit, I found myself jogging through town, the spire above the church like a compass needle drawing me magnetically towards the open doors. I quickened my pace as if this were a race and ran straight into Alec Menzies as he was re-arranging the guide books and literature on the shelves beside the entrance.

'Alice . . .'

'Why haven't you come to see me?' I demanded.

'I was waiting for you to come to me.'

'What if I hadn't come? What then?'

He furrowed his brow as he thought up some excuse. 'I knew you would come when you were ready,' he said.

'That's rubbish.'

'It's true. I prayed.'

His eyes were bright in the diffused light and I noticed the whites were very white. He smiled and that rare, singular feeling ran through me like an electric current: I was suddenly happy, happy to be there in the golden light falling through the strained-glass windows, happy, dare I say it, to be alive.

We went back to that same pizzeria and blessed the future sharing a bottle of wine – a rare indulgence. Alec drove me back to my flat and the following day a delivery van turned up with a new television. Alec bought me a new refrigerator and a washing machine. He made astonishing trucks from Lego when Billy came out, and he talked in an adult way to JJ, who appreciated that. JJ was chirpy and self-confident. He didn't need booze and drugs to make him happy. He just needed someone to talk to.

There were slips. Lots of slips. There were cocaine nights with Matt and binge drinking with Shirley. Poor Kato would still take the razor blade to my arms and the caring staff at A&E would stitch me up again. Even if the psychiatrists weren't always clued up on my condition, the staff at the hospital knew I wasn't self-harming to seek attention. They would call the church warden and he'd come and take me home, fill the new refrigerator with food, pop in next morning to make sure I was all right.

When Alec's wife took breaks in France, he stayed the night at my flat and we became lovers. We became lovers in as much as we had grown to love each other. I knew it was love because to my amazement I found the word 'we' cropping up on my tongue almost as often as 'me'. Sex was never going to be easy, but I liked being held. I liked the feel of Alec's hands on my arms, my back, his strong arm round my skinny waist. I knew he would never let me down. I had stayed away. I had tested him. He had waited. He was there for me. He was old enough to be my father. I was aware of the complexities, the Oedipal psychology, the gossip. But love isn't a collection of cells that can be studied under a microscope. Love *is*. It happens. Or it doesn't happen. For the first time in my life, I was normal, hopeful, contented.

Alec counselled me; he grew to know my family of alters. He saw me at my worst and I tried to become the best I could for him. Each time Alec discovered one of those threatening letters from the utility companies, the bank, the council, he paid off the debt. But the thing with debts is that as you pay them, more bills arrive on the doormat. Alec paid those too. He didn't believe in storing money just to earn more money. Money, he said, was a gift to be used and spread.

'You have to give to get,' he said. 'It's made round so that it goes round.'

Our friendship, our quasi-affair, went on for a long time; it seemed for years, as if we had always been together. Bit by bit, with Alec spending more time with me and less time at home, I was coping, improving. I was helping others with mental-health issues to face their problems through exercise routines. I felt as if I was one half of a couple and, at the same time, I felt whole. I felt free too. Alec had slowly but surely paid off all my debts.

We went on walking trips. I laughed as Alec marched over the Malvern Hills like a soldier. We stayed in sweet little hotels that always reminded me of the boarding house outside Liverpool where I had gone with Patrick O'Hay for that hopeless night of unfulfilled love. Alec taught me how to drive and, when I passed my test – Shirley at the wheel, naturally – we went to the best restaurant in Birmingham and spent more than £100 on one meal.

Then the bomb exploded and the walls came tumbling down.

What Alec hadn't told me was that the money he had been spending so freely had eaten away the inheritance from his wife's late father and was now wiping out his army pension. In September 2007, Alec's wife discovered what had been going on, packed her bags and moved to the cottage in Provence. She wanted a divorce.

Alec decided to stand by me. It was a strain. And he tried. He still came over, still stayed in my little council flat at the top of a steep flight of stairs. We still went to the pizzeria. He played with the Lego when Billy appeared. Things were the same but not quite the same. There was a subtle, imperceptible sense of change like autumn turning to winter.

Christmas was coming. We bought a tree and I decorated

the flat with paperchains made by the kids. Alec bought a big turkey. He never did things by halves. The army major and the loopy girl were similar in many ways. Like attracts like, in my experience, not the other way round. I spent three hours one afternoon in the shopping centre looking for the perfect gift for Alec and bought a yellow cashmere V-necked sweater that I thought would go very well under his tweed suit. Alec never wore an overcoat, no matter how cold it was. It's the Scotch blood, lassie, I was wearing a kilt till I was twelve.

I returned home with my surprise wrapped in tissue. Alec was sitting on the sofa with a grim expression. I knew what he was going to say. Multiple personalities give you multiple intuitions.

He was going back to his wife. It was Christmas. His children were in the south of France. It was the right thing to do. Of course it was. It was the right thing to do for that little family, but it left me feeling betrayed, scorned, hopeless and alone with the Christmas tree hung with miniature teddies and the ceiling strewn with home-made paperchains. Alec put his glasses back in their scuffed case and I saw tears running down his cheeks as he closed the door.

Like an echo, I instantly became Baby Alice. I snuggled up with Mr Happy and cried for forty-eight hours. I stopped crying when all the tears had gone. I was drained, empty and the voices that had been intermittent and distant were back, full-throated and venomous.

No one likes you. Everyone hates you. You're nothing. Do the world a favour and top yourself.

Fuck off!

I ripped the decorations from the walls and dragged the Christmas tree down to the bins at the back of the flats. I watched the season of good will go by through the bottom of a gin bottle and comforted myself with a sad sense of pride that I didn't call Andy and get a few grams of coke. I had good credit now all my debts had been paid.

Each day I woke after sleeping-pill nights with that black thing from my childhood growing big inside me again. I had survived being raped, buggered and abused; I had survived deep self-doubt, depression, seemingly careless psychiatrists and monstrous psychiatric wards.

Now this.

Kill yourself, Alice. Kill yourself. It's the only way.

'For God sake, fuck off.'

Kill yourself. Kill yourself.

Always the damn voices.

On 20 January I received a letter from Alec informing me of his change of address. He and his wife had sold their house and were moving to a more modest flat. He said he didn't want to lose contact.

Kato was enraged by the letter. He punched the walls. He kicked the sofa. He smashed the empty bottle of gin. His anger built up inside him for the next few days and on 25 January he snapped. He leaned over the bath and took a shard of glass to my arms.

Kill yourself. Kill yourself.

'Fuck off.'

Look at that blood. You've finally done the right thing.

'Fuck off and leave me alone.'

The blood poured down my arms, dribbled from my fingers and spotted the bath, the spots running together in a pool.

You've done it now. You've finally done it.

I shook my head to shake away the voices and, as I looked down at the red puddle against the white porcelain, I saw Kato's face transform into my own face and realized what had happened. I grabbed a towel to wrap over the wounds, but the blood was pumping out. I didn't know what to do. I felt weaker with each passing second. I finally ran out of my flat up the concrete stairs to Uncle Joe. He was playing the violin. I could hear it through the thin walls. I hammered on his door and collapsed into his arms when the door finally opened.

I had known Uncle Joe for years but only now as he called for an ambulance and tried to bandage my arms did I look at him closely. Only now did I *see* him: old, worn, caring, a refugee from Eastern Europe. I wasn't even sure exactly where he came from. A fellow human being who was there when I needed someone, as we should all try and be there when people need us. You can't change the world, someone once said, only yourself.

The wounds were deep and the blood kept soaking through the dressings and dripping over the lino in the small kitchen.

'Why you do this, Alice?'

'I don't know. I'm sorry.'

The ambulance arrived. I was carried down the stairs on a stretcher and listened to the siren wailing, imagining the traffic grinding to a halt as we raced through the streets to A&E. I was immediately placed in a cubicle, but the nurses couldn't stem the blood pumping from my arms.

What happened next is unclear.

What I do recall, and I recall it vividly, is coming face-to-face with Grandpa. I couldn't believe it. He smiled. I smiled back. He looked exactly the same as I remembered him that last summer when we sucked toffee together in his greenhouse. Quite aside from his visual presence, I actually felt Grandpa's embrace, tender and filled with love. I felt that hug and I heard him say:

'Not yet. It's not your time. GO.'

I was resuscitated and regained consciousness with those words echoing in my mind. There was six people gathered round the bed in the resus room: doctors, nurses and a man in a tweed suit with a green waistcoat squeezing a bag of saline through a drip and massaging my toes. Alec had come home.

I had lost, I was told, almost 50 per cent of my body's total blood mass and gone into hypovolemic shock.

'We lost you for a while there,' said the young nurse who took me to the toilet after I'd been stabilized.

For several moments I had had no cardiac output: my heart had stopped. If it had not been for some brain activity, I would have been clinically dead. A part of me had wanted to hold on to my grandpa, my beloved childhood soulmate, to cross to the other side, but I remembered feeling Alec squeezing my foot and looking relieved as I regained consciousness.

When my heart had stopped beating, it seemed as if I were passing through a white cloud into another place. Once I came face to face with Grandpa, I didn't want to lose him again. I really could have died. I did die. But I trusted Grandpa when he yelled at me to go, and I knew what he meant. It wasn't my time.

Alec took me home. He held me close. And he sobbed.

'I was really scared I'd lost you.'

Alec still had a key to my flat. He had arrived shortly after the ambulance had left and, when he found the blood and broken glass in the bath, he had rushed straight to A&E. He had come to tell me, as he told me now, that he had tried to patch up his marriage, but he had been living a lie.

'I will never let you down again. Ever. Ever. Ever,' he said.

The end had so nearly been the end, but in fact, that January day was a new beginning for the both of us. Alec moved in with me, leaving his new flat and the house in France to his wife.

Soon spring came and I was happy. I was loved. I was clean. I had survived.

Was I better? Would I ever get better? The ultimate aim of DID/MPD therapy is the integration of the alternative personalities. This has worked in me to some extent, but not entirely. There are good days and bad days. I don't use illicit drugs and medication keeps me more or less in balance. More or less. I still get flashbacks and nightmares, but I have Alec's love and a small circle of good friends who accept me for who I am. Even if I'm not always the same person.

It has been a long journey to reach this position. The alters suffered the pain of being abused all through my childhood and I forgive those alters who have inflicted pain on me as an adult. Of course I do. They are my friends. They still pop out when they shouldn't, but they are getting more considerate and I have, of my own free will, decided not to integrate them fully. Alec has supported me in this respect and is quite happy to assist Billy in building trucks with his Lego. Shirley is still partial to a Gin and Tonic and I share that taste for the drink with her, but not to excess.

Sometimes when I awake from a nightmare in the pitch black night I hear little JJ's voice saying everything's going to be all right. I put my faith in him – a ten year old child, as Grandpa would have said to be, 'wise beyond his years.' JJ, as well as the others, has helped me this far; and so because he sings *Everything's going to be all right*, I believe everything *is* going to be all right. I am certainly no longer as vulnerable as I once was. Even though sometimes I am Baby Alice and Alec sings me a lullaby as I settle to sleep. Other times I may be Samuel, or Billy, Kato or Shirley. But for certain, today I am Alice.

Afterword

In September 2006, I contacted the local CID to ask if I could have on official police notepaper a validation of the handwritten note given to me by the female DC who had dealt with my complaint against my father in 1999.

I spoke to a detective inspector, who picked up on the fact that I needed closure. He promised to call me back. Child abuse, child murders, child kidnappings and child slavery were more openly in the public arena and the police had departments investigating and dealing with these issues.

I was surprised to discover that my case had not been forgotten. True to his word, the inspector was on the phone later that afternoon.

'It seems to have been a very nasty case,' he remarked.

'Yes, it was. It still is,' I told him.

There was a pause. 'Have you ever thought about reopening the case?' he asked.

'Well, no, I haven't, but if that's a possibility then, yes, I would like to.'

He arranged a time to interview me at my flat. He arrived with a detective constable, a woman of my age who was serious, sympathetic and clearly trained to deal with such complaints. After talking at length, the inspector emphasized there was always the possibility that my father might not be brought to trial. However, the CID launched an investigation that was to last a further three months.

Today, Alice's 'alters' are partly integrated but she continues to receive regular visits from five-year-old Billy and ten-year-old JJ. She lives with her partner Alec.

Clifford Thurlow is the author of numerous biographies, most recently *Making a Killing,* the inside story of Captain James Ashcroft's eighteen months as a hired gun in Iraq. His biography of Carlos Lozano, *Sex, Surrealism, Dali and Me* has been translated into several languages and was the basis of Thurlow's sixty-minute Arts & Entertainments documentary on Salvador Dali made to coincide with the centenary of the artist's birth in 2004. Thurlow lives in London.

Visit **www.panmacmillan.com** to read more about all our books and to buy them. You will also find features, author interviews and news of any author events, and you can sign up for e-newsletters so that you're always first to hear about our new releases.

The inspector came to visit me again in December and broke the news that the CPS had decided that as there was no fresh evidence, the case couldn't proceed to prosecution. This was the second time I had been given such news and I was bitterly disappointed.

I reminded the inspector that I had requested a letter on police headed paper stating that the investigating team were confident that I had told the truth. I could use it as a reality check whenever I was frustrated at not being able to bring my father to justice. It proved someone in authority believed me.

Before leaving, the inspector asked, 'Have you ever thought about fighting your father through the civil courts?'

'No, I haven't,' I said.

'It's an option, Ms Jamieson. You can make a claim through the Criminal Injuries Compensation Authority,' he added.

The letter arrived as promised on official police notepaper. I put it on file while I decided what to do next. I had Alec for support now. He had joined my team and we were applying for a larger council flat.

We – 'we' – did consider taking out a civil action against my father, but Alec didn't want me to suffer being dragged through the courts. The police, likewise, didn't want me dragged through the courts, and I thought justice was poorly served.

I did, though, as the police suggested, make a claim through the Criminal Injuries Compensation Authority (CICA), a government body set up to award compensation to victims of violent crime, which includes sexual abuse.

After two and a half years of assessing the injury I sustained as a result of the abuse, by trawling through my medical and psychiatric records, and documents lodged in police archives; as well as calculating my loss of past and

future earnings had I completed my PhD, the CICA has
finally awarded me a substantial amount of money, – further
affirmation that I, Alice Jamieson, have given a 'truthful and
honest account', as the police duly noted.